TRAVELERS' TALES

THE
BEST
WOMEN'S TRAVEL
WRITING
2005

TRUE STORIES
FROM AROUND THE WORLD

D0113103

TRAVELERS' TALES

THE BEST
WOMEN'S TRAVEL
WRITING
2005

TRUE STORIES
FROM AROUND THE WORLD

Edited by
LUCY MCCAULEY

Travelers' Tales
Palo Alto

Travelers' Tales and *Travelers' Tales Guides* are trademarks of
Travelers' Tales, Inc.

Credits and copyright notices for the individual articles in this
collection are given starting on page 291.

We have made every effort to trace the ownership of all
copyrighted material and to secure permission from copyright
holders. In the event of any question arising as to the ownership
of any material, we will be pleased to make the necessary
correction in future printings. Contact Travelers' Tales, Inc.,
853 Alma Street, Palo Alto, California 94301.
www.travelerstales.com

Art Direction: Michele Wetherbee/Stefan Gutermuth
Interior design and page layout: Melanie Haage using the fonts
    Nicolas Cochin, Ex Ponto and Granjon.

Distributed by: Publishers Group West, 1700 Fourth Street,
Berkeley, California 94710.

ISBN 1-932361-18-9
ISSN 1553-054X

First Edition
Printed in the United States
10 9 8 7 6 5 4 3 2 1

For Hannah.

Our home is the universe.
Our task is anything we
set our minds and hearts to.

—MARY V. PATEL

Table of Contents

Introduction

*A*lmost ten years ago, when I was compiling my first anthology, *Travelers' Tales Spain*, I read stories about a pilgrimage called the Camino de Santiago—and I began to dream: of adventuring solo, lost in my thoughts amid the lush green hillsides ubiquitous in northern Spain; of the personal epiphanies that the challenge of pilgrimage could yield; of the camaraderie the Camino offers, among an international assortment of pilgrims carrying walking sticks and backpacks. Last fall, after years of planning my trip—postponed for a cross-country move, a marriage, a baby—I finally walked the ground of that dusty trail in northern Spain.

Since medieval times pilgrims have made their way to the town of Santiago de Compostela as a religious quest (an enormous cathedral towers over the grave, they say, of Saint James), but nowadays people make the journey for all kinds of reasons, often spiritual but sometimes purely for the beauty and challenge of the walk. As for myself, I was going through a difficult period in my life and the timing just felt right; travel and walking, in particular, have always been a way for me to reorient myself, to gain perspective.

I brought the baby (for reasons—based on the response from friends and family—that apparently only I will ever understand). I would be reasonable, however; I wouldn't do the entire 500-mile Camino. ("Not alone with a toddler!" friends who are mothers exclaimed.) I would take a few weeks and do only small sections of the trail, with a lightweight stroller, from "home bases" that I established in major towns along the path.

Right from the beginning, though, I was an anxious pilgrim. Rather than pausing to gaze at the velvet hues of Spanish wheat fields, at the rolling canopy of clouds at every stop, I occupied myself with diapers or powdered milk and bottles for my daughter Hannah. And rather than becoming lost in the transcendent experience of walking the ancient Camino, my primary emotion was fear of becoming quite literally *lost*. Constantly on the lookout for the next scallop-shaped marker that indicated the path—what if I'd strayed, and with *the baby?*—I wondered: When would this pilgrimage begin to feel "transporting"? When would a dramatic insight capture me in its grip? Where was my moment of epiphany?

Of course, the answer to my questions lay on the path itself. It was there all along; it was even spelled out in a sign that pilgrims see here and there along the Camino: "*Verse a si mismo*": Look inside yourself. If travel does anything it reminds us that in life as well as on the road, the markers we find don't always point us to the proper path of discovery—either of the self or the world. All we can do is take the next step—and understand that the way will become apparent only to the extent that we are willing to trust the journey itself.

For more than a decade, Travelers' Tales anthologies have been inspiring people to take that next step, to embark on the kind of journey that I felt inspired to make. The books have been dedicated to inspiring women, in particular: when the press got started it was among the first publishers to collect women's travel writing in a serious and consistent way. Since the first title in 1995, *A Woman's World* (edited by Marybeth Bond), press founders James O'Reilly and Larry Habegger have published seventeen women's titles, including this one, out of a total of some eighty books. This dedication to collecting and publishing women's writing (from a couple of guys, no less!) is just one reason I feel so proud to be part of their work.

The collection in your hands inaugurates a new yearly series of *The Best Women's Travel Writing*. In it you will find a wide range of stories and voices: of young women entranced by a foreign place for the first time, as well as seasoned travelers reconnecting with places they'd loved in their youths. There's a story of an American woman who in her golden years begins to live as the "Parisian" she knows she was born to be, and a story of a traveler who meets the Devil—a not-unknown character, perhaps, to any woman who has journeyed solo. There are tales of romance, as well as accounts of spiritual journeys in which women connect with places *within*. There are adventure stories, including that of a woman who kayaks alone 600 miles to Timbuktu, a sojourn no man had ever completed—and certainly no woman. And although only one story takes the title "Open-Road Therapy," in their own ways each of these essays is about the transformation that travel offers, about that moment of renewal and insight that eventually opens up through the act of journeying.

Happily, that moment did finally come for me along the Camino de Santiago. It was toward the end of my little self-made pilgrimage when I found myself deep in a eucalyptus forest. Stopping to dig out the Cheerios from my backpack, I suddenly noticed the profound silence that enveloped Hannah and me, and how the sunlight streamed through the narrow, towering trees. I let the scent of them fill my head, while from her stroller my daughter began singing softly to no one in particular. And it occurred to me that in that precise moment I was simply present. I was *there*, my thoughts no longer darting around with worry. I held myself still and felt flooded with a deep sense of well being, of joy to be alone in a forest in Spain with Hannah, despite all the naysayers and despite especially my own fears. Suddenly all the hardship associated with traveling solo with a child felt worth it. And even if for only a little while, rather than looking for the next marker I simply put one foot in front of the other along the path, each step leading me surely to the next.

I hope that this collection might inspire you to take your own next step. May it be along a path to some long dreamed-of journey.

—Lucy McCauley

Preface
by Mary Morris

Throughout my early years, I traveled. I went everywhere I could. I kept extensive journals, described incidents and events in great detail. But these jottings never left my journals. I never wrote about it. The fact is it never occurred to me to do so. I felt that my experiences as a woman traveler somehow weren't as compelling as those of my male counterparts.

I have always been aware that women move through the world differently than men, and I have written about this now a great deal, but at the time it seemed as if those experiences—the fear of dark alleys, the difficulty of carrying luggage, body issues, a general malaise when my bus would get in late and I wasn't sure where I'd be spending the night—were just what women had to put up with. Female troubles didn't seem to be the stuff from which travel literature was made. And I felt sure that the rest of the world wouldn't be particularly interested in it.

The truth was at the time that not many women were writing about their experiences on the road. There were the Victorian lady travelers, of course—those eccentric, courageous women, usually childless spinsters, who climbed the Himalayas and rode camels across North Africa. But for various reasons that have to do with the sociological circumstances of women after

World War I, women's travel writing, with only a few exceptions such as Rebecca West and Mary McCarthy, came to a halt. It seems as if some aspects of modern life, such as being combat soldiers, airplane pilots, and travel writers, had not yet trickled down to women.

In 1986 I was sitting in a restaurant in New York with my editor. I was between books. A novel I was working on wasn't going very well. And my editor asked me what I wanted to do next. I really wasn't sure. But the weekend before, The New York Times had come out with a special summer travel issue. They had reviewed twenty-seven travel narratives, all written by men. I was struck by this fact and I told my editor how odd I thought it was.

"Well," she said, "you travel all the time. Why don't you write about it?"

The obvious left me stunned. Of course I traveled all the time. I had those journals to prove it, full of travel experiences, tidbits, incidents, writings. All my thoughts as I'd trudged through the world. And yet these musings had never seen the light of day and this gave me pause. So like a good student I began to read some of those twenty-seven books the Times had reviewed. And I found them wanting. Or rather, they did not speak to me. My journey as a woman writer was as much inner as outer, as much about my emotional terrain as the landscapes I moved through. And yet as I read those books I found I learned about culture and history, about men and their missions. But the traveler eluded me.

That was almost twenty years ago and now everywhere I look women are traveling and writing about it. And not just writing about it as adventurers, but as writers who are going out and thinking about what it means to be a woman in the world. To lose your luggage or have to carry it. To travel incognito in a world that is dangerous to women (and in a sense what world isn't?). To be obsessed about your body and food in a world that is starving. To go shopping with women in another culture. To raise children in forbidden places.

Women are not only having their own experiences, but they are embracing them. And sharing them in their writing. There is an image seared into my brain that I have written about many times. There are certain moments and memories that make us who and what we are and this is mine. My parents were invited to a "suppressed desire ball." You were to go as your secret wish, your heart's desire. My mother made herself a costume of the world. It was the only thing she ever really wanted. To go to China, the Taj Mahal, to live in Paris. All of which eluded her. Instead of seeing the world, my mother became it.

Now, as women, we can not only see the world. We can become it in our own way as we bring our unique personal vision to what we see, what is around us. The journey, after all, like beauty, is in the eye of the beholder, and I am grateful that the women in this book have brought their visions to bear.

Mary Morris is the author of twelve books, including five novels, three collections of short stories, and a trilogy of travel memoirs, including Angels & Aliens: A Journey West, Wall to Wall: From Beijing to Berlin by Rail, *and* Nothing to Declare: Memoirs of a Woman Traveling Alone. *She has also coedited with her husband, Larry O'Connor,* Maiden Voyages, *an anthology of the*

travel literature of women. Her numerous short stories and essays have appeared in such places as The Paris Review, The New York Times, Travel & Leisure, *and* Vogue. *The recipient of the Rome Prize in Literature from the American Academy of Arts & Letters, Morris teaches writing at Sarah Lawrence College and lives in Brooklyn with her husband and daughter.*

KATHRYN KEFAUVER

♫ ♫ ♫

It Takes a Village to Please My Mother

In Laos, gratitude alights on a frustrated daughter.

NO ONE MEASURED THE TEMPERATURE IN LAOS—
it was hot, everybody already knew. The afternoon I left to meet my mother at the airport, it was hot enough that the engine of the *tuk-tuk* I'd hailed—a blue boxy cab of wood and metal welded to a motorbike—heaved off clouds of gray smoke, and then, with a swift hissing sound, erupted into flame. The driver, with his expression blank, puffed a flat cigarette and didn't accelerate much to cross two lanes of traffic. We parked by a storm drain, a gully of cracked dirt, and I waited in the patchy shade of a lone tree, a bodhi tree with gray stains of exhaust on the white hollowed out bark.

The driver swatted the engine with an oily rag and I

1

glanced at my watch. The thought of my mother standing alone in the dusty warehouse that was Wattay Airport, and of me, failing before our seven-day visit even began, expanded into rage at the entire country of Laos. There wasn't a word for "late" in Lao, so I spoke carefully to the distracted driver, hoping to convey the urgency of the situation without botching the tones of the language.

"I cannot go slowly," I said in Lao.

"*Bo penn nyang*," he said. "Don't worry" or "It is nothing."

My friend Phet had teased me for leaving an hour early—sixty minutes was barely a unit of time there. After nine months in Vientiane, I'd almost adjusted to perpetual delays and nonlinear transit. But a parental visit regressed me through time, like the hours lost crossing date lines, though with my mother it was years.

I handed the driver the agreed-upon fare and hailed another *tuk-tuk*. As I rattled toward the airport again, I remembered my first trip into Vientiane on this road as it unspooled in reverse: the grit and chaos of cars; the roar of motorbikes; bicycles and trucks milling every which way; dust swirling on the sepia-toned land; buildings slouching in decay. Roadside shops were empty while people slept in chairs, in the shade of a *tuk-tuk*, or on mattressless beds in open rooms. At the edge of the road, where the swell of traffic met the stillness of a crumbling sidewalk, an ox lumbered against the weight of a cart almost toppling with melons, pacing a man who walked with two dozen straw brooms lashed to his back.

All of this looked suddenly new to me, imagined through my mother's eyes, acclimated fifty-four years to Chevy Chase, Maryland, with brief intervals of Europe. My mother had talked for decades about a cockroach that scurried across her foot in my aunt's cabin.

"Don't take her more than three hours from a hamburger," the same aunt had warned me.

At the airport, Lao families wore their finest silk to greet their loved ones. I watched one reunion, a round Lao woman in pink polyester pants surrounded by four or five people in traditional clothes. At least two of them were sobbing. I wanted to be more like my friend Phet. Unlike myself, she didn't have a separate, unpleasant personality that emerged just in the presence of family. She and her mother slept in the same room, under one blanket, on a mat on the tile floor. Phet sat for hours with her frail, gray-haired mother, who was bedridden and scarred, with lesions down the top of her nose and across her cheeks in a ragged red cross. Despite her mother's railing, Phet fetched water, prepared soup, and dispensed pills without the slightest trace of impatience.

"The old ones," Phet said, "are sometimes this way."

Suddenly my own mother stood before me. Her black hair just touched the collar of a white blouse made of high-tech, sweat-wicking fabric. The elastic strap of a money belt surged over pressed khaki pants with four kinds of pockets and drawstrings over new-looking boots. "There's no jungle in Vientiane," I wanted to say, "it's a city," but I'd already told her that numerous times. We were not a hugging family, but I encircled her and her red backpack with my arms, inhaling her scent of Chanel and mild sweat.

She pulled back. "I was first through customs. I met a nice man on the plane. A diplomat."

"That's great," I said.

"I could see you with someone like that," she said.

"Hmm." I pressed my lips closed.

"Someone a bit older. He doesn't live far away—
Phnom Penh I think."

"Let me take your bag," I said.

"Careful," she said.

"Jesus, you have cement in here?"

"That's my new G4," she said, referring to her Apple
laptop. "Hold still." She unzipped the smaller, outermost
pocket of the backpack, extracted a pale green compact,
and snapped it open to check her makeup. I grabbed
her other bag, an enormous suitcase on wheels, and she
walked next to me, inspecting her nose and cheeks. At
the curb, I bargained with a *tuk-tuk* driver as if my life
hinged on the extra seven cents.

"We're almost there," I said, as we turned on the unpaved lane toward the center of my village. The entire
ride, my mother had barely spoken. She clung to an
overhead bar with one hand and covered her salmon-
pink lipstick with the other.

"That's where I work," I'd shouted over the roar
of the engine when we'd passed Communist Party
Headquarters.

"I can't hear you."

"I work there. That's where I teach."

"Stop straining your vocal chords. You need to use
your breath more efficiently." My mother was a speech
therapist.

"I'm not straining."

"Yes, you are."

"I'm not."

"You're yelling," she said.

My house was the last on a row of small but still
Western-looking hybrid houses of wood and stucco. It

was relatively plush with two bedrooms and a porch shaded by mango, lemon, and rambutan trees. Beyond my window, the lane converged on a vast rice paddy, and flanking this sea of green, most of my Lao neighbors lived in ramshackle one-room houses on stilts.

"What do you think?" I said.

"About what?" she said.

I paused. "About the house."

"It's a house," she said.

"I have my own lemon tree," I gestured toward it like a game-show host. I'd confessed to Phet that the sight of fruit growing on trees still amazed me, and perhaps I expected my mother to be similarly impressed. Instead she stared at the waist high mound of rotting garbage in the lane, into which a wandering goat plunged its mangy head. The rooster, which usually just rested on top of the pile, squawked angrily at the goat. "That's our alarm clock," I said.

My friend Chantala emerged from the one-room house across the lane, a house on wooden stilts leaning slightly to the left.

"Mahmah!" she said, jogging down the rickety stairs, "*Sabaidi!*"

Chantala *waid* to my mother, raising her hands in prayer position high in front of her face, as one would for monks and for elders. My mother nodded vaguely in reply, eyeing a black water buffalo in the rice paddy.

"She's afraid of the buffalo*,*" I explained in Lao.

Chantala grasped her shoulder reassuringly, "*Bo yan, bo yan,*" *do not fear,* "We take care of you, Mahmah."

My mother swayed, her eyes squinting in the sun, smiling in Chantala's direction.

"She's tired," I said, and steered my mother inside. She looked over her shoulder at the buffalo, which was still as carved obsidian except for the doleful whipping of its tail.

Inside, my mother froze in her bedroom, "How do you turn on the light?"

"Look, a light switch. On. Off. Just like America."

I checked my watch. Less than an hour had passed.

"I'm going to lie down." I crossed the hall and stretched out on the bed in the room across from my mother's. I'd spent the week before her arrival unable to sleep, awake at odd hours trapping millipedes beneath a plastic bowl.

"How do you work the shower?" she called from the bathroom.

"You turn the knobs," I shouted, sinking lower into the bean-filled pillow and lower in my self-esteem. I imagined Phet looking on with a stern expression. Moaning, I hauled myself up to help.

Later, I unfolded a mosquito net over her bed and flopped onto the thin mattress next to four *Mac Addict* magazines and the silver G4. It should not have surprised me that she brought her laptop. At some point her fondness for Apple computers had taken a devotional turn. She needed the newest technology for her work, and I had often been the beneficiary of barely used machines. Still, I thought toting a laptop around Laos was an excessive display of wealth, and even if it stayed inside, it would steal her attention for hours. I would savor that quiet time, I told myself, I need not compete. When I moved the computer to a bedside table and covered it with magazines, she glanced at me as if to say something, then decided against it. She continued unpacking a cornucopia of REI accessories: an elastic clothesline, an iodine dropper, a headlamp, miniature bottles of bug repellant, a plastic compass, packets of drugs, and a first aid kit with a red cross on the white plastic top.

"We're not going on safari," I said.

Then I seized one item I'd requested: a University of Michigan baseball cap. I'd asked for the nicest one she could find in navy blue and gold.

One night at Phet's house I'd looked through her glossy photos. She kept them neatly stacked on the cardboard boxes that furnished her room, boxes that doubled as tables and dressers. In one, Phet was a teenager posed next to a young Thai man. They weren't touching, but they stood flirtatiously close, shoulders landsliding inward.

Phet had sighed at the photo. "He is a Thai rock star— I liked him so much. I tried to get him to give me that hat, but he liked it too much too." With a fingernail blocking his face, Phet sounded out the syllables, Michigan.

"That's where I went to university," I said.

Phet coveting a Michigan baseball cap redeemed everything I'd found distasteful about the school, which was often embodied in people who wore U of M accouterments most avidly. I associated those hats with frat boys in t-shirts that read "I drank 'til I puked at Phi Delta Chi" and sorority girls in my lit classes who participated only to garner recommendations for law school. My sense of superiority to them lingered for years, long after they'd graduated and gotten steady jobs, and I flailed in a directionless morass that culminated in a move overseas.

The hat seemed exotic to me now, too.

Each day of her visit, my mother and I shared a table in an air-conditioned bakery glassed off from the heat, the dust, the din of traffic. Everyone knew it was run by Canadian missionaries, that in this Buddhist Communist country, this particular foreign couple was hiding Jesus behind shelves of glazed cookies and kiwi pie. Still, it was the only place to get tuna and tomato sandwiches, and therefore a favorite spot for expats, military, and development people. I'd taken my mother to several noodle shops, but she insisted that the water, and therefore the broth, might not be clean. I'd pursed my lips as she doused her soup with iodine.

After lunch we trudged from temple to temple, monument to monument, market to market. My mother took pictures.

Our last stop was the Morning Market, a sprawling, open-air warehouse structure of rows and rows of things to buy, from cheap Thai radios to ground bones of lemur. I watched the wood-slatted floors for spiders while she rummaged through the silk and the carvings.

"Mom," I said, "don't take out all your money in public, O.K.?"

"Why not?" she asked, holding a wad of American dollars in one hand.

"That's like millions of dollars on the Lao scale."

She looked around. The long row of vendors was nearly deserted. An ancient-looking woman slept on a table, her head resting on a stack of bright fabric.

She shrugged. "It seems safe to me."

"It's not dangerous," I said, "it's just not...never mind."

"I could use a *siesta,*" she said.

We were quiet on the ride home. We read in separate rooms.

"Mom, please remember my English students are Lao communist officials, O.K.?" It was day five of her visit.

"Kathryn, you have told me that ten times."

"I know, but I need you to understand."

"What's there to understand? I understand."

As we approached the dingy gray government office where I taught, I feared for the rapport with my Lao students that I'd built over months. I'd learned the hard way the intricate delicacies of speech in a culture that valued harmony above all, including clear communication. My mother, in contrast, said whatever came to mind.

A few monks were cutting across the parking lot, their orange robes stark against black umbrellas that protected their heads and shoulders from the blazing sun. A gaggle of children cried, *"Falang! Falang!"*

"What are they saying?" my mother asked.

"It means foreigner. Or French person, which covers all non-Lao. Or mango."

I was so accustomed to this call I barely heard it now. But my mother waved, and the children ran away shrieking.

Inside, we stopped in the bathroom. My mother adjusted her lipstick, and I glimpsed myself in the mirror, barely recognizing my wide-eyed face, which was stiff with shame at my own *jai-hon*, as the Lao would say, my hot heart, my impatience.

In the small, windowless classroom, the air-conditioner roared, and several of my eight students in the advanced class were already seated—a rare display of punctuality. All had their daily props: Khingsavan with his dog-eared dictionary and magnifying glass, Nisith in his gray cadre's uniform, Ping with her miniature mouthwash bottle and three sharp pencils. They rose to shake my mother's hand.

"We are happy to meet you, Mahmah," they said, with emphasis on the last syllable.

She didn't seem to notice this sudden familiarity, but it soothed me. Also, I was startled, remembering the limpid, vague handshakes when I'd first arrived, no one meeting my eye, words trailing into whispers.

Nisith fetched a glass of cold water for her. I handed back their tests, asked them to provide correct answers. My mother scanned a copy of the test with eyebrows furrowed.

"Question ten is pretty unclear," she said.

"O.K., who wants to start?" I ignored her.

"On page three," she insisted.

"Ping, why don't you start?"

"You could choose answer A or answer B," my mother said.

"Could you raise your hand please?"

"It's ambiguous," my mother said.

"Am-big-u-ous," Khingsavan said, reaching for his dictionary and magnifying glass, inserting his nose in the front pages of the battered book.

"Mahmah, can you spell, please?"

"Ping, please start," I said.

My mother whispered to Khingsavan, "A-M-B," almost as loudly as Ping answering my question.

She was quiet again until we got to page three, question ten. Her objection pertained to the meaning of the word "lawyer."

"Lawyers do all kinds of things," she said, a cavil concerning my father, not the test. "What about lawyers in Laos?"

"We don't have," said Nisith.

Since I couldn't silence her, I suggested conversation practice for the last fifteen minutes of class. My throat was suddenly sore.

"Is there anything you would like to ask about Laos?" I said to my mother.

Her hands were folded in her lap, and my students seemed riveted. For an instant I saw my mother as they might, a quirky stranger with a face like mine, riling their teacher to unprecedented efforts of feigning calm.

"Is it true," she said, lowering her voice to a conspiratorial tone, "that there's opium grown in the Golden Triangle?"

There was an awkward silence, even the air conditioner seemed to hum more softly. I stood in front of the whiteboard, open pen dangling in mid-air.

"No," Nisith said finally.

I glared at my mother, the look she used to give me when my fingers snuck onto the plate to bulldoze my food toward a fork.

"But I read that," she insisted.

"A long time ago," Nisith said.

"Maybe," Khingsavan said, "we ask questions to Mahmah."

I sat down, considered resting my head on my fore-arms, as the Lao sometimes did at their desks. Some days it was like culling water from a cactus, getting these students to speak, but my mother had tapped the secret root.

"Does Kathryn write to you many times?" Nisith asked, the little smile on his face spreading to others.

"Well, actually..."

After this, only parts of the exchange caught my attention.

"Mahmah, Kathryn marries a Lao man, what do you think?"

"That's fine with me—I told her the only thing she can't do is buy a Windows computer."

No one knew what to make of this.

But the worst was at the very end: "If Kathryn stays another year, you come visit again—yes?"

"I certainly will."

Phet came over after her French class.

"Mahmah!" she shrieked, and wrapped her arms around my mother's waist. My mother's arms lifted upwards as if to reciprocate, then stopped. But Phet did not let go; she wedged her head onto my mother's shoulder, which had contracted upward. "Welcome. I am so happy to meet Kathryn's Mahmah."

I fetched water from the kitchen. In sweltering Laos, this was standard etiquette.

Phet sipped at her glass, but my mother shook her head.

"It's bottled water," I said. "Clean."

Still, she doused it with iodine, pinched her nose to stifle the flavor.

"I'm going to lie down," I said. I stretched out on the floor, beneath the chopping green fan on the ceiling.

I felt calmer in that position, and I noticed how exhausted my mother looked: hair swirled in every direction, her skin too pale. I also noticed how beautiful Phet was, in a long silk skirt and a tailored blouse, and that she spoke near perfect English, her sixth language.

My mother talked to Phet about our visit, about the famous temples, the restaurants with Western food, the monks, the markets, the *tuk-tuk* drivers, and the gaping holes in the road. Phet told my mother about her studies, and I listened, until my mother asked if she preferred Windows to Mac.

"Mother," I snapped. "There are about one hundred computers in the country."

Phet looked at me as if she'd never seen me before, and turned back to my mother. "Computers are good for Laos, I think, all the different kinds."

My mother agreed.

As Phet gathered her bookbag, my mother stepped into her room and returned with the Michigan hat. Phet received it in both hands, her palms and fingers loose, as if it were a sacred relic, as if it were a scarf for prayer.

"Ohhhh." She stroked the shiny threads of the word MICHIGAN. "I love it."

She lowered it carefully onto her head, searched a dark window for a faint reflection of the blue and yellow cap with her traditional, pastel silk clothes. For a moment we three stood together in that reflection, smiling. I looked down, away from my own smug grin.

That's when I saw it: the inch-long millipede dashing toward my mother's room. Without a word I turned to run to the kitchen. I would trap it with the bowl I kept for just that purpose. But there wasn't time; the gray insect breached the doorway. It zigzagged across the bamboo mats, heading for a pile of my mother's laundry. I thought briefly of stomping it but my feet were bare. I grabbed a Mac Addict magazine from the bed and swatted. Finally the millipede's legs ceased their flailing.

I dropped the magazine, sank to the bed, put my head on my knees.

"I'm so sorry," I whispered at the floor.

I listened to the voices in the other room.

"Thank you," Phet was saying. "Thank you for the gift."

"It's nice that someone appreciates," my mother said.

"We have *baci* for Mahmah," Chantala said the next morning, clapping her hands together, "before you go."

Since I'd arrived in Laos, I'd been dying for a *baci,* a ritual that accompanied important passages: birth, death, weddings. It was something that happened on the Buddhist holy days, or after a sickness or a theft, or flanking a journey—as was the case with my mother. The soul could slip away when a person was far from home—and the *baci* was a ceremony to call it back.

The last morning of my mother's visit, I gave Chantala some kip for the food. A few hours later, other women from the neighborhood came over with knives, cutting boards, baskets of vegetables, eggs, papayas, and two squawking chickens.

"It's too much work," I said.

"You go teach," Chantala corralled me out the front door.

After class, I invited my students to the *baci,* not expecting anyone to come on such short notice.

"For Mahmah?" they asked. "We come."

That evening, I walked into the house utterly drained—into the most elegant occasion of my whole life. Five women had purged the neighborhood of silver bowls and glasses and candlesticks, covered a long table with a white cloth and platters of food: a tray of sliced mango, papaya, and kiwi; a mound of baked egg rolls; bowls of sticky rice; papaya salad and steamed fish.

Chantala had gathered my students, as well as some village elders and former monks, to preside over the *baci*: three silver-headed men with coppery skin and

sporadically toothed smiles. On white plastic chairs in
the front yard, they sat with the air of benevolent gang-
sters, of ownership and assurance.

I fetched water for them, still shocked that I was host-
ing this event.

I found my mother in her bedroom, half-dressed and
fretting over her open suitcase. "Mom, people are here so
don't parade around in your underwear."

In my own room I shucked off my sweat-soiled
blouse and buttoned up a fresh one. I layered deodorant
on, avoiding the mirror. I emerged to find my mother
sitting with outstretched legs, feet pointing at the *baci*
centerpiece.

"Mom, you can't sit like that," I said, racing toward
her.

With a glazed, petulant look she folded her legs
Indian-style.

"But that's more comfortable," she said.

"Too bad," I whispered, "it's not just impolite, it's
profane. It would be like someone using a little crucifix
to scratch their butt, or dig in their ear."

On the floor we formed concentric circles around
the elaborate two-foot-tall sculpture of orange flowers,
surrounded by boiled eggs, bowls of rice, ripe papayas,
and containers of holy water. Three-inch white strings
dangled in thick clumps from the blossom stems, in
addition to six or seven long strings, which went to my
mother, me, Phet, Nisith, Khingsavan, and one of the
village elders. We grasped these strings with our palms
pressed together. Chantala and the other women sat
behind us, touching our shoulders. Everyone either held
a string or touched a person who did. Phet's face was
serious beneath the Michigan cap. Chantala grinned

when I turned around. The moment we were all linked, a sudden quiet replaced the steady creek-sound of continuous talk.

The elder chanted in Pali, voice rising and falling, sometimes spinning words rapidly, other times drawing one out over several notes. The singsong, somewhat random rhythm gave it a prayerful sound. Some words were said over and over, invoking the power of repetition, of form, of tradition, interrupted only by the word *Leslie,* my mother's name, with emphasis on the final syllable drawn out, *Les-leeeee, Les-leeeee.* At the sound of the foreign name, everyone smiled.

Towards the end of the *baci,* the elder asked a question and everyone called out in response. People closed their eyes and laughed as the elder hurled drops of holy water onto our faces.

"Lesleeee, Lesleeee," everyone cried.

My mother averted her eyes, but her face was soft and her cheeks were flushed.

For the last part of the *baci*, everyone untied the smaller strings from the centerpiece and moved around the room to tie them on others' wrists. The string held the spirit in, and had to be worn for at least three days— but my students later would wear them for months. The person tying made a wish out loud for the person receiving the string, and secured it with a knot.

"I wish you health and happiness."

"I wish you long life."

"I wish for your dreams to come true."

"I wish you to stay another year," said Khingsavan, my quietest student.

I glimpsed my mother across the noisy room; people surrounded her. I suddenly recognized how far she had come, literally crossing the earth to see me. I felt something like tenderness, as if it had flowed into me through the vein of the string that had linked us all, as if I'd borrowed it from the group.

I exchanged wishes with my students, my neighbors, my friends.

Through the meal and several rounds of toasts, my mother looked tired but content with a traditional *pa-bian*—the prayer scarf my students gave her—draped over one shoulder.

"She's never been to a party this rowdy," I explained to everyone in Lao. "No one is allowed to make her drink rice whiskey or she might fall over."

So Phet and I picked lemons off a tree in the front yard to squeeze and sweeten in water for her. My skin tingled in the balmy air and the fruit felt unbearably real in my hand—as if it were more than an ordinary lemon. I felt a rare awareness, recognizing that some things will happen only once in a lifetime.

It seemed my mother felt it, too, as she strummed the strings on her wrist and sipped lemonade far later into the night than she usually stayed up. I could have tied a string around her wrist, shaped so much like mine, and said to her, "I wish for you to know that I love you." But I didn't. I wouldn't. But even in my failure to love her well, I provided people who could—agents of love, a detoured message that arrived nonetheless.

At the *baci,* I heard Nisith say to my mother, "I wish that you don't forget us, the people of a poor country."

The next morning, these words echoed in my mind as I used my mother's camera to photograph her with Chantala. In the background there was the rice paddy, flat and green, the orange sun, the listing house. My mother clasped her hands in front of her, her forearms bright with strings. A month later, my sister wrote that my mother still wore them, dirty, tattered, around both wrists.

Kathryn Kefauver is completing her Masters of Fine Arts in Creative Writing at the University of San Francisco. Her work has been published in The Christian Science Monitor, San Francisco Examiner, *and the* South Florida Sun-Sentinel. *She lives in San Francisco.*

KIRA SALAK

ॐ ॐ ॐ

Mungo Made Me Do It

She set out alone for Timbuktu on a river journey no
man had ever completed—and certainly no woman.

*I*N THE BEGINNING, ALL MY JOURNEYS FEEL AT BEST
ludicrous, at worst insane. This one is no exception.
The idea is to paddle nearly six hundred miles on the
Niger River in a kayak, alone, from the town of Old Ségou
to Timbuktu. And now, at the very hour I have decided to
leave, a thunderstorm bursts open the skies, sending down
apocalyptic rain, washing away the ground beneath my
feet. It is the rainy season, in Mali, for which there can be
no comparison in the world. Lightning pierces trees, slices
across houses. Thunder wracks the skies and pounds the
earth like mortar fire, and every living thing huddles in
its tenuous shelter, expecting the world to end. Which it
doesn't. At least not this time. So we all give a collective
sigh to the salvation from the passing storm as it rumbles

east, and I survey the river I'm to depart on this morning. Rain or no rain, today is the day for the journey to begin.

"Let's do it," I say, leaving the shelter of an adobe hut. My guide from town, Modibo, points to the north, to further storms. He says he will pray for me. It's the best he can do. To his knowledge, no man has ever completed such a trip, though a few have tried. And certainly no woman has done such a thing. Earlier this morning he took me aside and told me he thinks I'm crazy, which I understood as concern, and so I thanked him. He told me that the people of Old Ségou think I'm crazy, too, and that only uncanny good luck will keep me safe. What he doesn't know is that the worst thing a person can do is to tell me I can't do something, because then I'll want to do it all the more. It may be a failing of mine.

I carry my inflatable kayak through the labyrinthine alleys of Old Ségou, past the huts melting in the rain, past the huddling goats and the smoke of cooking fires, past people peering out at me from dark entranceways. Old Ségou must have looked much the same to Scottish explorer Mungo Park, who left here on the first of his two river journeys 206 years ago to the day. It is no coincidence that I've picked this date, July twenty-second, and this spot to begin my journey. Park is my guarantee of sorts. If he could travel down the Niger, then so can I. Of course, Park also died on the river, but so far I've managed to overlook that.

Thunder again. Hobbled donkeys cower under a new onslaught of rain, ears back, necks craned. Naked children dare one another to touch me, and I make it easy for them, stopping and holding out my arm. They stroke my white skin as if it were velvet, using only the pads of their fingers, then stare at their hands, looking for wet paint. I stop on the banks of the river near a centuries-old kapok tree, under which I imagine Park once took shade, I open my bag, spread out my little red kayak, and start to pump it up. A photographer, who will check in on me from time to time in his motorized boat, feverishly snaps pictures. A couple of women nearby, with colorful cloth wraps called *pagnes* tied tightly about their breasts, gaze at me as if to ask: Who are you, and what do you think you're doing? The Niger, in a surly mood, churns and slaps the shore. I don't pretend to know what I'm doing. Just one thing at a time now: kayak inflated, kayak loaded, paddles fitted together. Modibo watches me.

"I'll pray for you," he reminds me.

I balance my gear and get in. Finally, irrevocably, I paddle away.

Before Mungo Park left on his second expedition, he never admitted that he was scared. It is what fascinates me about his journals—his insistence on maintaining that all was well. Even as he began a journey that he knew from his first experience could only beget tragedy. Hostile peoples, malarial fevers. Hippos and crocodiles. A giant widening of the Niger called Lake Débo to cross, like being set adrift on an island sea. It can boggle the mind, what drives some people to risk their lives for the mute promises of success. It boggles my mind, at least, as I suffer from the same affliction. Already I fear the irrationality of my journey. I fear the very stubbornness that drives me forward.

The Niger erupts in a new storm. Torrential rains. Waves higher than my kayak try to capsize me. But my boat is self-bailing, and I stay afloat. The wind slams the current in reverse, tearing and ripping at the shores, sending spray into my face. I paddle madly, crashing ahead inch by inch, or so it seems, arm muscles smarting.

A popping feeling now and a screech of pain. My right arm lurches from a ripped muscle. But this is no time or place for an injury, so I try to ignore the metronome-like pulses of pain. There is only one direction to go: forward. Always forward.

I often wonder what I seek when I embark on these trips. There is the pat answer I tell the people I don't know—that I'm interested in seeing a place, learning about its people. But then the trip begins, and the hardship comes, and hardship is more honest: It tells me that I'm here because I don't have enough patience yet, or humility, or gratitude. So I've told the world that it can do what it wants with me if only, by the end of the trip, I have learned something. A bargain, then. The journey, my teacher.

The Niger has calmed, returning its beauty to me: a river of smoothest glass, a placidity unbroken by wave or eddy, with islands of lush greenery awaiting me like distant Xanadus. Tiny villages dot the shores, each with its own mud mosque sending a minaret to the heavens. The late afternoon sun settles complacently over the hills to the west. Paddling becomes a sort of meditation now, a gentle trespassing over a river that slumbers.

Mungo Park is credited with being the first Westerner to discover the Niger, in 1796, which helped to make his narrative, *Travels in the Interior Districts of Africa*, a bestseller. But I wonder if the sight of his "majestic Niger" was enough reward for the travails he suffers: the loss of his possessions, the brutal confinement by the Moors, the half-starved wanderings in the desert. Before quinine was used to fight malaria, travel to West Africa was a virtual death sentence for Europeans. Colonial powers used only their most expendable soldiers to oversee operations on the coast. It wasn't uncommon for expeditions to lose half their men to fever and dysentery if the natives didn't get them first. So Park's ambitious plan to cross what is now Senegal into Mali, then head down the Niger River to Timbuktu, hasn't a modern-day equivalent. It was beyond gutsy—it was borderline suicidal.

Park wrote that he traveled at the rate of six or seven miles an hour, but I travel at barely one mile an hour, the river preferring—as I do—to loiter in the sun. I eat turkey jerky and wrap my injured arm, part of which has swelled to the size of a lemon. The Somono fishermen, casting their nets, puzzle over me as I float by.

"Ça va, madame?" they yell. How's it going?

Each fisherman brings along a young son to do the paddling. Perched in the back of the pointed canoes, the boys gape at me, transfixed. They have never seen such a thing. A white woman. Alone. In a red, inflatable boat. Using a two-sided paddle. I'm an even greater novelty because Malian women don't paddle. It is a man's job. So there is no good explanation for me, and the people want to understand. They gather on the shore in front of their villages to watch me pass, the kids screaming and jumping in excitement, the men yelling questions in Bambara, which by now I know to mean, "Where did you come from? Where is your husband?" And, of course they always ask: "Where are you going?"

"Timbuktu!" I call out to the last question. It sounds preposterous to them, because everyone knows that Timbuktu is weeks away and requires paddling across Lake Débo and through rapids and storms. And I am a woman, after all, which makes everything worse.

They shake their heads in disbelief. We wave goodbye, and the whole ritual begins again at the next village.

I might be the pope, or someone close. But in between is the peace and silence of the wide river, the sun on me, a breeze licking my toes when I lie back and rest, the current as negligible as a faint breath.

Timbuktu lies somewhere to the northeast, as distant and unimaginable to me as it must have been to Park, who first read about the city in *Geographical Historie of Africa*. Written in 1526 by a Spanish Moor named Leo Africanus, the book described Timbuktu as a veritable El Dorado. The city was indeed a bastion of wealth, the pearl of West Africa's great Songhai Empire, home to a university, one of Africa's largest and grandest mosques, and a population that may have reached fifty thousand. Timbuktu throve off its location as a crossroads of commerce between the great Saharan caravan routes and the Niger River Basin. It was there that men traded Saharan salt for the gold, ivory, and slaves that came from the south. The Arabs gave the Niger the name Neel el Abeed, "River of Slaves." Slavery still exists here, tacitly, though some anthropologists and Malian officials claim the practice was abolished when France colonized Mali in the late 1800s. But I carry two gold coins from home, and if I ever get to Timbuktu, I intend to find out the truth, and then, if possible, free someone with them.

Unbeknownst to Europeans of Park's era, Timbuktu's exalted stature ended in 1591, when a Moroccan army crossed the Sahara with the most sophisticated weaponry of the time—muskets—and sacked the golden city. The raid marked the beginning of a decline from which Timbuktu never recovered. Still, ill-informed Europeans embarked, one after another, for an African El Dorado that no longer existed. There were only two ways to get there: you could risk enslavement or death by trying to cross the Sahara from the north, or brave the malarial jungles of West Africa and then travel up the Niger. Park's first journey ushered in the frantic "Timbuctoo rush" of the early 1800s. The River of Slaves became a highway into a lethal region that was known as the White Man's Grave.

In the middle of the night, I wake with a start: the bear bell on my kayak is ringing—someone has discovered my boat. From inside my tent I hear two men whispering; I can see the beam from their flashlight flickering anxiously about the dark shore. I had hoped that the bell would prove an unnecessary—if not paranoid—precaution, but here we are: the middle of the night, two strange men going through my things, and only a can of Mace and some martial-arts training between me and potential theft and/or bodily harm. But the men don't know that I'm alone. And they don't know that I'm a woman. So I get up, arm myself with a section of a paddle, and burst out of my tent, yelling "Hey!" in a deep voice.

It works. They flee in their canoe. Sighing in relief, I watch in faint moonlight as they disappear around a bend.

But it's not over yet. About ten minutes later I hear their voices again. And now I see their flashlight beam coming toward me across the savanna. I run to take down my tent and stuff my gear into the kayak. In a matter of minutes, I shove off. I stroke to the middle of the river, then stop paddling. The only sound is the lapping of the quicksilver waters against my boat. No sight of land, no suggestion of people. Just darkness. I'm scared to make a sound. All I can do is float along to wherever the river wants to take me

I decide not to camp for a while. After a day of paddling, I approach the village of Siraninkoro, inhabited by
traditional herders called the Fulani. A few women, large
washtubs balanced on their heads, see me and run to alert
the rest of the community. Soon everyone who can walk,
run, or crawl is awaiting me onshore. I use Park's 200-
year-old narratives as my guide and do exactly what he
did when he arrived in a new village: I find the chief and
give him a generous gift. I sit beside him on his mat and
ask if I can spend the night, then accept his calabash full
of foaming cow's milk straight from the udder. Things
haven't changed much in 200 years.

The women surround me. They wear large gold disks
in their earlobes, and their hair is styled into ornate corn-
rows. Their skin is light, a dark blue tattoo accentuat-
ing the area around their mouths. Here, in this remote
village, women wrap brightly patterned *pagnes* around
their waists to cover their legs and buttocks—areas
Malians consider sexual—and leave their breasts bare
with wonderful nonchalance.

They want to know where my husband is and how
many babies I have back home. I try to explain through
signs and broken Bambara why I have neither, but it takes
some time. We're still discussing it as we eat dinner. I'm
afraid we might be discussing it all night, but at last the
women declare that it's bedtime. We all lie down side by
side on foam mattresses spread outside the huts. Mosquito
nets stretched overhead blur the stars. Fleas hop on my
skin; chickens jump on us. I fall asleep to the sound of the
old folks snoring, goats nibbling at our feet.

Always, at some point in these trips, I suddenly wake
up to the reality of what I'm doing. I discover, quite

unexpectedly, that I am, say, alone in a little red boat en route to Timbuktu. Somehow this comes as news to me, and I'm forced to pull over and ponder the implications. Timbuktu is so far to the northeast that it hides on another section of my map. My god, I think, but always when it's too late. As is the case now: At least fifty naked children are sprinting over a hill and descending upon my boat. *"Toubabou! Donnez-moi cadeau!"* they scream. Hey, whitey! Give me a gift!

Their excitement turns chaotic. Hands pull and grab at the things in my kayak. I take out a bag of dried pineapple slices and throw them in the air, and the mass of bodies flies toward the treats, kids fighting and tearing at one another. I have never seen anything like it, and I paddle away as if for my life.

I wonder when Mungo Park's moment of realization struck. When he was captured by the Moors and a woman threw urine in his face? When he was so destitute that he was forced to sell locks of his hair as good-luck charms? Or perhaps it didn't come until the second journey, when he found himself in a rotting boat, forty of his forty-four men dead from disease, Park himself afflicted with dysentery. "Though I were myself half-dead," he wrote in one of his final letters, "I would still persevere; and if I could not succeed in the object of my journey, I would at least die on the Niger." Why didn't he turn back? What was wrong with the man?

But I'm beginning to understand Park. Once the journey starts, there's no turning back. The journey kidnaps you, drugs you with images of its end, reached at long last. You picture yourself arriving on that fabled shore. You see everything you promised yourself. For Park, it might have been streets of gold, cool oasis pools,

maidens cooing in his ear. For me, it is much simpler:
French fries and air conditioning.

And now another storm is coming, a strong wind
blowing directly against me. Dark clouds boom and
rattle while great Saharan winds churn up the red clay
and paint blood trails across the sky. I rush toward shore.
The winds get worse, the river sloshing with three-foot-
high whitecaps. As I lean forward to secure my bags,
a huge wave broadsides my boat, flipping it. I fall out
and swim to the surface to see my kayak bottom up and
speeding away. I dive for it and grab its tail, turn it over,
and retrieve my paddle, only to see my little backpack—
the one with my passport, money, journal—starting to
sink nearby.

It is as if my worst fears are being realized, one after
the next. But by treading water and holding onto the
kayak, I'm able to retrieve the backpack. Pulling myself
into the boat, I fumble to get oriented in the waves, then
paddle toward shore with all my strength. Thunder bel-
lows, lightning flashes. I make it to the bank, rain shoot-
ing from the sky with such force that the drops sting my
skin. I huddle, shaking from adrenaline, and take a tally
of what I have lost: two water bottles and some bags of
dried fruit, but, mercifully, nothing else. The Niger has
won my submission.

I reach the town of Mopti, everything soaked from my
kayak wipeout, and not quite recovered from it myself.
I'm wasted. I meet a local man named Assou, a friend of
the Peace Corps folks in town. When I tell him what my
trip has been like so far, he says I obviously didn't know
about the genies that inhabit the Niger—every Malian
knows about them—which explains why I've been hav-

ing problems. He says it's essential that I enlist these spirits in my cause of reaching Timbuktu, or who knows what tragedies might befall me. At his urging, we head inland to the Bandiagara escarpment to see Yatanu, a Dogon sorceress.

We reach the village of Nini, a collection of mud-brick dwellings and thatched granaries high on a rocky plateau. Dogon women crouch in beehive-shaped menstruation huts in order to protect the village from the devilry of their periods. Assou instructs me to follow the path he takes so as to avoid stepping on taboo ground. Dogon boys gape at me as we pass, their navels protruding from distended bellies like stubby appendages.

We climb the slope to the huts perched above, searching for Yatanu. Assou has never met this woman, but he's heard about her: She's at least seventy years old and is one of the Dogon's most powerful and feared sorceresses. It's hard to get a consultation with her because she doesn't like most people, but I've brought along a village officer to help the cause. Yatanu is unique among her fellow witches. When she was ten, her parents, sorcerers themselves, cut open her left arm and put a scarab beetle into the biceps, then sewed the skin back up. The beetle died, but presumably its spirit remains. Yatanu converses with it to obtain knowledge about people's lives.

Yatanu appears before us: a toothless and wizened woman, breasts lying flat against her chest, a scrappy indigo *pagne* tied around her bony waist. She stands in the shadow of her hut and stares at me. Assou tells her that I'm here to ask for a consultation—will she grant me one?

She steps forward into the sunlight, sits on her haunches, and studies me. Smiling nervously, I look into her eyes, clouded with cataracts. She says something in Dogon to the village officer, who then translates to Assou, who translates to me: "She likes you."

Sighs of relief all around. I give her a wad of money and ask my question: "Will I get to Timbuktu?"

She puckers her lips and nods as the question is translated. She places her left arm tightly against her chest and speaks to the muscle where the beetle spirit supposedly lives. All at once, the muscle leaps up; a large object seems to strain and lurch beneath the skin. I've never seen such a thing, nor has Assou. Our mouths drop open.

Yatanu reports her findings: "You'll get to Timbuktu."

Back on the Niger, the days fill with the slow progression of one village after the next, one grove of palm trees after another to break up the monotony of sand and shore. I stay with different groups: the Fulani, the Somono, the Bozo.

All of it takes me to Lake Débo, finally, and the crossing I've been dreading, just as Park dreaded it two centuries before. I see it as the most treacherous part of the journey, where all sight of land will be lost for an entire day. If a storm should catch me, overturn and separate me from my boat, I could drown.

I start the crossing in the early morning, hoping to beat the wind and storms that usually arrive at midday. It's not long before the horizon shows only a meeting of sky and water, the waves sizable and unruly. But perhaps there is something to be said for Yatanu's assistance, because there is no hint of a rising storm.

A river steamer passes me, so loaded with people and baggage that water nearly spills over its gunwales. The ship overshadows me like a giant, her crew cheering and howling, the passengers craning to get a look at me in my tiny boat as I paddle beside their swift vessel. I follow the distant white buoys that guide the boats across, reaching one and then the next, hoping to catch sight of land. The heat becomes intense; my thermometer reads 106 degrees. But I don't stop.

Finally, after seven hours, I'm relieved to see land and the broad channel of the Niger ahead. Hippos peer at me from the shallows, blowing air from their nostrils. Lake Débo barely stirs behind me.

The days become frustrating. I constantly fight the river, its curves and twists seem to take me nowhere. I call it "uphill paddling," the battle against winds that kick up waves and batter me against the high clay banks. But at least my body cooperates; muscles appear on my arms, compensating for my injury.

After another difficult day, I approach a prosperous-looking village to buy a meal and lodging. Stopping at villages is always a crapshoot. What tribe will I get? Will they have food to sell me? Will they like me?

I'm greeted by the usual crowd. Kids swarm around, yelling excitedly. They tell me this village is called Berakousi and that it sits at the spot where the Koula River enters the Niger. I ask what people they are and am told they're Bozo. Fishermen.

As I search for the chief, it quickly becomes evident that I'm not wanted here. I'm particularly troubled by some young men, one sporting a black t-shirt with Osama bin Laden's face printed on it like a rock star's. They harass me in broken French. What man allowed me to travel here by myself? Would I like to have sex with them? I ignore them, but I'm nearly knocked off my feet by the crowd of pushy onlookers.

The chief is in the fields, so I sit on a wicker chair to wait for him, refusing numerous requests from women who want me to breastfeed their babies. I wait and wait. The sun is almost gone. It's too late to go elsewhere, the river too choppy and mercurial along this stretch to make night paddling safe. The villagers are still milling about me when the chief appears. He surveys me, frowning. I give him a wad of money as *cadeau,* explain as best I can that I'd like to buy a meal and sleep on a patch of ground nearby. He slowly nods. The young men sit around me, demanding money, too. One tells me that he wants the flashlight that I've just removed from my pack. I seem to be the subject of a heated conversation, of which I can understand only the word *toubabou*—whitey.

One of the chief's four wives announces that she has food for me. I thank her and give her some money, and she drops a bowl in front of me. Inside is a rotting fish head, blooms of fungus growing on its skin.

"*Mangez,*" the woman says. She puts her fingers to her lips.

And I'm so hungry and fatigued that I do: I crack open the mottled skin and pull out bits of white meat. Everyone laughs heartily, and see that this is a joke, feeding me the dog's dinner. When I finish, I notice that Osama and company have requisitioned one of my pens. I decide to let it go. One man sits close to me, his face inches from mine, and speaks threateningly. The chief—my usual benefactor elsewhere—does nothing. When the man wraps his hand about my wrist, I wrench my arm away, holding up a fist.

"Don't touch me," I say.

The villagers laugh. Scolding myself for losing my temper, I get up, put on my backpack, and head to the river. Can I still get out of here tonight? But it's darkness all around, and the Niger churns madly at its confluence with the Koula. I'm stuck.

I sit for hours on the dark shore, slapping mosquitoes, hoping the villagers will get bored and go back to their huts. It feels like a true Mungo Park moment: "I felt myself as if left lonely and friendless amidst the wilds of Africa," he wrote in one of his last letters. When I finally return, the village has cleared out. One of the chief's wives smiles in pity and brings out a foam mattress for me to sleep on. I lie down and wrap myself in my tent's rain fly. It is one of those nights that I know I must simply get through, that promises no sleep.

Each day the land along the shore seems to get drier. Trees have all but vanished, and only scant brush dots the horizon. The people are mostly Songhai now, living in mud-brick homes with ornate windows and doorways and praying in sharp-angled and refined mosques.

I spend a night in a village and wake up with the rooster calls, day only a gray suggestion to the east. My stomach lurches; only two days to my goal, and now this. Some kind of dysentery, though I can't say which— amoebic, bacillary? I'm hoping it's the latter, which is easier to cure. A group of village folk have risen, and they watch me, *tsk*-ing. Poor, sick white woman. The children watch, silent and uncomprehending, as I take down my tent and load up my kayak, I will get to Timbuktu even if I have to crawl.

Back on the river, I alternate between vomiting and paddling; my thermometer already registers 110 degrees. The sun burns in a cloudless sky, and there is no hint of a breeze. The luckier villages have a single scraggly tree to provide shade. I pass village after village, impressed by the tenacity of the Niger as it cuts through the sands, a gloriously stubborn and incongruous river.

I wonder what Park felt on this stretch. His guide, Amadi Fatouma, the one survivor of the expedition, claimed that Park and his men had to shoot their way through these waters. Which might explain why, at every turn, entire villages gather to yell at me. Gone are the waves of greeting that I experienced at the beginning of my trip. Inexplicably, the entire tone of this country has changed.

One more day, I can get to Timbuktu by night, but it's quite a distance on a river so sluggish, with my body so weak.

I start at first light. I have no food left, so I don't eat. Great dunes meet the river on either side, adobe villages half-buried beneath them. I am now in the land of the Tuareg and the Moors. They crouch close to the water and stare at me from their indigo and black wrappings, none returning my waves. Park admitted fearing the Moors most, plagued by nightmares of his captivity among them.

I share Park's trepidation, especially when an island splits the Niger, creating a narrow channel on either side. People can reach me more easily; there is less opportunity for escape. And this is the most populated stretch of the river to date. All I can do is paddle hard, the villagers screaming and scolding me as I pass, some swimming after me. I have no way of knowing what their intentions are, so I follow my new guideline: Don't get out of the boat—for *anything*.

When I stop to drink some water, a group of men leap

into their canoes and come after me to demand money. With a can of Mace in my lap, I manage to out-paddle them but more canoes follow their example. It's like a macabre game of tag, and while I can usually see them coming and get a lead, one man is able to reach me and hit my kayak with the bow of his canoe. I know one of us will have to give up, so I pace my strokes as if the pursuit were a long-distance race, and he soon falls behind.

It is more of the same at the next village, and at the next one after that, so that the mere sight of canoes onshore gives me fright. No time to drink water now—to stop is to give them an incentive to come after me. Head aching, I round a bend to see the river widen; I don't see any villages. I stop paddling and float in the middle of the river, nauseous and faint. I squint at the Niger trailing off into distant heat waves, the sands trying to swallow it.

"This river will never end," I say over and over. Still, I must be close. I begin to paddle like a person possessed. The sun falls, burning dark orange in the west, and I see a distant square concrete building. Hardly a tower of gold, hardly an El Dorado, but I'll take it. I paddle straight toward it, ignoring the pains in my body, my raging headache. Timbuktu! Timbuktu! Some Bozo fishermen are watching me. They don't ask for money or *cadeaux*, yelling instead, *"Ça va, madame?"* One man stands and raises his hands in a cheer, urging me on.

I round a sharp curve and approach Timbuktu's port of Korioumé. I pull up beside a great white steamer named, appropriately, the *Tombouctou*. All at once, I understand that there's no more paddling to be done. I've made it. I can stop now. The familiar throng gathers in the darkness. Slowly I haul my kayak from the river.

People ask where I came from, and I tell them Old

Ségou. They can't seem to believe it. I unload my things
to the clamor of their questions, but even speaking seems
to pain me. Such a long time getting here—three weeks
on the river. And was it worth it? Or is it blasphemy to
ask that now? I can barely walk; I have a high fever. I
haven't eaten anything for more than a day. I would give
a great deal right now for silence. For stillness.

We will never know if Mungo Park reached
Timbuktu. According to his guide, he was repelled
by the locals. In 1827 another Scottish explorer, Hugh
Clapperton, heard a tale that Park had made it to the
golden city and was received warmly. Regardless, Park
ended up dying on the Niger as he had prophesied,
getting as far as Bussa, near modern-day New Bussa,
Nigeria, before he disappeared.

Timbuktu: the world's greatest anticlimax. Hard to
believe that this slapdash latticework of garbage-strewn
streets and crumbling dwellings was once the height
of worldly sophistication. The pearl of the desert, the
African El Dorado is nothing now but a haggard out-
post in a plain of scrub brush and sand.

I walk the dusty streets. It is 115 degrees and barely
noon. I bow under the weight of the sun, and every ac-
tion feels ponderous. I pass donkeys scavenging in rubbish heaps and dodge streams of fetid wastewater trailing
down alleyways. I visit the former homes of Scottish
explorer Gordon Laing and the Frenchman René Caillié,
both of whom risked their lives to get here. They must
have been just as disappointed. Caillié, the first European
to reach Timbuktu, in 1828, and return alive to report on
it, wrote that the city and its landscape "present the most
monotonous and barren scene I have ever beheld."

Tourists, mostly flown in on package tours, wilt in the sun as they trudge through the streets in search of whatever it is that Timbuktu had promised them. I imagine they, too, are disappointed, though this end of the world knows enough to sell them air-conditioned rooms and faux Tuareg wear at inflated prices. I see that Timbuktu is better left to name and fancy. It is not meant to be found.

History pervades the place, with slavery one of its most secretive and enduring institutions. It occurs among the Bella, a people who are the traditional slaves of the Tuareg. If you mention the idea of slavery in Mali to some experts, though, they say that Mali's constitution prohibits it. They insist that the Bella are now paid workers with civil rights, including freedom of movement. In short, they're not slaves anymore.

Others in Timbuktu tell a completely different story: that the Bella are slaves in fact, if not by law. They are still a form of property that the Tuareg refuse to give up; Bella are often raped or beaten by their masters and are forced to turn over any money they earn. So is it slavery, then, or is it not?

Before my trip, I was perplexed by a recent human rights bulletin posted on the Web site of the U.S. State Department. It included reports of de facto slavery in Mali. Why had an entire group of people remained the equivalent of slaves in a country that claims slavery no longer exists? Was there no recourse for them? I mulled over the feasibility of actually freeing someone—in itself a controversial act. Some people familiar with the region suggested that I would only be duped by those involved in the negotiations. Others argued that, at least on a psychological and economic level, the Bella would remain hopelessly tied to their Tuareg masters, so that anyone I freed would be left without a means to make a living at all.

But suppose I really could free someone? Just suppose. And then, what if I gave that person enough money to start a business and become self-sufficient? Wouldn't it be preferable to a dehumanizing, often brutal life of servitude? After much soul-searching, I finally concluded that it was worth a try.

So I pay Assou's travel expenses to come up from Mopti and help me with the negotiations, since he grew up in Timbuktu and knows the right people. He won't accept any payment for his assistance: He wants to free someone as badly as I do. Assou is fond of saying that "what you do for others, you do for yourself." Back in Mopti, he told me a secret—though he's Songhai by birth, he was breastfed by his mother's Bella friend. "The Bella are in my blood," he said. "I am one of them." It is a daring admission for him to align himself with this outcast group: Some Malians use the word "Bella" as an insult.

And now a breakthrough: Assou has found a Tuareg master, Iba Zengi (not his real name, we're told), who is willing to sell a Bella or two, but everything must be done in secret, because slavery doesn't officially exist in Mali. Assou will pass on my money and pretend to be the one in charge of the negotiations, or none of this can happen. He has told Zengi that he's freeing the women as part of his college research, and that I'm coming along to help him take notes. Assou has not let on that I'm a writer.

Assou and I arrive at the Bella village, where we sit in the midst of small thatched huts. The people gather around—old and young, children half-clothed, women cradling infants. Assou admits he doesn't know which Bella Zengi will choose to sell. I study each of them and try to imagine what it is like to be them.

There is a brief wait. Zengi lives elsewhere, among his own people; the Bella in this village report each day to him and his family for their work duties. A car arrives, and Zengi steps out. He is cloaked in indigo wrappings, the Tuareg man's traditional desert clothing. I can see only his eyes as he daintily holds the bluish material over his nose and mouth, as if afraid of catching a cold. He sits on a mat before "his Bella," as he calls them. He strokes and pats an older man as one might a favorite pet.

I have Assou ask if these are his slaves.

"Slavery is illegal in Mali," he says calmly.

"But they are 'your Bella.' Are they paid monthly wages?"

He answers that he gives them a place to live, animals to raise, the clothes on their back. When one of them gets married, he provided animals for the bride price. This, I'm to understand, is their "pay." I turn to a middle-aged woman sitting nearby. "If she wanted to leave and not come back, could she?"

As Assou translates my question, Zengi's veil falls for a moment, revealing a trace of a smirk. "Either I kill her, or she kills me," he says. That is to say, Over my dead body.

I ask Assou to find out who is to be freed and whether my money is sufficient for the purchase of one or two people. They talk for a while. Zengi will free two women, household helpers whom he can spare, since he has three others and enough Bella babies to fill future vacancies. Their price is to be considered a bargain and a sign of Zengi's beneficence: the equivalent of $260, more than the average Malian household income for one year.

He motions to a couple of young women standing at the edge of the crowd. They approach with apprehension. "These are the women," Zengi says. He orders them to take a seat on the mat before me. One holds a sickly-looking baby girl.

I tell Assou, "Ask him if he can include the baby with her mother.

A brief discussion ensues. "He won't," Assou says.

"Then ask him how much the baby is." I can't believe such a sentence has come out of my mouth. Assou asks, but Zengi is shaking his head. Assou leans closer to me. "He's already giving us a favor by selling two people. It's best, when a person gives you a favor, not to ask for more."

Which I take to be a warning. I stare at the little girl and wonder what will become of her, but there is nothing to be done. While I know that her mother can still live in this village and will not be physically separated from her child, the girl will remain bound to a life of servitude for Zengi's family as soon as she is old enough to work. A numbness comes over me. Better not to feel anything. I stand and tell Assou that I'd like to get this over with. Pay Zengi his money. Buy these people already.

Zengi follows us behind a hut—he doesn't want "his Bella" to see him receiving money for their family members. Assou hands him the bundle of bills. The man pockets it and leads me back to the crowd. With a regal wave of his hand, he directs the two women toward Assou and me.

"Go with them," he says. "You belong to them now." The shocked looks on their faces are hardly what I expected. Hell, I don't know what I expected, but definitely not this. The two women obediently follow us as we walk away from the throng. I have no idea what to say to them and ask Assou to tell them that I did this—bought them—so that they'd be free, earn wages, live without having to bow down to anyone.

The women just stand in front of me. Fadimata, who has the sickly baby, is smiling, but the other, Akina, looks like someone has just smacked her in the face. I hand them each a gold coin, worth about $120 apiece. As well as some Malian money. I have Assou tell them that this money is meant to help them start a business, get a footing somehow.

The women nod. Fadimata thanks me, but Akina looks down, silent. I don't understand what's wrong, so I ask if we can go somewhere to be alone. We head into a hut and sit on the sandy floor. The women sneak glances at me; Fadimata holds her—Zengi's—baby.

"So will you start a business now?" I have Assou ask them. Fadimata says she'll buy some millet or rice and try to sell it in the market. Though she'll probably stick around this village to be with her baby, she'll be self-sufficient. Any money she makes from produce that she sells in the market will be hers.

"Did you like working for Zengi?" I ask.

"No," she says immediately. "I want to live my own life and have my own business."

"What do you think about your baby belonging to Zengi?"

"I have no choice." She caresses her daughter's head.

When I ask Akina if she like working for Zengi's family, she shakes her head, refusing to look at me.

"Did they hurt you?" I ask.

Softly, she says that they beat her. Fadimata nods in agreement: they beat her, too.

I really don't know how to ask the next question, but I feel I must. Did the Tuareg men ever take them...rape them?

The women are silent.

I have Assou tell them that they're safe, that I'm their friend.

"It didn't happen to me," Fadimata says. "But it happened to my friend. She told me."

Akina nods in agreement, but she says nothing. I sense that the women are withholding something. Akina looks scared; she fingers her dress, frowning.

I have Assou ask her if she's O.K., and she looks into my eyes for the first time. "I feel shame," she says, "about what happened."

And it comes out that she's ashamed that she was sold like some animal. She's ashamed to be sitting in front of me.

"No," I say. "Tell her not to." I reach over and take her hand. She stares at me; we've got tears in our eyes. I keep squeezing her hand. "Tell her not to feel ashamed."

Assou tells her, and her whole countenance relaxes. When I ask her to tell me how the Tuareg have hurt her, she stands and her hands come up and down with an imaginary stick, as if trying to drive it through someone's body. Her expression is one of pure rage, pure hatred. Both women tell me that they were beaten daily, for no reason.

I ask them what guarantee there is—if any—that Zengi won't reclaim them the minute I leave.

"No, he can't," Fadimata says. Akina nods in agreement. "We have his promise. When he told us to go with you, that is a guarantee that means 'You're free.'"

I can only hope they're right. In a society that refuses

to acknowledge its slavery, there can be no official papers drawn up, no receipts. If Zengi is honorable, upholds his part of the bargain—as the women assure me he will—then they have nothing to worry about. And the fact that they are already planning their futures, telling me about the millet they will buy, is enough to reassure me. For now. At any rate, perhaps they won't be beaten or humiliated anymore.

When I get up to leave, I shake their hands as they tell me that God will bless me, will take care of me for what I've done. I'm glad to see their happy expressions, though I don't know what to say. Maybe Fadimata can buy her baby from Zengi if she makes enough money? I don't have words.

I go with Assou to the Djinguereber mosque. I want to see the door that, according to local legend, can end the world if opened. This mosque, Mali's oldest, was built by the great Songhai king Mansa Musa in the fourteenth century. It has survived virtually intact and now sits on the edge of town, its spiked minarets reaching skyward, garbage swirling about its walls.

We have the mosque to ourselves; the caretaker is busy with tourists on the roof. Inside it is dim and cool. Faint light trails down from skylights, exposing the clouds of dust kicked up by our feet. It is hugely empty here, where the mud-brick walls reveal the pressing of ancient hands.

The special door is in a wall along the far side of the mosque, hidden behind a simple thatched mat. Assou tells me that no one is shown the door anymore. He doesn't know why. Perhaps it's too dangerous. .

"I want to see what it looks like," I say.

Assou laughs nervously. "I never met someone as curious as you."

"I'm serious."

"Then go look." But he is scared.

I creep forward and gently pull back the mat. And here it is: the door that can end the world. It is made of wood, the middle part rotting away. It looks unremarkable, like a piece of faded driftwood. Suddenly, impulsively, I stick out a hand and touch it.

The world doesn't quake. The waters don't part. The earth continues on its axis, churning out immutable time.

"The world hasn't ended," I declare, my voice echoing off the far walls.

"You must open it," Assou says, laughing.

And I could open it, standing here as I am, the caretaker blithely unaware of the roof. For an insolent moment I pretend I hold the world in my hands. I think of Zengi and the slave women. I think of the Bozo fisherman cheering me on to Timbuktu. It is such a kind yet cruel world. Such a vulnerable world. I'm astounded by it all.

Kira Salak is a contributing editor to National Geographic Adventure *and is the author of* Four Corners: Into the Heart of New Guinea *and* The Cruelest Journey: Six Hundred Miles to Timbuktu.

ℛ ℛ ℛ

The Making of My Maman

Who *was* this chic, seventy-something woman
whom the author once called "Mom"?

*I*T STARTED, AS THESE THINGS DO, WITHOUT A LOT OF
hoopla. It was my mother and I arriving at the Place
de la Concorde during her first-ever trip to Paris. There,
suddenly, she flung her arms out wide and squealed something that caused every Parisian within earshot to turn.
"I'm back!" she announced to the startled throng. Well,
it was at that moment I became convinced: In a previous life my mom had lost her head to the guillotine that
once stood in that very spot. Now, she has lost her head
in a different fashion. Or maybe it's her heart. At seventy-
something, this mother of five, grandmother to seven, and
lifelong Francophile is cashing in her fantasy and becoming a French *madame*.

Who knew she had it in her, this utter oneness with a

45

buttered baguette for breakfast (it used to be plain toast), this bliss while browsing Monoprix, this absolutely transcendent expression she gets when she says to the pear man at the market in something that's actually French, "*Deux belles poires, s'il vous plait, monsieur*." My mom. Now she is my *maman*.

She has learned to tie a scarf, become a connoisseur of lemon tarts, and to see her charming them in the stalls of Saturday's *marché aux puces* at the Porte de Vanves is to see my mom—excuse me, my *maman*—inhabiting a character who must have been there all along, I suppose. Maybe it just was hidden within the harried housewife of classic California suburbia, the French-themed person that lurked beneath the surface of the well-to-do, stay-at-home mom possessed of passions, apparently, far beyond the obvious: beautifully prepared meals and a house that, thanks to her own mastery of a mop and certain vavavoom with a vacuum, tilted toward the immaculate.

I don't know, maybe there were hints. How her garden behind our modest wood-shingled house had to have precisely pruned rows of shapely, pointy things, gravel paths and a fountain—a formal style I later would learn channeled Versailles. How she said "lingerie" unlike anyone else's mom, or even store clerks or TV—pronouncing it the authentic French way (*lahn-je-ree*) even though she never had been to France, much less learned a word of French or even met an actual French person. These were things, she said, she "just felt." And it is not like translated French books and romantic French films fed her imagination. From the day she met my Army officer-turned-stockbroker dad on a blind date, married him two weeks later and gave birth to babies one, two, three, four, and, after a brief timeout, five, her life was an all-consuming whirl of wifedom, children, and housework. Even if she *had* had the slightest second to herself to study a foreign language or culture, she would have used it first to collapse, exhausted.

"Endless drudgery," she called it all. But we knew underneath the sometime whining she loved it (didn't she?). Home and family, after all, were her pride of accomplishment.

So today when my *maman*, who keeps a tiny, pink apartment in Paris's chi-chi 16th *arrondissement*, doesn't just say, but *wears* sexy French lingerie, I wonder how she was born one person—my mom—only to become another: this mom-object of such major admiration (from me) that I would be beyond thrilled if I could be even a tenth as fabulous as she. How can becoming a French *madame* do that?

Well, anyway, this is what happened. First there was the espadrilles and boat-neck, striped t-shirt thing. Maybe it was how Jackie Kennedy always was photographed in St. Tropez wearing the fetching, oh-so-French summer outfit (with white jeans), but my mom (who *loved* Jackie Kennedy, didn't we all?) wore espadrilles coming and boat-neck, striped t-shirts going, even if it was only to the grocery store. Then there was the *coq au vin*. Maybe it was how Julia Child on TV cooking class would reminisce of her days at the Cordon Bleu while slapping around her chicken breasts, but my mom (who *loved* Julia Child, didn't we all?) started revising our meals. *Coq au vin, remoulade, vichyssoise, tapenade*: not overnight but slowly, as surely as the Tour Eiffel lights the Paris night with romance, even magic, family dinners required a French accent to describe.

By the time she was in her fifties she finally, *finally* put down the Hoover long enough to take her first trip to

France, it was pretty much over. My mom was quite far gone as my *maman*.

She could claim with pride a small, remaining shred of dignity (*trés* small) after being worked over for years by the terrifying Mme. Bliss, the French language teacher who was none too impressed with my mom's...well, let's just say *issues* with the *imparfait* (for one). She now was routinely going by Jacqueline, her French given name, instead of Gadgie, her father's nonsensical childhood nickname for her—which my mom would use, but never my *maman*. She had our foyer, sunroom, and bathroom floors all rehabbed in black and white tile (*see,* Malmaison), named our wire-haired fox terrier Pierre, and never, *ever*, even if she were flat out postal with hunger, eat so much as a bite between meals. Of course, a French *madame* is like that: emerging from the boulangerie she might bite off the butt end of her baguette before lunch or dinner to avoid a faint, but dive into a sack of Cheetos? *Horreur!* I would learn things like that later, of course, after my mom was well into her *maman*inization.

So after her first trip to Paris and the *I've lived before, but I was French!* incident at the Place de la Concorde, my mom could not get enough of it. Like she was picking up the misplaced bits of a soul that long ago had shattered and was scattered by the winds of time; like she was ecstatically sticking each one back in place until her essence again was shining, happy, whole. She did a trip of French cathedrals, another of museums, a third of spas—Vittel to Evian. There was the chateaux tour, the art trek, the ancient villages drive-by event. If she didn't pray to the Virgin at Lourdes (she did), she was buying a bikini in Biarritz that was oh-so-Brigitte Bardot. If she wasn't getting teary at the beaches of Normandy (she was), she was flipping over the faience of Quimper, lost in downtown Dijon, or found to have friends in Provence.

Over the years each trip would leave my mom a little more *maman*-like. Her hair, for instance. My mom's graying brunette bob that in the youth-obsessed U.S. was dyed (to its eternal shame) a shade not found in nature became in my *maman* a glossy bob of silvery pride, its *au natural* hue (as encouraged by her Paris hair people), a halo of honor for her ageless grace. Her shoes went down a heel height—the better to speedwalk Paris cobblestones—her handbags up in quality, and her closet...why, if my mom were to get a load of her closet, practically bare but for a few—a very few—exquisitely tailored things, she would wail *I have nothing to wear!* But not my *maman*. *She* finds her dribs and drabs of outfit take her from day to hot date with my dad (I don't want to know about it) in something that before her Frenchification my mom tried for for years sans success: total chic.

Weird, no? Or as my *maman* would say, *non?*

And it's not like my mom's transformation is limited to such frippery as style. No, the more and more my *maman* emerged after mastering the many mom-challenges of life in France—the art of just saying yes! to rich French pastries daily without packing on pounds, say, or the science of shampooing, leg shaving, et al. with a shower nozzle that has an agenda of its own—the more I was convinced: I am the daughter of a *madame*! A *madame* almost as authentic as if once upon a time in another life she had been ruled by a Louis or two. Or has she? Who else holds family as the raison d'etre of a happy life, and has made long Sunday lunches a weekly ritual? Or infuses grace in moments, charm in hours, and meaning in years of loving and generous efforts on behalf of those she loves—never forgetting that nothing says love like a perfectly made *tarte aux pommes?* My *maman,* that's who.

Oh, my mom could navigate her seventies convinced it's time to slow down, stick close to home, be content to look back—a lot—at a fruitful life best enjoyed these days through the adventures of her grandchildren...*not.* My *maman* will have none of it. Racking up Air France miles, she is; jetting between San Francisco and Paris with a vengeance bred of the overwhelming need I'm guessing she lost at the guillotine: that is, to fly along Rue de Passy in the rain on her way to the *métro,* her shoes French flat, her handbag French fine, and her part-French heart totally at home.

We miss her when she's there, of course. But knowing my *maman,* with dad, is snug in her itsy-bitsy Paris *pied-a-terre,* which vacation schedules permitting we always are invited to share, is to thrill to my mom knowing a happiness—no, a *bliss*—that I sure hope one day to find for myself.

The day I was born, long before she became my *maman,* my mom named me Colette. I should have seen it coming.

ಜ್ಞ ಜ್ಞ ಜ್ಞ

A native of the San Francisco Bay Area who has lived and worked around the world in such places as New York, St. Moritz, and Paris, Colette O'Connor graduated from the University of California, Berkeley with a degree in journalism. Her award-winning lifestyle features, travel pieces, book reviews, interviews, and essays have appeared in numerous publications, including the Los Angeles Times, The Washington Post, World Traveling, *and* America West. *She is the editor-in-chief of* Flying Adventures: The Private Aircraft Owners/Passengers Travel & Lifestyle Magazine.

≈ ≈ ≈

The Devil and Hare Krishna

Sometimes without warning
a traveler can fall off the path.

*B*Y THE TIME I LEFT THAILAND AND RETURNED TO Malaysia after three months in Asia, one month in Australia, three months in New Zealand, two months in Fiji, and six weeks traveling west across the States from Ontario to Hawaii, travel had begun to wear me down. The Road's soft green moss and feathery fractured light had receded. Now the Road clawed up at me with jagged edges. I'd been gone a long time, gone from where, I couldn't say anymore. I wanted to go to a place where I could stay, to a solid place that would wrap itself around me like a well-worn jacket. I knew Fiji was that place. I had to find a way back to Taveuni, reverse my journey, retrace my sodden steps, do what wanderers rarely do: return.

I would need another teaching job. A flight to Fiji would be expensive, even from Southeast Asia, cheap-flight center of the world. I decided to go to Georgetown on the island of Penang, Malaysia's chief port city and old colonial center for artists, dissidents, intellectuals, and dreamers. From the ferry I squinted at the glare of Penang's tall buildings of gilded glass. Cities are selfish, greedy, reckless, hard-boiled, dirty, and they don't give a damn. But I needed a city. Penang would help me return to Fiji. With Fiji's silky sunsets and easy smiles idling in the back of my mind, enduring another city would be a cinch.

A cinch.

The first person I met in Penang was the Devil. The Devil just happens to be a taxi driver, among other things. He also wears polyester hip-huggers, red flip-flops, and a half-unbuttoned shirt exposing two gold chains dangling low on his chest.

Nonetheless, I never would have imagined the Devil could display such concern for anyone other than himself. Actually, I would never have imagined the Devil existed at all, but there he stood, waiting for me at the ferry dock, happy to make my acquaintance. He had taken English lessons. I could tell.

"Where did you learn such excellent English?" I asked, not yet knowing whom I was addressing.

"International English School, in big ta-wa building."

"Tower building? Do you think they need teachers? I'm an English teacher."

"Yes, need teachers. Need you."

I tossed my backpack into his cab and off we sped in the direction of the big ta-wa building to find me a job. Arriving in Malaysia was much easier the second time. It just takes practice.

Except we weren't going to a big tower building.

As we drove through the city, the Devil asked me all kinds of questions about my travels and about me. He seemed to know the right questions to ask. Not everyone does. After twenty minutes we reached a building on the outskirts of town, but it wasn't tall. It was long and snaky, flat, with slits for windows.

"What is this place?" I asked him.

"Just to look he-ah first. Maybe you want work he-ah instead teach English. Pay betta this place."

I noticed his English had deteriorated.

"But what is it?"

"Come hinside."

On most days of our lives, even while traveling, we follow fairly predictable paths, not in a ho-hum way, but thoughtfully, with intent. We're happy, or as happy as the next person claims to be, but then without warning we fall off the path. We find ourselves in another world, an underworld existing alongside our happy-go-lucky world of relative normalcy. We don't know our way around down there because it's dark and frightening and new, although it's always been there...waiting.

It was difficult to see anything once the doors closed behind us even though daylight still polished and graced the world outside. Dark ruby lights revealed figures casting shadows onto a plush red rug. Women, or possibly just girls, were harnessed into leather miniskirts, low-cut

Lycra tops and pink pumps as they lounged on bar stools and couches and sipped bright red drinks from tall glasses with straws, like Barbie dolls. Barbie dolls gone wrong. They glared at me. Heavy rouge and gummy neon lipstick concealed their ages, and their souls. Men with facial scars and sleeveless black t-shirts stood guard, crossed-armed. They glared also. This was the first room in what appeared to be a long line of rooms. A waiting room. Twice, from a room beyond, screams broke out into this vile deposit of lethargy and seemed to charge the air with perverse expectations. Then the feeling would die.

I considered the fact that I'd entered a brothel. Either that or the movie set of a cheap porno flick. Or possibly hell itself.

"What are we doing here?" I asked as I stood gawking, although I knew the answer.

"You can work he-ah. Good job. Good pay. Own-ah good friend to me."

This was a ghastly thought. I wanted out, although secretly the place fascinated me. Who were all these women? Where did they come from? Why were they here? The creepy blackness of the place began to seep into my skin. He stood blocking the doorway.

"I'm leaving," I told him.

He aimed his dreadful face at me and released his horrific smile and that's when I understood his true identity for the first time. "No, you no leaving."

"Yes, actually I am." And I did, once I barged past him and out the door. But that was only the beginning of the Devil in Penang. And my dark underworld.

I tried to erase the underworld from my mind as I asked someone directions to the center of the city. After three months in Asia, I'd learned how to ask questions.

Rather than pointing in a specific direction and saying "Is this the way to town?"—which inevitably leads to a "yes" answer even if it's the wrong way (because they don't want to disappoint the person asking and make her look foolish)—I would say, "How do I get to the town?"

Nearby, I found a discount travel agency where I checked on fares to Fiji. The fares didn't look good. Everything in the city was more expensive than I expected. In the travel shop I met a Portuguese traveler named January who told me about a place where travelers could stay free. The place even had a beautiful garden and free food. "What's the catch?" I asked him.

"It's a Hare Krishna temple," he said, embarrassed, "but it does not mean you have to be one, a Hare Krishna follower, not necessary. I'm not one and I am there now three weeks. They don't care."

He didn't have a long draping orange robe and a shaved head and I saw no sign that he'd been bestowing flowers on strangers at street corners. No vacant glassy overjoyed look in the eyes either. He looked ordinary enough, for a traveler.

"Are you saying it's a non-pushy Hare Krishna temple?"

"That is what I say to you. It's very good place. Ten travelers are there now, none of us Hare Krishna converted people."

I thought it wouldn't hurt to take a look. My first impression of the temple was that of old-world elegance gone awry. A mass of tangled thorny trees hid most of the building from the road as if keeping the temple a secret. Behind a tall black iron gate, I could see stone-carved Hindu statues meditating beside a fountain pool. A small Indian woman in a sari smiled at us as she tended a garden of flowering trees and curvy vines. "Hare Krishna," she said, bowing in our direction.

Inside the temple, recorded music of harps and flutes floated into the downstairs lounge. January led me up the stairs to the women's dorm and there I met Katja, from Yugoslavia, who gave me the lowdown on the place. Katja had been staying at the temple for over a month because she was studying tai chi somewhere nearby. She told me four women travelers staying in the dorm at that time were wonderful and I'd like them all. "Oh, and Margaret lives here, too. She's Hare Krishna. Margaret's bossy. And screwy." I liked the way Katja pronounced screwy in her Yugoslavian accent. In fact, I liked everything about the Hare Krishna temple. It felt homey.

Then I met Margaret. Margaret looked to be in her mid-forties and she reminded me of a great blue heron. Her tall, shockingly thin body with its crudely cropped hair on top and faraway lost eyes behind magnified glasses gave her that hungry water-bird quality. Something vaguely icy about her chilled the dorm room when she swept through it. "Hare Krishna," she said when she stalked by me. She said this as if by command rather than in spiritual greeting. She told me that to stay at the temple I would have to work an hour each day performing some duty, and I would be expected to attend the nightly meetings after dinner to discuss spiritual matters. There was also the morning ritual. She didn't elaborate on the morning ritual. I asked if I could work in the kitchen and she handed me a broom to sweep the dorm and said I could. Margaret and I would be bunk mates, an intimidating thought, so I figured breaking the ice might be wise. She told me she grew up in a small Bible-belt town in Missouri where she married young and had three children and never left the state until she was thirty-five. Then one day she found herself in Hare Krishna's main temple in West Virginia. Everything changed for Margaret after that. She did whatever her guru told her to do. She left her husband and three kids and came all the way to Asia, to the Penang temple—to do exactly what, I hadn't figured out yet. Was she happy? This was no longer a relevant question. She couldn't remember happiness back in Missouri, only a lot of laundry, long and nerve-shattering drives to little-league games, and a husband who liked beer better than he liked her. At the temple she felt a calm and cooling flow wash away her old life.

We ate a delicious vegetarian Indian dinner that evening as we sat circled on the wooden floor of the dining room. I met the other authentic Hare Krishna followers, and all the rest—the travelers. I had more in common with the travelers.

That night, five of the travelers and I went out on the town. I found my new friends to be a happy collection of eccentrics, which suited me just fine. Christof, a twenty-year-old Berliner, had just spent a year traveling through China. Christof was an eager intellectual, witty, and he made me laugh. Kirstina from Denmark had arrived from a Buddhist temple in Thailand where she had spent a year meditating in silence. Penang was her vacation for conversation. We talked about traveling, as travelers always do, and they told me about an eccentric traveler who had just left the temple. "A weird Irish guy" was how Katja described him.

"Did he yell out 'Hey you!' all the time, and then give you a corny piece of his philosophy?" I asked.

"He did that all the time. That's all he did. Nobody could ever talk to him. In the middle of a meal when everyone was quietly eating, he would shout out, 'Hey, we're all in this together, we're all wandering rootless nomads.' Or else he would just shout at one of us. He would say, 'Hey you, do you risk looking like a fool for love?' Something like that. Then he would go back to eating and not look at anybody. You know him?"

"I can't shake him. He's everywhere. But I'm glad. I like his corny pieces of philosophy."

The six of us found an old colonial hotel filled with students and foreigners drinking and dancing under a high ceiling and chandeliers. Malaysia's racial mix of Muslim Malays, Chinese, and Indians seemed to work well in Penang, especially in this nightclub where everyone laughed and intermingled. Music from every part of the world blared out of the speakers and our little group danced for hours. I noticed a table of Penang university students sitting beside the dance floor. They were laughing at us. The students seemed particularly amused by Christof, who was a fabulous and expressive dancer. When a slow and hard-to-dance-to song came on, Christof began to perform tai chi-like movements as if every note of the music commanded a different muscle in his body. He closed his eyes in ecstasy. This was too much for the students at the table; clearly they had never seen the like of it and a couple of them snapped pictures. Then one of the students, an especially bold and inebriated one, came up to join us. The student had horn-rimmed glasses and stood right beside Christof, studying him. Then the student too began to dance. Soon he was imitating Christof's every move, and by the end of the night, the student danced as beautifully as Christof. As he was leaving he shook all of our hands, told us we had changed his life, then turned around to fall flat on his face. In a graceful, expressive way, of course.

By the time we left it was after three in the morning. The curfew to be back at the Hare Krishna temple was ten in the evening. Hare Krishnas believe the body and spirit are at war, all desires of the body are bad, and going out dancing is just plain evil. We had to sneak in over an iron gate and tiptoe upstairs past a snoring Margaret.

It was probably four in the morning when I fell asleep. I hadn't even begun to dream when I was awakened by an annoying clanging from downstairs, followed by the rude deployment of far-too-bright fluorescent lights in our dorm. Margaret's doing. "Get up, all of you, and come downstairs," she said. I guessed this was the morning ritual I'd heard about and I seriously thought about ignoring it. At five o'clock, my personal morning ritual has always been sleep. Margaret must have sensed my less-than-enthusiastic devotion to her religion because she poked me in the stomach with a long twiggy finger and told me to be downstairs in two minutes. Were we living like medieval Catholic monks here? After some groggy reflection, I considered going downstairs after one hour of sleep a relatively small price to pay for free room and board. Besides, I might finally figure out what Hare Krishna people actually do other than stroll airports. The secret study of Margaret was alone worth the price of a night's sleep. I dragged myself down there with the others.

What I found downstairs at five in the morning at Penang's Hare Krishna temple were twenty people circled on the floor banging on pots, pans, and little tin drums as they chanted the Hare Krishna chant over and over for exactly one hour. The real Hare Krishna people, orange-robed and baldheaded, chanted and swayed with love and vigor in their hearts, while the rest of us just clanged a little on the pots and pans to keep from nodding off. After the hour of clanging, all of the travelers ran back upstairs to sleep until noon. That part surprised me more than anything: they let us go back to sleep, to deprogram. If they really wanted to brainwash us, surely this wasn't the way.

That day I found my job teaching English. Not in a big ta-wa building either. I met an English woman who was shopping in the textile market downtown for batik material to take back home. She told me she had just quit her teaching job at an adult language school and would introduce me to the school's director. After taking a cab back to the temple to change my clothes and retrieve my resume and certificates from my backpack, I hurried to meet her and off we went to the school. The director said I could start teaching the next afternoon.

I arrived back at the temple that evening in time for my kitchen duty, where I was taught how to make *rotis* from a sweet saried woman from India who chanted the H.K. song the entire time. I didn't mind, though. She had a nice voice. Besides, I found it rather soothing and pleasant after the harried and noisy city.

Most of my students at the English school were businessmen intent on getting only the gist of the language to carry them through business deals, which seemed like a sign of linguistic decline. My few female students were usually too shy to speak. As in Japan, many Malaysian women are trained to be subservient and to coddle their men. They aren't expected to have opinions of their own.

But after class, after the men left, the same women would let loose, giggle shyly, and then laugh wildly, as they told me the most astonishing things. That was my favorite part of teaching there. Conversations with the women always stopped just short of feminism, which some of them considered dangerous. They liked hearing about my life, however, and always asked me plenty of questions, especially the old standard: "Why aren't you married yet?" I would tell them marriage sounded like too much work and they would laugh and agree with me. Often they would express candid opinions in English that they would probably never say in their own language. I learned a lot from those women.

The men in the classes often puzzled me. Many Asian men think of Western women as not quite real, a little barbaric and aggressive, certainly sexually permissive, and possibly alien. One man in a conversational class asked me, quite seriously, "Please tell, in your cold country, is it warmer for white women to do things upside down?"

The days flew by like golden butterflies: up at five to bang on pots and then back to bed to restore my head, then off to teach for six hours before my dash back to roll *rotis,* followed by extraordinary Indian cuisine and long talks with the travelers, sometimes meditation and tai chi lessons next door, then off to the nightclubs to dance, later to sneak in and be scolded by Margaret, and, finally, sleep until the clanging commenced. Days of noisy joy.

Then one day I saw the Devil again. I was looking over lychees in the market after school when it happened. His nasal, churlish voice had branded itself into my skull and there was no mistaking it. As I squeezed fruit for freshness he spoke into my ear from behind, which made me wince, gave me goose bumps. "My friend, you want job now? Good pay. You like it there. Come back." I squeezed too hard and squashed something, some innocent piece of fruit; juice squirted all over my hand and I ran away. "Come back, lady. I give you the job." I could hear his raspy voice calling after me for three blocks before I lost him in a crowd of teenagers gawking at bootleg CDs from a street stall.

The Devil figured out where I worked and, eventually, where I lived. Not that it could have been too difficult for him to track me down. He was the Devil, after all. Or so I made myself believe. Ordinary humans didn't move through the world the way he did. In the streets I'd see a multitude of confused souls walk by and I knew he played no part in this confusion. He carried something else inside him, something more terrifying. I saw it the first day we met. There in the tiny irises of his eyes was all the evil I had ever seen, heard of, known. It suffocated all traces of human vulnerability, wiped out the history of compassion, bloodied centuries of human weakness for love. Nothing in my life had prepared me for such a discovery. Avoidance was crucial but, for unknown reasons, impossible. I would see him all over town, hear his inhuman footsteps behind me, and storm clouds would gather in my chest in silent terror. Sometimes I could have sworn he was just ahead of me, waiting at a café or inside a store. He would always attempt a smile but it was never genuine. His smile curdled blood. It lived in a viper's den and only came out when it wanted something. "Come take the job, lady." I would watch the ugly words fall out of his mouth like drool. I tried to take different routes to work, come back home through different neighborhoods. I even stopped eating

lunch at my favorite little neighborhood restaurant which
served coconut-milk fish soup. I hated him for that.

I remember walking into a batik fabric shop one day
to have a dress made. I'd been there many times to admire and touch delicate material that smelled like sandalwood incense, and I liked the way the shopkeeper's
eyes enlarged when he heard gossip. The man loved to
eat and his laugh was deep and reassuring. On that day,
when I turned to greet the friendly shopkeeper, I looked
straight into the face of the Devil. There he sat behind
the counter on the shopkeeper's stool. Surely they
weren't friends. The Devil parted his lips back to show
me his stained and collapsed teeth, and his glazed eyes
pierced mine too thoroughly. Across the counter, where
the shopkeeper had eaten a thousand curried *rotis,* I felt
the Devil try to X-ray my vital and most secret core. I
opened my mouth to speak, to demand to know what he
had done with the shopkeeper, but no words came out.
I felt paralyzed as if in a nightmare, unable to move or
speak. "May I help you?" he asked. I shook my head. As
I flew out the door I heard him laugh and I swear the
laugh came straight from the rotting depths of another
world not nearly as likable as this one.

After that I tried to think only good thoughts in an
attempt to keep him out of my life. I vowed to meditate
in the quiet garden sanctuary at the temple. I would
cleanse myself of any darkness hiding inside, darkness
the Devil must have sensed. I might even pay attention
at the morning rituals.

Unfortunately none of this worked, despite all the
new-agey books written on this sort of thing.

The day he knocked at the Hare Krishna temple to
ask for me, Margaret answered the door. I'm glad she

did, too, because anyone else, blissfully unaware of the diabolical nature of the visitor, would have come and found me working in the kitchen. But Margaret told him I was "doing my service to Krishna." That sent him scurrying, perhaps akin to holding out a cross or garlic to frighten vampires. He certainly didn't try to whisk Margaret off to the big ta-wa building to convert her into a prostitute. I'm sure he could see that Margaret's soul was tied up elsewhere.

Encountering the Devil was rather amusing at first. Actually no, it was never amusing. Unsettling was more accurate. Then it became strangely alarming. For some reason I couldn't tell my friends about it. I'm not sure why. Perhaps a part of me was fascinated by what lay inside the big ta-wa building. I've always been intrigued by worlds populated by lost and dangerous souls. After weeks of teaching and banging pots every day, leading a well-ordered life, part of me wanted to step down off the path again, just for a while, and explore the darker places, the places not understood.

Unreasonable thoughts grabbed me with claws, pulled me. I followed. I found a job hostessing in a semi-sleazy nightclub. Those jobs are easy to find if you're looking for them. This was nothing like the big ta-wa building, of course, but it was part of the underworld nonetheless. Daylight couldn't reach it. Had Margaret and the other Hare Krishnas known, I would have been chased and chanted out of their temple with the musical pots and pans banging on my heels. Fortunately, Margaret and the others seemed to live in a land of air and clouds, far more serene than this one, so they never noticed my unusual hours. A second job would hasten my return to Fiji, I told myself.

Hostessing paid even more than teaching and it fit into my schedule perfectly. Dancing at the colonial nightclub with my non-Hare Krishna friends would have to go, but other than that sacrifice, nothing changed. Not in the beginning.

For the first couple of weeks in the sleazy nightclub, thick layers of cigarette smoke rolled through my head like fog. Living in such a haze, I didn't have to think too much about what I was doing. My job was mindless. I made silly nonsensical chit-chat with men at their tables, heard the same questions over and over and gave different answers every time, and even poured drinks. I stopped short of lighting their cigarettes—I was only willing to go so far. It wasn't a bad job. Sometimes I even enjoyed it. I liked the other women I worked with, foreign travelers like myself who were there for the money, or a lark. We couldn't believe how much money they paid us just for showing up at the joint. We laughed at them. We thought the joke was on them.

You have to understand: we had to see it this way.

I tried to take a philosophical view of my life in Penang. Everything I did was to get back to Fiji, I reasoned, but my days were so filled, little time remained for introspection. That can be dangerous.

One day as I walked along a busy street, I realized the Hare Krishna chant had hijacked my head. It hit me that there was a good chance I'd been humming it for hours, possibly days. When I tried to turn it off, I couldn't do it. In defiance, it only got louder and more inane. I tried to hum something else to push it out—a Fijian love song, Neil Young, a show tune, Judy Garland, a Christmas carol, but Hare K. was too powerful—like a rude guest at a party who won't shut up.

Hare Krishna
Hare Krishna
Krishna Krishna
Hare Hare
Hare Rama
Hare Rama
Rama Rama
Hare Hare

It never stops. It goes on like this forever. As far as I could tell, this chant is all they do. This *is* their religion.

I got a little panicky. I searched the street for a sympathetic spirit, someone to talk to, but all the faces were stark and shut down, the faces of a crowd. Hundreds of faces passed me by and I could shut none of them out. What chants played behind those faces? I wondered. It was that time of dreaded dead, hot stillness that settled every afternoon, when life hangs in heavy suspension, waits for a break. The world was too bright, too glaring in blues and whites, jerked apart by the steel gray of tall buildings. My eyes craved darkness. A naked little man passed me as I crossed a busy intersection. The tiny loincloth around his waist wasn't working for him and everything lay out there for the world to see. I kept turning around to check if I'd seen it right. A bus was stopped at the crosswalk and when I looked up I saw that the bus driver and passengers were laughing at the naked man and my reaction to him, so I smiled and laughed with them. When I turned around again to watch the little man walk away into the crowd, I realized he was not sane in any known sense of the word. But I'd forgotten what sane and normal were supposed to mean. My world was slipping into the absurd. I could feel my old self draining out of me. Further down along the street I saw the Devil waving at me through the traffic, and something happened that should have surprised the hell out of me. But it didn't surprise me, not then.

I waved back.

It was that very night that life as I'd known it stopped making sense. Later I suspected the day had been to blame because daylight isn't all innocence and yellow roses in the sun. That's how days get away with things—tricks of light. As usual that evening I went to the night-club to hostess at nine o'clock. The first hour was dead boring, which wasn't unusual at all. I had to make small talk—minuscule talk—to a group of Japanese business-men who could hardly speak English as I watched them try to outdrink each other. I was getting paid for this and it was turning my stomach. Over at the bar I joined my friend Belinda, from Ireland, and a German woman, Stella, who had only started working there that night. Stella was tall and busty and could shoot vodka down her throat with an ease that would have had the Russian army quaking in their boots. She was a man-hater, too. She wasn't even pretending to be feminine like the rest of us. "The men in this place, they have brains like little turds; I vant to spit in their noodles, pee in their drinks." I was glad Stella was there that night because I needed to hear someone rant and rave. Her spewing venom about men might chase Hare Krishna out of my head.

"You think this is a vile place, you should see the big ta-wa building," I told her.

"De vhat? Vhat is dis?"

"It's the parking lot for hell. Makes this place look like a Doris Day bakery."

"What is this place?" asked Belinda.

"Some weird kind of brothel, really repulsive, frightening."

"Where is it?" asked Belinda.

"On the edge of town. I was only there once. When I first got here."

"Is it all one level and long?"

"Yeah, that's how I remember it. Why?"

Belinda's pretty face aged ten years right in front of us. She stood up off the bar stool and her sunken eyes looked into mine. Her eyes had black flecks I'd never noticed before.

"I was there, too."

Our bodies shivered in mutual disgust, in camaraderie, like war buddies might do reminiscing about a particularly horrendous battle. I ached to ask Belinda about the Devil, to ask her if she knew him. But speak his name out loud? I hadn't said his name aloud to anyone, not even myself, except when he invaded my dreams and made them nightmares. I'd yell at him then, in my dreams, tell him to get lost, go to hell, go home. What name he chose for himself on this level of reality, I didn't know. How could I even describe him? Other than being the Devil, he was fairly nondescript, ordinary. I couldn't ask her. She would think I was crazy.

Wait, I was crazy. Krishna was seeing to that.

"How did you get there, to that place?" I could feel my pumping heart as I spoke the words.

"Oh, this disgusting taxi driver. Creepy, he was. I didn't ask him to take me there, either."

"I know."

In Belinda I had found my sympathetic spirit. Thank God, the Devil wasn't hungry for my soul alone. He was an actual breathing person, cruising the city in polyester, not an annoyance hanging out in my head along with the H.K. chant. Of course he was real. Hadn't I seen him out on the streets every day? Why hadn't I told anyone? I felt a lightness take over me, like a white soft-feathered gull sweeping up into the blue of the sky. I wasn't mad and I wasn't bad. It struck me that the weeks leading up to this moment had been a mixture of lunacy and dreams, nonsense, and chaos, all jumbled together now into a curious sensation of joy. I felt as if I'd awoken from a long disturbing sleep.

"We must go to dis place. I vant to see it," said Stella.

Stella, architect of daring ideas, Bavarian woman of vision, eager to stampede what most of us are afraid to contemplate. The world could learn much from Stella.

We took a cab there the next evening. Belinda seemed to know the way. I didn't ask her why. We were dressed to kill, I in my black miniskirt, gold tank top, and lace-up leather sandals, Belinda in a plunged-neck sequined dress, and Stella, long and tall, in cut-off jean shorts and a t-shirt. Like falling stars we shot through the moist night toward the big ta-wa building: Belinda, for reasons she wouldn't elaborate on; Stella, presumably to bomb the place; and me, I can't be sure. It was something I had to do, something that made sense in a world where all sense had been lost.

Although I had tried to shove the big ta-wa building into the backyard of my mind, it had never really gone there, and when I saw it again, lying there in the half-light, I felt caught up in something large and intoxicating. The big ta-wa building was real and alive, bigger and more impressive than I remembered. An awakened surge I hadn't felt in weeks bolted through me, signaling a new

adventure pulsing through my bloodstream. A strange
wind filled my hair. I looked at my two companions as we
walked to the entrance and it felt good to be caught up in
this drama with others. I didn't see our shadows on the
pavement and I wondered if it was true that in the dark
of the night, we become our shadows.

We found the door locked and for an instant I was
glad of that. My feet were getting cold. Some form of
humanity, or what I hoped was humanity, was inside,
however; we felt and heard it leaking out. I knew I had
to go inside because as a wandering sightseer of this
world I had paid my admission at birth and had long
since given up my card to live by the rules. There's no
need to live normally. We can chase our whims, however
misguided they may be, and venture out into the amuse-
ment and mystery of the world. We're allowed.

Music that sounded as if it came from a giant tin
can crawled out of the crack under the door, music for
adrenaline junkies who aren't fussy about how it sounds.
Deep voices and screams dominated the clamor escaping
from the place and I considered turning on my quasi-
high heels to run back to a safe place that would give me
a peaceful easy feeling. Stella wouldn't hear of it, being
from Germany and not a child of the seventies. Stella
was steel wool ready to scour. At the bottom of Stella's
long and bronzed muscular legs grew two significant
feet sturdily wrapped in tough German sandals of un-
abashed comfort which she employed to kick the door.
They worked well, those German sandals, because a big
man opened the door immediately, a man bearing scars
and tattoos. I remembered him by his feeble attempt to
corral his thinning hair into a ponytail. We sat down at
the bar. It was dark.

I wasn't surprised at the identity of our bartender that evening. Who else could it have been but the Devil? For half a second, his smile even looked almost authentic. Stella took him up on his offer of free drinks—she didn't know where he came from. "Hot today, no?" She commenced her chit-chatting repertoire learned the night before at her new job.

"You think this hot? Much hotter where I live." The Devil didn't really say that, but he should have. He wasn't quick enough. Instead, he just smiled, or pretended to. This is a secret: the Devil isn't that bright. But neither, apparently, was Stella. The Devil was chatting her up and she was going along with it.

Belinda nudged me. "Laur, we've got to do something. This is dreadful, this place. Why are we here? This is disgusting. This is sick and wrong."

Belinda was right. Stella was throwing back booze. Frightening people glared at us. I looked around the room and for the first time since I started working in the nightclub, the tame nightclub, I felt truly nauseated at the idea of women wooing and pampering men for money, however ancient the dynamic might be. "Shouldn't we have gone beyond this by now? How is this still happening in the late twentieth century and why are we a part of it?" I had to yell. It was loud in there. Belinda gave me a blank stare. This was no time for philosophizing.

By now, the Devil had joined Stella on our side of the bar and the two of them were playing drinking games.

"Back home, I all the time vin the games for drinking." I thought I heard some slurring in there but I couldn't be sure. Stella banged her empty glass down on the counter for another round.

Something had to be done. Things had gone too far already.

It occurred to me that I had been in a situation like this before, in another part of the underworld lit by similar dark ruby lights. A place I wanted to escape. Morocco perhaps. I wondered if there exists out there in space some sort of giant cosmic Silly Putty that duplicates our awful comic ways, again and again, through the folds of time.

I still wasn't thinking clearly.

Belinda, on the other hand, apparently was, because she dumped a glass of beer on the lap of the Devil. I was impressed. And inspired. I called him a snake. That's when Stella began to laugh uncontrollably. She's under his control, his evil command, I thought. Or she's piss drunk.

"Why you do that?" demanded the Devil. "Why you hate me?"

We didn't answer. We didn't have to. A tiny woman with sparks in her eyes had arranged her body that evening to fit into a zippered vinyl contraption that set her legs free at the thighs where they could do as they pleased until they reached a pair of child-sized red spiked heels jailing her little feet. She and her outfit stormed over to us at the bar, where she flung her drink in the Devil's face. Belinda must have inspired her. The Devil's head shot back and his face dripped like melting plastic. When the tiny woman saw what she had done, she laughed along with Stella. What came out of her was more of a cackle than a laugh, which surprised me, from such a pretty little thing, possibly a mere teenager. Other women laughed also. I wondered who the Devil was. Then the music stopped.

All eyes in the room, eyes of young women, set their gaze on us. Just moments earlier their eyes had been aloof and flooded with an apathy that knew certain experiences had isolated them from other women in the world and there was no going back to simpler times. But now these same eyes seemed to flare up, come alive with mirth and rage and youth. The Devil didn't like it. He squirmed on his bar stool.

Everything went dark after that. Someone must have killed the lights. But it didn't matter just then about the darkness, because the light I had seen in a few of the women's eyes had been overwhelming, something I needed to see. Like a camera flash, the image had impressed itself on my brain in one shining instant of intensity. I saw that life burns like fire inside these seemingly captive women and I knew they wouldn't allow the Devil their souls.

The room was dark, though, and in darkness we forget that light slants golden and cuts through fog and our hearts every morning. We forget all manner of lightness. That's how a gathering panic filled the room that night. I heard glass shattering, shouts and cries in different languages, heckling laughs. Heat seemed to rise from the floor where shards of glass lay.

"Let's get out of here," I said.

Nobody answered me.

In the blackness I made my way through the swarm of soft bodies and scent of cheap perfumes. Where had Stella and Belinda gone? I couldn't get a grasp on what was happening. The big ta-wa building was in the grip of madness, or was it always like this? It sounded as if people were throwing things, but others were laughing hysterically. Had we incited a riot? I found myself

laughing inwardly for following the strange path that
led me this way. But now I wanted out. I wanted my old
life back. If only I could find a crack of light to escape
through, I thought, then everything would be all right.
But no cracks could I find. I reached out in front of me
and touched skin, skin of someone who said something
in an unfamiliar language, and her voice was shrill and
fraught with angst. Where were my friends? Would I ever
get out? What could I do?

I did the first thing that came to me, the only thing
to do in a situation like that. I chanted Hare Krishna
until the cows came home. Would it ward off the Devil?
Would it have me committed? Would it make Margaret
proud?

Krishna's powers must have finally come through for
me because I suddenly found the exit door. I found Stella
and Belinda, too. And the Devil. They were all outside
talking. Chatting, to be precise. Stella was throwing her
brand of radical feminism at him and she didn't appear
the least bit intoxicated. The Devil seemed to be taking it quite well. Although I was relieved to be back out
into the freedom of the soft night air and a rising vanilla
moon, I felt a little disappointed. How anticlimactic. I had
wanted to find Stella in one of those rooms from beyond
with a whip in her hand, beating the Devil silly while he
cowered on his haunches and apologized for the nuisance
he had been making of himself. The thought struck me
that he might not be the Devil after all, but a bored man
of meager inspiration and a lousy sense of ethics. This was
only a fleeting thought, however. I'm not religious but I
know the Devil when I see him.

I decided to leave Penang. I said good-bye to the
friends I had met throughout the city, in the market

and restaurants, at the nightclub, the English language school, and the Hare Krishna temple. Margaret was the last person I saw as I left the temple in the fading dusk with my backpack. She was on her way home from a day of soliciting money on a street corner and she smiled when she said good-bye. It was the first time I had seen her smile since we met. Perhaps she was happy to see me go. Or perhaps we had touched each other's lives in a way I hadn't realized.

Wanderers of the world often sweep through one another's lives and many collide. But as time passes we become familiar with the others' strange ways and notice the outer differences less and less. After layers of the heart are peeled back, none of us is really that different from anyone else.

"Hare Krishna," she called out when I walked up the road.

"Hare Krishna," I called back.

Krishna lay down and died in my head that day. He's never tried to make a comeback.

Just in time, I made it to the night ferry for the mainland. He was there at the ferry dock, of course, letting loose his smile of slime. Whether he was waiting for me or waiting for new prey, I couldn't say. A cold shudder rippled up my back as I watched him while we pulled up anchor. But I was safely away from him. I had money and my ticket for Fiji. I had Fiji in the palm of my hand and the Devil could never find such an out-of-the-way place.

Out into the velvet darkness I sailed away to disappear into a thick slice of midnight. Does the Devil have night vision? Not if you stay in the shadows.

ᔆ᠆ ᔆ᠆ ᔆ᠆

This story was excerpted from Laurie Gough's Kite Strings of the Southern Cross, *shortlisted for the Thomas Cook Travel Book Award in the U.K. and silver medal winner of* ForeWord Magazine's Travel Book *of the Year in the U.S. She has written for* Salon.com, the Los Angeles Times, the Globe and Mail, Canadian Geographic, *and for several anthologies, including* Wanderlust: Real Life Tales of Adventure and Romance, AWOL: Tales for the Travel Inspired Mind, *and many* Travelers' Tales books. *Her new travel book,* Kiss the Sunset Pig, *will be published in 2006. She lives in Canada.*

❧ ❧ ❧

Where Size Matters

Booty is in the eye of the beholder.

I HAVE A SMALL BUTT. IT IS ROUND AND, ALTHOUGH IT juts out a little bit, it is by no means a focal point. It fits into the pants of my generation just fine, which is probably why I never gave it a second thought. When a body-conscious friend would ask me if her butt looked fat in a particular pair of black pants, I would grimace, "It looks fine." As a friend, I tried to be patient and understanding, but in fat-butt insecurity situations I could never muster much sympathy. That is, until I myself began to teeter on tiptoes, peering around at my rear in a grimy mirror in a bathroom in Senegal, asking myself, "Does my butt look scrawny?"

My time as a study-abroad student in Senegal was marked by many revelations. One of them was this: For the first time in my life, my butt was hopelessly inadequate.

It did not swagger or jiggle or swing as I walked through the neighborhood. My pants did not cling seductively to the curves of my caboose. My cheeks did not pillow into a heart beneath me as I sat down because, sadly, they had nowhere to go.

The Senegalese women I knew generally did not have this problem. Their curves tucked at the hips and then expanded gently like cushions beneath them to absorb the shocks produced by the potholes and cracks tripped over by the wobbly mini-buses we rode to get around town. My female friends leisurely sauntered around the *quartier* so that each hip cocked out one at a time and in the release, bounced back just so. Men nearby, from the businessman in the sleekest tailored suit checking his watch to the older gentleman in a knit cap slumped on a bench by the curb, perked to attention as my friends would slowly glide by. In Senegal, the female posterior is an object of reverence and it did not take long for me to realize that there was very little of my backside to revere.

Nor did my gluteus inadequacy escape the attention of my Senegalese host family. The mealtime chant, "*Il faut manger! Lekkal!* It is necessary to eat! Eat!" was a standard tune around our communal bowl. My host sister, Kiné, ensured that the metallic bottom of my triangular portion of the bowl was never exposed by pushing rice out from the center and piling more vegetables and fish in front of me. Sure, these daily interactions were motivated by the Senegalese tradition of heaping hospitality, but this did not stand alone. My family explicitly informed me that they planned to send back an improved, more attractive Wendy to the States, a softer Wendy, a more substantial Wendy, a Wendy with a big butt.

My American friends who were more generously endowed in the booty department were subject to a different kind of scrutiny. They endured daily catcalls of lustful admiration from both strangers and friends. Exasperated, self-conscious, and vulnerable, they would respond, "You just can't tell an American girl that she has a big butt, even if it is a compliment!" "Well, you are not in America anymore," the backside enthusiasts would reply. This being a pretty good point, I began to observe changes in my friends' behavior. My once-insecure friends returned from the market with the spandex-like jeans that were the rage among our Senegalese female peers and wore them to the red-plush-mirrored, TV-movie-esque nightclubs of Dakar, to shake and grind defiantly on the dance floor. Where earlier in the year, an unidentified man hissing about the size of a friend's derrière would cause her to drop her shoulders and head and to tighten her mouth, in time, she might be inspired to thrust her shoulders back, fix her eyes ahead, and even smile.

As a group of enlightened American women we were sure we would never concede to this brand of what many would consider objectification, and we certainly never expected to revel in it. Yet, as the Senegalese tell it, catcalls are not merely the vessels of lust or oppression, but an opening for appreciation of the luscious mystery of the female form. Although my backside was rarely in the streetside spotlight, my general appearance stirred many a hiss and holler as I walked to the university, the bakery, or the bus stop. When I complained to my Senegalese host sister, Boundaw, how I hated all the attention, she looked at me with a smirk, "Oh, I like it very much. I'll take yours." In my first vulnerable, doubt-wracked months, I would have gladly handed Boundaw all the anonymous compliments the exotic appeal of my white skin and blond hair garnered; yet, somehow what initially felt like a daily assault became a daily affirmation. In fact, when I received fewer side-walk accolades, I wondered, "What? I don't look cute today?" At least, that's how I felt on the powerful days. The golden-tressed lioness days. The days when I could talk to anyone, shake their hand, and canoodle their baby. But there were other days when the stifling heat and poverty choked my fearlessness, when I didn't want to see the young mother with pink scars on her ankles and a newborn in her arms, parked in the dirt, begging for food or spare change, and I didn't want her, or any-one else, to see me.

In Senegal, women are often marginalized in the general economy, but they are fierce participants in the rickety streetside one. Almost every household offers a mother or a daughter to the curb to sell mango slices, toothbrush twigs, bags of sugared peanuts, frozen *bis-sap* juices in plastic baggies, and *fonde*—sugary balls of doughy goo. *Jaay fonde amul pertiman.* Or "Sell *fonde*, have no loss." This is the first line of a song about *fonde* and sexual politics. It is sung in every courtyard, market, and high school, essentially wherever women congre-gate to gossip and tease and cook. The song instructs: don't worry if you don't sell your *fonde*, it is really bet-ter if you eat it yourself, because it will fatten up your behind. The underlying message of this anthem is that a chunky bottom will catch the attention of a handsome beau or sustain the interest of a husband who is eas-ily distracted and who would otherwise bring another woman into your house as his second wife, the recurrent nightmare of wives trapped in Senegal's polygamous tangle. In this way, *"jaay fonde"* has entered the popular lexicon to mean a chubby rear and to be *"jaay fonde"* is to be healthy, feminine, and sensual. Beyond sexual desire, *"jaay fonde"* is an imperative; your Senegalese mother will tell you so.

In a Senegalese marriage, there are several interconnected assumptions: the husband will provide for the family, the wife will bear many children, and said wife will balloon to twice her previous size. A large wife is the unambiguous symbol of a family's prosperity and an indication of a husband's ability to bring home the mutton. The Senegalese dietary staples of starchy white rice, baguettes, and fatty vegetable oil sold by the gallon contribute to this triangular prophecy. I met a Canadian nutrition student who studied diabetes and anemia among women in a community outside Dakar. Many of the women she spoke with were ultimately unwilling to risk losing weight by using oil sparingly and cooking with hearty, healthy Senegalese couscous instead of rice. Somehow, a healthier lifestyle was not worth the risk of shedding social status and straining marital satisfaction.

If sexual norms are created, not out of desire or arbitrary preferences, but out of functional necessity, then in Senegal, wide childbearing hips have been selected generation after generation to pop out babies to fill the fields of millet, maize, and then sugar cane and rice, and then cotton and peanuts. As the Sahara Desert has crept with sinister silence into Senegal, as droughts have struck tired soil and villagers, agrarian life has been weakened. Young men and women flood the cities, hopeful that industrialization will hit before famine does. In the city, where material expectations swell, modern mothers and

fathers with gainful employment have begun to choose
a car, a cell phone, or a television set over more mouths
to feed. A digital and glossy assault of skinny women has
already been launched from Occidental headquarters.
Could *"jaay fonde"* go out of vogue as the anticipated
wave of modernization selects butts like mine? Perhaps,
when Dakar freezes over. Besides the fact that most
Senegalese laborers are still engaged in a farm economy,
my imagination cannot begin to stretch around a Senegal
without *"jaay fonde."*

Returning from Senegal, I saw new beauty in my
friends' behinds and the wide hips of my mother's pear-
shaped frame. I know that I shall never look at any butt
the same way again, and if my new aesthetic preference can defend itself against the circus of shrinking
American women, I do believe *"jaay fonde"* will endure
among those nursed from the start on its mysterious
succulence.

After six months or so in Dakar, every time I turned
my back, I began to rouse chuckles and comments from
my host mother about my ballooning butt. Soon, my tai-
lor remarked with a raised eyebrow that my hips were
a couple of centimeters wider than before, to the amuse-
ment of everyone in the shop. Next, my sister pinched
my rear and exclaimed, *"Oooh, am nga jaay fonde leggi!*
You are *jaay fonde* now!" Despite the reinforcement of
a chorus of similar comments, I have to be honest with
myself: my butt never actually grew; these remarks were
really just subtle affirmations of acceptance and affection. Before last year, I would never have imagined finding myself in a society where to say, "your butt is big,"
is to mean, "we like you," but I did. When such compliments were given, however true or false or in between

they may have been, I smiled and blushed and the blush spilled down into the slight swagger in my hips and the bounce in my butt. And I admit it, after almost six months back in America, I still stick it out a little bit.

A native of Madison, Wisconsin, Wendy Wright Soref recently graduated from Cornell University. She now teaches second grade in Hughes, Arkansas.

MARISA LOPEZ

✿ ✿ ✿

A River Runs Through Me

Navigating the "chakras" of India's landscape,
a seeker stumbles onto the dark side.

S OMEONE ONCE TOLD ME THAT INDIA IS LIKE A MAP
of the human body. You could say, then, that my
journey began in India's ass and ended up in her third
eye.

Traditional ayurvedic medicine, the form most widely
practiced in India, follows the blueprint of the seven
chakras, or main energy centers in the body, stretching
from the Muladhara Chakra at the base of the spine to
the Sahasrara at the crown of the head. Traveling on my
own, I began to see and experience how seven key cities would mirror these vital hubs as I traced the bumpy
course of India's vertebrae, one chakra at a time. What I

didn't know then, was that India would also be tracing mine.

The lower chakras are found in the region of the anal and sex organs. Often negatively associated with primal desire, addiction, and self-gratification, they are rooted in the physical body. As the chakras continue upward along the spine, they carry the spirits of personal strength, love and compassion, creativity and communication, intuition, and finally, enlightenment; the higher one goes, the more detached the ego, and the more connected he or she is to the cosmic One.

I first arrived in India's lowermost chakra, at the southernmost tip of the subcontinent. The port city of Kanniyakumari, ironically meaning "virgin maiden of the sea," immediately struck me as overtly sexual and dirty. Here, men gawked, calling out "Hiii baaaby," even touching themselves in front of me. I witnessed rampant elephantitis and leprosy, I ran from spiders the size of my hand scaling my bathroom walls, and I grimaced at the garbage floating out to sea. As base as it was, I loved the notion that my body was traveling inside a larger body, and each energy center I visited would exhibit its own lessons and distinct personality.

After over three months of travel, the crux of my awakening came about in Varanasi, India's sixth chakra (or "third eye"). The third eye is the doorway to intuition, where internal wisdom or consciousness overrides external judgment and sensation. It made perfect sense for Varanasi: It was here that I had to look far beyond the surface of things, and here that I had to look inside myself to find out where I ended and the world around me began.

Varanasi, said to be India's holiest city, is older than Jesus, more intense than any place I have ever been. Her energy—for she is definitely feminine—can be felt in the electrified air, in the way the pink light of sunrise dances on the Ganges River and paints the whitewashed walls of the temples; in the bright hues of the silk and gold-threaded saris women wear, in the hazy halo glow that is everywhere.

Here, life and death commingle, and it's not uncommon for bloated bodies of cows and dead babies to drift downstream and interrupt an otherwise perfect sunrise on the Ganges. From my boat, I watched mesmerized by the beauty of the locals as they bathed rhythmically in her holy waters—waters that are said to contain a higher concentration of bacteria than anywhere in the world.

In this land of extremes, cows crowd the streets like a traffic jam, chewing the neat piles of garbage left there for them and shitting as they please. Like the slow buckling rhythm of her animal inhabitants, Varanasi is remarkably calm: It may be the first place I've been to in India where shopkeepers and rickshaw drivers did not harass me constantly. The people here are charming, not to mention psychic. They remember you after having only seen you once, they can read your face, your hand, your energy so well it's spooky.

Varanasi was the quintessential India I had always imagined. Now that I was there, I felt intoxicated by her perfume of frankincense and honey, shit, marigolds and curry, and burning flesh. I wanted to taste her smells, ride the wave of her intensity, and consume the light and darkness that enveloped me as I lost myself in her narrow alleys. With a gut feeling that my purpose here went far beyond tourism, I canceled my other travel plans to the north of India and Delhi, and rented a little room for eight dollars a week, run by a musical family.

I tied bells to my ankles and studied Kathak Dance every afternoon with Saraswati, named after a goddess, in her kitchen. I spoke with astrologers, and spent hours slipping raw silk through my fingers and sipping *masala chai* through my lips. I ate up dreamy afternoons painting the magnificent light of the city as it faded from copper to lavender and pink. In the evenings I attended *puja* ceremonies and live music concerts of flute, sitar, *sarangi,* tabla, and sarod. Just before bedtime, I followed the locals down to the river, and copied them as they placed a tiny candle in a leaf, and surrendered their dreams to the current with a soft and silent prayer. I went to sleep each night imagining the Ganges as she sparkled with hundreds of little wishes like mine.

In my conversations with other travelers, I learned about a yoga teacher there (I shall call him by disguised initials, S.P.), who once read someone's palm and successfully predicted he would die in a traffic accident, which happened one week later. He not only had a knack for reading the future, but he had also traveled as far as Los Angeles to massage and heal a handful of Hollywood celebrities. Intrigued by his psychic powers and distinguished reputation, I signed up for yoga on a nearby hotel rooftop, where S.P. taught everyday at dawn.

The class opened with the Gayathri Mantra, a heart-wrenching tune that beckons the rising sun and celebrates birth and life and the coming of a new day. Ironically, this was all taking place in a city where bodies are cremated for twenty-four hours a day in the open, and where millions come honorably to die. The pure sound of our chanting, coupled with the ghostly ashen sunrise around me filled my body with awe and sudden electricity—my hair stood on end; my feet hardly touched the ground. Although S.P. spoke gently, his gaze penetrated me.

The other students in the class—all Western women—were visiting his studio in the evenings for massage therapy. Like most healers in India, S.P. practiced ayurvedic massage, designed to move energy, or *prana*, between the body's seven chakras, via channels or pathways called *nadis*. By matching the blood and guts of the physical being to their corresponding chakras and *nadis,* the intuitive, two-layer approach this type of massage takes can go so far as to simultaneously heal disease and the emotional trauma that caused it. When my teacher approached me one day after class about partaking in his three-part massage series, I said fine.

I really knew very little about ayurvedic massage, aside from the one I once had by a woman at an ashram in the south. I remember a greasy wooden table and the smell of dank earth, oily circles and figure eights, and a tingly sensation when it was done. I was naked, and it was messy. The swamis at the ashram used to speak of the power of ayurvedic massage to cleanse, heal, and release blocked energy. By opening the *nadis*, as in deep meditation, *prana* is able to flow more freely up the *kundalini* (the serpent energy that lies coiled and dormant at the base of the spine), now and then resulting in a greater consciousness than one human can handle. My teachers used to warn that such a profound release of energy could make you vulnerable, and in some cases, even crazy.

The ashram was very strict regarding same-gender massage, and now I was getting anxious about putting myself into a man's hands. I should tell you that in India among Indians, men do not massage women, and women do not massage men. In this conservative society, where you're more likely to find two men holding hands than a married couple displaying their affection publicly. Given his credentials, however, it seemed that S.P. would have had enough experience in the West to know and respect the boundaries.

He began our session by placing his thumb on my wrist's pulse. He told me, "You were born in October. You are twenty-six years old." Then he continued, "Somebody did something bad to you when you were fifteen." A shudder ran through me. He had my attention.

He then told me to lie on my stomach so that he could begin with the first chakra, at the base of my spine. As his thumb held my coccyx, my heart beat more quickly. My pelvis tingled. I was sweating. As he made his way toward my second chakra, the reproductive organs, I winced.... I was becoming suddenly, incredibly turned on. Oh God. While my mind screamed one thing, my body wanted another. Was this normal? Where exactly was he taking me?

Sensing my discomfort, he shifted gears to chakra number three: the navel, or Mannipura Chakra, known also as the fireplace of one's energy. In geographic terms, this is Hampi, a tropical paradise in India's southern interior, which I had visited twice. Next came the heart chakra, located in the realm of my breasts. He moved to my throat, and massaged my ever-widening third eye: Varanasi. Finally, our ritual ended when he poured thick green oil onto my head and rubbed it in a hypnotic, circular motion. We were done.

I floated home to my rented room that night, zapped by my own untapped energy and flooded by a whirlwind of memories, present and past. I was very curious about everything, but I didn't know how much more I could take and still be able to maintain my composure.

The following morning in class, I noticed that he looked at me more often than usual. The sun was still sleeping, and the sky was filling with crows. The whole scene was becoming creepy.

I decided I would continue with my second session, but I wanted to do a little more research before we began. I needed to learn the rules of ayurvedic massage so that I would know where and when to put up my boundaries. I had already broken the first rule, according to my guidebooks and the many locals I interviewed: never get massaged in India by a member of the opposite sex.

Throughout the day, I consulted the other women in the class, to find out exactly what I should and shouldn't expect during my massage. When I brought up the odd nature of my first session, blushing, they all said the same thing: ayurvedic massage is intense, it moves energy through the seven chakras, it goes places that may seem a bit strange (one woman told me about a friend who was given a vulva massage on the beach), but in the end, they all assured me that S.P. was not an impostor, but a master of his trade.

On Day Two, I arrived feeling more open, ready to see what new discoveries we would make. He began by telling me that I am laden with negative energy in my second chakra region and said that he would have to focus our work there especially. He said over and over again that he could help me. Heal me. Then, I broke rule number two: Never get massaged by a man in India without your clothes on. I don't know what I was thinking. I wanted to trust him so badly...

As we began, time and place quickly dissolved. I lay there imagining Varanasi and her ultra-feminine beauty coursing through my body.... *I was fifteen again.* I was picturing the flame from a candle, the dance of colorful saris.... *The door was locked; I was pinned to the ground.* The swirling smell of incense burning.... *There was a hand over my mouth.* The lapping of the Ganges against the ghats; the sun setting on bobbing corpses...*I loved this man.* And the ritual leaves floating downstream. I hadn't noticed what was actually happening to me in that room until long after it had begun. His entire arm was in me.

I shot up, horrified, heart beating, pleading "No!" but no sound would come. I put my clothes on and took my things and ran. I ran through the crooked streets of dark Varanasi, so fast the bony cows were frightened. I ran past small crowds of leering men drinking tea, past puddles of filthy water and shit, past women carrying buckets of stinking liquid on their heads, and lost children crying in the night.

From the tangled guts of this cobble-stoned city, I found my way back to my room finally. I lit a candle, and as I watched it flicker against the rundown walls of my chamber, I started to cry. I cried for all of the times in my life I had been objectified by men. For the staring and catcalling, for my inability to control my sexuality, and my inability to control people's attraction to me. For all the times I had wanted to be known for my mind and not for my beauty. And most of all, for the violent experience that carried me into my adulthood too soon, when I was barely still a child.

The next morning I awoke later than usual, feeling empty. It was a good empty. Clean, devoid of the emotional turbulence of the night before. I would even say that I felt happy. In my head I was repeatedly chanting the mantra of Gayathri.

I have to believe that my teacher crossed a line and was wrong. Yet in a perverted way, he had also helped me. When it happened, I had felt violated a second time, ashamed, filthy. Looking back today, I thank India for confusing me to the point of clarity. For dirtying me to the point of making me clean. For helping me tear the heads off my demons like the goddess Kali, and for challenging my being right down to its *nadis*. The re-opening and closing of an old wound had opened my third eye. As my own self-awareness set in, I knew that something in me had shifted: for the first time in eleven years, I could feel my heart again. I felt stronger, whole, unashamed, and free.

Varanasi, her pedestrian streets zigzagging in no particular direction, was both a body of blocked pathways and a network of fluid energy. She was the dancer and the smoldering corpse, the dead and the living. I was stretched emotionally to the point of snapping, lost in the space between present and past, and blinded by a thick fog of gender and cultural expectations. Little by little as the air cleared, I began to define my own boundaries. It was a test of my strength as a woman in a world made of men, which I lost and then won.

The following year when I returned to India to earn my yoga teacher's certification, the head swami initiated me and gave me a spiritual name: *Ganga* meaning "intuition," "flow," and "emanating from the Ganges." He touched my forehead with *kumkuma* (a red tumeric powder signifying auspiciousness), and it blinked. With gratitude, I cried, knowing that I had finally arrived on the other side.

ঞ৹ ঞ৹ ঞ৹

Marisa Lopez is an avid traveler and adventurer who feels that life is too short and the world is too big to sit still for too long. From Laos to Taos, she has trekked the Himalayas, belly-danced in Poland, taught yoga in China, and guided hiking trips in the Pyrenees. Since contracting wanderlust in her early twenties, she has taken up three languages, organized cultural exchange programs for artists, exhibited her travel photography in NYC and New Mexico, and has published her travel essays in India and Nepal. Attempting to settle down, she recently moved to Northern New Mexico, where she managed the Taos Mountain Film Festival. She now lives on the Mediterranean coast of Spain.

෴ ෴ ෴

State of Grace

On a nostalgic trip to the land of quirky
serendipity, a traveler stumbles on wolf-whistling parrots,
oversized reptiles, and minor celebrities.

LOUISIANA IS A STATE OF OFF-KILTER OCCURRENCES,
a place where odd, alluring things big and small can
happen at any minute. Maybe that's why exiled French
Canadian peasants were pulled there, as though by a giant
magnet, in the 1700s, eventually becoming the often-
eccentric people known as Cajuns. And maybe that's why
the roguish French pirate Jean LaFitte was drawn to the
place, and dug it so much that he helped U.S. forces fight
the Battle of New Orleans during the War of 1812.

And perhaps that's really why I was compelled to go
to college there in 1984, though at the time I thought I
was heading to New Orleans because Loyola University's
promotional materials were pleasing to the eye.

Looking back now, I think we—the French Canadians, Lafitte, and me—were all pulled in by some peculiar aligning of planets over the boot-shaped state. Either that or a strange confluence of psychic energies all blowing in there simultaneously, creating a most humid and idiosyncratic atmosphere. Against good judgment, I left there in 1998, but those same undeniable forces now draw me back to that wacky, random place at least once a year.

Early this month, Marty and I trotted down to New Orleans for the annual Jazz and Heritage Festival. Of course, quirky things happened just about every day, starting with our first morning, when we awoke to what sounded like horny construction workers outside our window. Over and over again, I heard the my-you're-sexy whistle coming from the backyard. But how could there be construction workers back there? I began to feel flattered.

Eventually curiosity pulled us out of bed and out onto the back deck. The sound, we saw, was actually emanating from a parrot—a big, exotic, non-native green-and-red parrot perched in a lush tree. Apparently it had just arrived, out of the blue. Tracy and Joe, our hosts, were in awe, but it was a mild awe, because, after all, this was Louisiana. Weird and unexplained is the norm here.

We giggled about the parrot, got dressed, and headed to Jazz Fest, a crowded, sweaty celebration of local music, food, and crafts held at the city's racetrack. We'd plopped ourselves down on the ground near the Congo stage and were eating red beans and rice out of Styrofoam when I looked up to see a pockmarked guy shuffle by in surfer booties, raggedy shorts, a dress shirt and tie, and a baseball cap. I recognized him—sort of.

"Hey Marty, look. That's the guy from—well, um,

I believe that guy played Gandhi in *Gandhi*. It's Ben Kingsley, I think. Oh, I don't know."

And then the guy was gone. It probably wasn't anybody, I reasoned to myself. What movie actor would dress like that? Besides, he looked kind of...batty.

We soon wandered over to the Fais Do Do stage. (*"Fais do do"* is Cajun French for "dance party," but literally translated it means "go to sleep." Apparently that's what Cajun moms used to tell their kids just before they went off to dance with Cajun he-men). That's when we saw it—a crowd gathering under an outsized oak tree several yards away. It wasn't a stage; it wasn't a food vendor or a craft tent. It was something spontaneous. We didn't think; we just moved toward it, blindly but with verve.

Once we'd pushed through the crowds and arrived at the tree's base, we saw what all the hoopla was about: a wedding, a tiny wedding. Someone was playing guitar and singing "Going to the Chapel," and the whole crowd was beginning to sway and sing. I clasped my hands together in delight. Oooh, a wedding! I hadn't attended an earthy, outdoor wedding since my own last September. Never mind that we didn't have a clue who these people were.

I craned my neck and saw that the bride was about forty-five and had short gray hair, a ring of flowers atop her head, a gauzy dress with a gold belt, and flip-flops with big green leaves on them. The beefy groom looked like a biker-cum-Southern gentleman with his linen suit, Panama Jack hat, walrus moustache, and red, mottled nose. Except for one kooky onlooker in a full-length, black, habit-like outfit and straw hat, most everyone had on shorts and tank tops or Hawaiian shirts. It was impossible to tell the guests from the rude onlookers such as ourselves.

We'd only been interloping for about thirty seconds when a kindly old bearded guy leaned in and said, "Did you see the movie *Con Air*?"

Talk about a non sequitur, I thought. "Yeah, why?"

"Well, the groom was the pilot in that movie."

I clasped my hands with even greater delight. Oooh, we'd stumbled upon a minor-celebrity wedding!

"And did you see *Monster's Ball*?" the guy continued.

"Yep," I said, holding back a squeal.

"That guy there speaking now? He played the detective Halle Berry talks to after her son is hit by a car."

Yowza, this was a minor-celebrity wedding with a minor-celebrity guest! I stood on my tiptoes to see more, but there were four or five layers of people in front of me. Between shifting, sweaty shoulders, I did catch a quick glance of a pasty white guy with dark hair, looking like a good ol' boy of privilege in his blue seersucker blazer. Marty recognized him as the *Monster's Ball* detective. Since he'd only been onscreen for about five minutes, I didn't. But still, I was enchanted, and thus unable to walk away.

The old guy leaned in again. "See that man in the ball cap right there? That's F. Murray Abraham, a friend of the couple."

I angled myself forward to see. Whoa! It was the guy I had seen shuffling by the Congo stage with the blue dress shirt on and skanky shorts, the guy I thought was Ben Kingsley and batty. I peered at him for a minute, then in a whoosh got a mental download of a scene from *Amadeus*, a movie my pal Sam and I had watched over and over when it came out the summer before I shipped off to college. I turned to the old guy.

"He played Salieri in *Amadeus*, right?"

"Right," he said. "And the professor in *Finding Forrester*."

After staring at F. Murray Abraham like an idiot for five minutes, my attentions returned to the base of the tree. There, the minister—a woman in a see-through white hippie shirt, a sports bra, and tropical pants slit at the upper thigh but connecting again at the ankle—was saying something that was probably profound, but I couldn't hear it. Then a guy with a guitar took her spot and began playing.

Our informant leaned in again. "That's Paul Sanchez, from the band Cowboy Mouth. I think he's somebody's brother."

God, what next? An orderly from ER? The would-be rapists from the alley scene in *Training Day*? A roadie for Nickelback?

Pretty soon the bride and groom were saying their inaudible vows and then hugging everyone, except us. The crowd disbanded. We walked on, feeling that the rest of the day, despite all the great music and amazing vittles that were to come, would surely be a letdown after that serendipitous event.

Alas, the day managed to measure up in its own way, especially when we saw Phish kids in rags and dreadlocks dancing in their flowing, soaring style to the likes of wizened old country singer Ralph Stanley. It was the oddest of juxtapositions. Another highlight was seeing earringed *60 Minutes* newsman Ed Bradley randomly walk onstage to say hi to New Orleans singer Charmaine Neville. And only in New Orleans would I feel comfortable seeking shade behind the children's tent, spreading out a blanket there, and taking a nap.

The next morning, after staring up at the still-present parrot for a spell, Marty and I, hankering for the bayou, headed southeast to the swamps. First stop, Earl's Bar to rent us a canoe. Miss Debbie, the bar's sassy proprietress, had told me on the phone that she kept a large pet alligator in the yard, adding that she regularly hand-feeds it. I wanted to see it. I wanted to touch it. Unfortunately, the creature was busy breeding. "But you can meet August," Miss Debbie said, scurrying over to an industrial white bucket in the corner, pulling out a baby alligator and handing it to me.

August—named for the month Miss Debbie stole him from his nest—was about eight inches long and crawled all over our hands and arms like an excited iguana that a zookeeper might hand a sixth-grader on a field trip. August seemed so delicate, so harmless. How macabre Mother Nature is that she would grow this fragile being into a prehistoric man-eating monster.

A half hour later, Marty and I were gliding along the calm surface of the monsters' home, examining every floating tree branch in hopes that it was an alligator, big or small. We spied turtles, a startlingly white egret, weird cobwebs, fish jumping, blue herons with crazy-wide wingspans flying low along the water, loads of spooky Spanish moss hanging from bald cypress trees, whole fields of plant life that looked like solid ground but were really all water. And because the bayou does not hesitate to please, before too long we saw a few alligators, four- and five-footers with their eyes sticking up above the water's surface, looking at us like we may or may not be trouble. Each submerged silently when we got within about seven feet.

An hour in, we hit the mother lode. About fifty feet ahead of us we spied that telltale cutting of the water.

From that far away, it looked like a giant olive-green dog tranquilly paddling. But we knew better. We quietly sped up to reach it and got close enough to see the massive alligator just swimming along, minding its own business. It was huge, plenty big enough to knock our boat over and tear us to ribbons if it wanted. We inched closer, gaining on it. Surprisingly, the beast didn't seem to notice us—that is, until my camera shutter clicked shut. With that, it submerged with a splash. We sat in our canoe exhilarated, but wishing I'd waited longer to shoot.

A few minutes later I was flapping my arms about my head to ward off some flies when *kerplush*, off flew my watch, landing in the water and sinking like a stone. I was dumbstruck. That watch, a Christmas present from Marty, had held onto me tightly for almost a year and a half, without fail. What would cause it to take its leave in the middle of beast-infested waters? Did it want to see how much I cared? I looked at the water's brownish-green surface and achieved closure right away. It was a special watch, but if the marshlands wanted it, they could have it. After all the entertainment those waters had provided me over the years, it was the least I could do. And now, the bayou would never be late.

We'd felt a little weird skipping Jazz Fest—it was what we in town for, after all—but at a bar later, Joe's sister, a nurse who works at the festival's first-aid tent, quelled our worries. Standing under a knock-off of the famous Blue Dog painting (this particular blue dog was not sitting peacefully under a tree, but was being taken advantage of in the worst way by a German shepherd), she told us that a small disaster had struck earlier in the day: Hordes of Phish kids who'd ingested bad 'shrooms flocked to the tent and began beating up the nurses. I was glad I'd spent the day communing with enormous reptiles.

That night, Tracy and Joe told us they'd seen a sign on a pole announcing a missing green parrot named "Jamie." They'd called the guy, who came and coaxed the bird down from the tree, and left a bottle of wine as thanks. Jamie was gone. That was our cue to move along, too.

Later, hurtling back to Washington on an airplane, I began to ache with nostalgia for my former home, that land of serendipity and eccentricity and people gamboling about and huge flying cockroaches and threatening reptiles, a place I'd left because there were no good jobs and no good men. I read the *New Orleans Times-Picayune* and happened upon an article about the city's new mayor, a guy who apparently lives in a house festooned with 1,200 amber ashtrays. And that did it— it sent me over some mental precipice, nearly compelling me to leap into the cockpit and demand that the pilot turn around. Louisiana was where I belonged, dammit.

But I didn't. Instead, I looked down at all the yellow and black crawfish gunk gathered under my fingernails, and vowed to leave it there as long as it would stay.

இ இ இ

Suz Redfearn is a freelance reporter and essayist based in the Washington, D.C. area. Her work has appeared in Salon, Slate, The New York Times, The Washington Post, *and* Men's Health, *among other publications.*

.⃰⃰ .⃰⃰ .⃰⃰

Hungry Ghosts

In Thailand, an American Buddhist nun confronts
personal demons who come back to haunt her.

*D*URING THE HOT SEASON THE MOUNTAINS ARE DRY
and the monks wear bright orange robes. In the
middle of the night I awake to the crackle of activity.
Bare-shouldered monks in only their under-robes dart
past my window, disappearing into the forest on our
side of the stream. Their dogs tense, bristling. Circles of
light jump along the dark pathways, carrying with them
flashes of white, the suggestion of women's voices, high
and rapid.

Pranee, the youngest *maechi*, stands high on the
mountain face, beating the earth with a broom. Her *guti*
is on fire.

During the hot season the dry underbrush surrounding the *wat* frequently bursts into flame, the unfortunate

side effect of the slash-and-burn farming techniques the local villagers use in the deep forest.

For some reason no one remembers, the *wat* was built at the forest entrance, a physical reminder of the reciprocal relationship most *wat* and villages seek. To enter, the villagers are always marching along the row of *maechi guti*, barefoot, faces blurred under dustings of black ash and red soil. In the indigo work shirt and straw hat of the Thai farmer, red checked scarves ringing their necks and machetes wedged into waist sashes, they are eerily reminiscent of the Khmer Rouge, who still wander free, not so far away. I see them on the path outside my *guti,* the occasional flash of square white teeth, and remind myself that they are farmers, not killers. I hear them in the predawn darkness, laughing and chatting in northern dialect, and again upon their return in late evening. This odd commuter trail.

When the water buffalo aren't being used in the rice fields, the villagers husband them back near the waterfall. The *wat* provides free grazing land as well as a deterrent to theft. In a Buddhist country, who would be bold enough to steal a buffalo and walk it through a gauntlet of living merit fields, along gardens of eggplant and holy basil, under the bower dripping with frangipani and jasmine, past the reception area with its bamboo cages of songbirds?

The day Ajarn Boon and I visited the *wat*, the day I decided to ordain, I remember being struck by the sunlight, the heat, the activity, the feverish colors of the monk's side of the stream. "It is called Wat Thamtong because of the caves," Maechi Roongdüan had explained. "*Tham* means caves, *tong* gold." *The Temple of Golden*

Caves. I had no idea that at night it would be the *maechi* side bursting into flame.

That day as I stood panting from the hike beneath a blistering sun, I made a decision to ordain. A decision based on desire, but it was a hunger burning in me all the same.

The poorest local farmers don't have water buffalo or even flat farmland to work. They are the ones who claim the jungle, hacking and burning the thick undergrowth, frequently leaving patches to smolder. So all hot season, *maechi* climb the mountain with brooms and buckets of water to put out the night fires before they reach the *wat*.

The burning is not intentional on the part of the villagers. Maechi Roongdüan explains: "Just as every day the leaves fall and we must sweep them, so too the villagers must farm in order to eat. It is life."

I can smell the burning of Pranee's *guti* now like a scorched pot. I wonder if I, in my poorly managed robes that keep unfastening themselves from this Western body, can be of help. Me, with my poor night vision and dried-up contact lenses. Or will I just distract as usual—the fragile foreign *maechi* giving everyone more to worry about? In my own country, I am surely more useful.

I take one agonized step toward Pranee and her burning home.

Maechi Roongdüan appears on the path with a bucket in each hand, the contents lapping softly against the plastic sides like bathwater in a tub. "We thought of waking you to help," she says, "but this time Ajarn Suchin sent the monks across the stream to help."

As usual, her face is wide, smooth, her smile rippling gently like a stream. "*Mai pen rai,*" she trills the Thai's favorite phase. *Don't worry.*

I sense rather than hear a sudden intake of breath, a collective unvoiced gasp like the absence of wind on a hot day. Maechi Roongdüan spins around, the water in the buckets scattering in an arc of droplets around our bare feet, staining the earth dark red.

A monk stands stranded high on the rock face, encircled by a ring of fire. Hungry, glowing flames the color of his robes lick at his calves and thighs. It resembles some horrific circus act. Pranee, still keeping the vow of silence, stares. Her face is orange and fluid, reflecting the monk like an unwilling mirror.

An early memory pushes its way into my consciousness: the black-and-white image of an elderly monk steadily pouring petrol on himself in a busy midday street and then setting himself alight. Flames roaring up his body as he sits immobile, chanting, palms clasped together. Women and men charge forward, faces and bodies dropping before him, prostrating themselves over and over. The air fills with wailing.

I scream and my mother rushes into the living room, a jar of home-canned peaches in one hand. She swoops down and scoops me under one arm, heading for the hallway. It is too late. This becomes one of my earliest memories.

Am I only a toddler, inexplicably watching Vietnam's Buddhist Crisis of 1966 as it unfolds on American television screens? Or is it years later, perhaps a war documentary with footage of Thich Quang Duc, the seventy-three-year-old monk who performed the first self-immolation the year of my birth?

My mother cradles me in the hallway, preventing me from seeing the rest of the story: the flickering black-and-white monk becomes a charred skeleton. His ebony bones list to the side, slowly, slowly, hands still locked together in a *wai*, brittle limbs collapsing, fluttering like a negative of leaves, like a river of red paper after the Chinese New Year. His prayers linger on the smoky air.

I go to bed early. This is one of my earliest images, this charred monk, and the Napalm Girl running down the road, arms outstretched, skin dripping off her body in sizzling strips, and the plump, golden peach orbs swirling, suspended in clear viscous liquid. I have nightmares about Southeast Asia for years.

Two decades later, I stand rooted to the foot of a fiery mountainside in Thailand. All around me, monks and *maechi* spring to the aid of the young monk, slapping the earth before him with straw brooms, forming a human chain up the mountain, passing bucket after bucket from the stream. The thick air sparks and glows. Water spatters at the monk's feet with great hisses.

Maechi Roongdüan nods briskly at the rescue, and I remember to breathe. The air rushes out of my lungs.

"See? It's just like trying to extinguish our *kilesa*." *Cravings.* She sounds almost triumphant. She hoists the lap-lapping buckets of water and disappears up the side of the mountain, leaving me alone on the dark path.

The next day, holding a finger to her lips and whispering so that we don't get caught talking, Pranee shows me her replacement *guti*. Unlike the standard wooden hut built on stilts to discourage cobras and other invaders, it is a small, dim cave in the side of the mountain. Just large enough for a lumpy pallet on a bed of rocks.

I pull back the stiff tarpaulin curtain, dip my head inside again and again. The murky stone walls resemble an underwater grotto, full of dark crevasses. I draw back, terrified, thinking about creepy crawly things and how superstitious most Thais are.

Pranee scoffs. "Ghosts are for idiots!" she declares, her sunny, scrubbed face lighting the rock. "The only place they exist is in the mind!"

She tells me about her old life. Her parents farmed up-country. She was one of seven children. Maechi Roongdüan lets her and Theew, the swan-necked twenty-one-year-old, speak together occasionally because "silence is most difficult for the younger ones."

Later that evening she gets permission to visit me and waits on the walkway outside my *guti*. She tucks a few fading snapshots into my palm: one of her parents in farmer dress, one of herself in her primary school uniform.

"Will you go back?" I ask.

"Maechi Roongdüan is my mother now," she answers. "And the others are my family."

She tells me about the time Maechi Roongdüan took them for a week-long meditation retreat to an abandoned crematorium. According to my Buddhist texts, graveyards, crematoriums, and corpses are all traditional settings or subjects for meditating on *annica*, the impermanence of life. Pranee explains that the place was stifling hot and *maechi* kept fainting during meditation. After three days, everyone except Maechi Roongdüan wanted to go back.

"She wants us to know about bodies," Pranee says, her eyes glittering with an emotion I can't place. "About death."

Restless after the enforced seclusion of the rainy season, Maechi Roongdüan takes all of the *maechi* on a *thudong*, a pilgrimage, to a local teaching hospital.

On the drive I gaze at the road, memorizing the colors of the Thai countryside, the emerald, jade, rose, aubergine, celadon. Before I realize it, we are standing in a chilly hospital room crowded with unsteady medical students, *maechi* in solemn white, and a few locals who seem to be here just for the fun of it.

The cadavers arrive on wheeled cots: a man with the skin of his head already folded back like a disassembled android, revealing red and blue veins of circuitry; a yellowing woman with a long pelt of hair clinging to a flap above her severed ear; a child. Though the room reeks of formaldehyde, I worry that I will be able to smell the stench of decay. It's like my certainty at the dentist's that the Novocain will wear off any minute, revealing the white-hot agony of the drill. Of course, it never happens, but the fear is so strong I interpret every sensation as pain.

Fingering stainless steel instruments with dusted latex gloves, the students tell quiet jokes and get to work, peeling the man's face off to get at his skull.

"That's all we are," Maechi Roongdüan says, lining us up and coaxing us forward. "Flesh and bone, some breath."

Breath. Breathe. In and out, in and out. My breath clings to the pale gray walls, to the metal trays, to the wheeled cots, leaving tiny droplets like perspiration. A sheen of my panic coats the room. I learn that a dead body is far worse than a live one.

I remember the body I did not see. Freshman year at college I worked with refugees from Laos newly arrived in the United States. Entrusted with two families, my volunteer partner and I were supposed to befriend the children and help the parents navigate the confusing waters of U.S. immigration and social services. We were supposed to convince them that America wanted them.

The families had been settled next door to each other in a rundown apartment building in Dorchester, Boston's most segregated neighborhood. The nearest T stop was in the white part of town, several long blocks away. The first time we visited, the children scolded us for arriving so late in the afternoon. "Bad people come out in dark," they warned us. "You leave by four!" My partner, queasy from an encounter with a rat in the bathroom, nodded.

Next time, we came in the morning, tripping across a minefield of hostile glares from white men outside the Irish pubs dotting the street. We arrived to find one of the sons, a teenager who worked the graveyard shift as a busboy, sprawled on the sofa, face swollen and head bandaged. "The bad people catched him as he walk home," the kids explained in hushed tones. "They thought he Vietnamese."

"We help America against Vietnam," the father protested, his one good eye searching ours with milky urgency. "That why we must to leave." He spread his fingers, palms up. "We lose everything for U.S.A."

My partner and I squinted in sympathy and left early, sunk in the realization that the family needed more than we had to give, hoping my partner's pale skin would keep the red-eyed, red-faced men at bay.

I began to develop stomach pains on Saturday mornings. Friday nights I dreamed about the long, jolting T ride to Savin Hill. The trudge down gray streets speckled with dog shit; the gauntlet of drunken men; the apartment smelling of urine and *gapi*, fish paste; the hunger of kids convinced that I didn't love them enough, convinced that each visit would be my last.

One Saturday morning I called my partner and told him I was sick. It wasn't working out; we weren't helping anyone. I spent the day huddled in bed, as I'd done in response to most things since arriving at college.

That evening the television news reported that a black man had been killed at Savin Hall. The camera showed our T stop and the street we walked along each week. The reporter explained that white men from one of the local bars spotted the man waiting for the train and taunted him with racist epithets. They then got baseball bats and chased him onto the railroad tracks, where he ran headlong into an oncoming train. He was killed instantly.

"Well, he shouldn't have been here," a white-haired grandmother-type snapped at the reporter. "This is our neighborhood."

I huddled under the covers, my rage a cancer gnawing at my gut. Through pain came understanding, as I realized that the kids' terrified accusations were true. I didn't love them enough. I didn't love anybody enough to let go of fear.

Suddenly I am face to face with a beautiful, rotting boy. All around me, Thais whisper in a vocabulary of sensationalism I can't quite understand. The boy died in some mysterious, violent way. His body is being preserved until the trial is over.

I am failing to exercise. Instead of focusing on the impermanence of the body, I find myself wondering about his short life. What are they whispering behind their fluttering, birdlike hands, their white masks? I hear the word *pa,* father. Did his father kill him? Is that the reality my vocabulary cannot embrace?

My stomach lurches, and at the edges of my consciousness I recognize my old friend—rage, nearly a stranger
now. For Buddhists, there may not be anything sacred in
the bodies of the dead, but the presence of tourists in the
room, gossiping, brings hot bile to my stomach.

I smell the gases leaking out of my pores, sour. Gold
Bond medicated powder ringing the necks of the female
medical students. Acrid rubbing alcohol clinging to the
tips of instruments cutting through flesh. Focus on that!

The dead boy looks like he's asleep. He has waxy,
veined eyelids; his lips and skin are blue. A grotesque
decomposition eats its way down the side of his head like
fancy embroidery. Focus on that.

Macchi Roongdüan is at the front of the room the
whole time, wanting to see what is what, sticking
her hands inside someone's open chest. She is not just
Pranee's mother—she is mine, staring unflinching at the
exposed flesh of man.

"Look at her," Pranee whispers. "She's not afraid of
anything!"

I focus on Pranee's eyes. They glitter with the intensity of a malaria victim, dark and sure.

ॐ ॐ ॐ

*Faith Adiele, a graduate of Harvard Collage and the Iowa Writers'
Workshop, is assistant professor of English at the University of
Pittsburgh. This story was excerpted from her book,* Meeting
Faith: The Forest Journals of a Black Nun. *She lives in
Pittsburgh, Pennsylvania.*

ɷ ɷ ɷ

Bananas and Eggs

A Chinese-American struggles with her dual identity.

𝒫ROFESSOR GUO, WITH A DEVILISH SMILE ON HER face, teases, "Ying Shang-Fen, you are a banana: yellow on the outside and white on the inside. Dan is an egg, white on the outside and yellow on the inside." She giggles—her shoulders vibrating with each breath.

Dan and I laugh, exchanging a tense smile. I am a foreign exchange student in my junior year of college, sitting in a classroom in Harbin, China. For Dan, my academic competitor who is remembering the Chinese characters we are learning at a faster pace than I am, this joke means very little. He is a Caucasian male, fascinated with Chinese poetry and the hidden secrets tucked within an unknown land. His yellow yoke gives him more flavor—an added understanding of another culture beyond his upstate New York origins. I, on the

112

other hand, am being questioned completely. *White* on the inside? The blood of thirty-three generations of Yings, government officials, goldsmiths, bean-curd factory owners, miraculously replaced by the veins of Anglo-Saxon Vikings. My grandmother is not a banana, neither are my seven aunts, five uncles, nineteen cousins or my parents. In one innocent joke, I become an orphan to my family—a girl mutated by Western culture into a being no longer whole.

Ever since I was born, my Chineseness has always been in question. When I was a baby, my skin was too white— my hair too curly. When I grew older and began to surpass my brothers in height, everybody wondered why I was so tall and what I was eating. In the summers I was too dark—a Filipina girl. When I majored in English, I was too Westernized, not becoming a doctor or engineer that made money. When I began to travel, going to places more Chinese and more traditional than any of my Hong Kong relatives had ever visited, I was just plain strange. But never once, after spending years living in China learning Mandarin and Cantonese, immersed in Chinese history books, did my family ever consider me Chinese. And now this doubt extended beyond my family and to my university professors. I sat there in the hard wooden chairs of our gray-plastered classroom, reciting the latest vocabulary words, wondering what made my whiteness project so openly.

When our Mandarin class is through, Dan and I say goodbye to Professor Guo. We are a class of two, the others slowly elevated into a higher grade. We were Conversation Class C—the lowest level with the least Chinese experience. When I first took the placement test, I was placed among the advanced speakers. They were convinced that my yellow face knew the answers to the basic Chinese questions, but I was too nervous to speak. Eventually, they figured out that nervousness wasn't the reason I didn't speak—I simply didn't know that much Mandarin.

Dan and I walk down the three flights of stairs, avoiding the jungle of construction. Men carrying long, wooden sticks turn the corners, nearly decapitating us. We jump over bags of spilling sand and puddles of water—over stairways with missing steps and through clouds of white dust. This is Harbin Institute of Technology, the ninth-ranked university in China—I wonder what number ten looks like.

When we open the heavy metal front door, pushing aside a thick blanket hung from the ceiling, the icy winds of the Harbin winter sting our cheeks. I zip up my winter coat, wrap my scarf tighter around my neck, and tug down on my knitted hat. The silence caused by the frigid winds, and mouths wrapped by woven scarves, creates a sullen atmosphere on the 50,000-student campus. Dan unlocks his rusted blue bike that he bought for four dollars on the street, back when the weather was humid and he had envisioned long bike rides through the city. With dimples on his bearded face, he offers me a ride on his bike rack. The winds blow against my exposed skin as I think of the icy patches, open manholes, dangling cable wires, and random debris that scatter the road between here and our off-campus apartment. But then I imagine a warm cup of instant coffee waiting for me in my heated bedroom. I climb on. My fingers grip below his seat, as we sail off.

Along the way we pass a tightly-bundled Professor Guo, who beams with romantic imagination—her two favorite students riding away, teetering on a barely workable bike. For the past few weeks, our conversation topics have been love, past relationships, and what kind of person we would like to marry. Unsubtly, Professor Guo has been trying to match us up. We don't have the heart to tell her that Dan is happily dating Jenna, another girl in the program, so we continue the classes pretending that we don't know her intentions. Now as we pass her, we wave back, returning an equally bright smile.

Like a set of dominoes, the curious stares turn one by one to follow us as we flow through the pedestrian-lined streets. A girl with her school bag looks up with large eyes. A mask-covered street cleaner, broom in hand, pauses as she follows us with her gaze. The heavily layered men digging ditches within the frozen dirt stare at the strange sight traveling on wheels. No words are spoken, just a pause—a red carpet laid for the unusual royalty about to pass. They think: Who is that white man? Is he Russian? And what is he doing with a Chinese girl? Is that a Chinese girl? (They look closer, attempting to peer past the scarf covering half her facial features.) Yes, she is. The same oval eyes, straight black hair, round face, she must be one of us. Then what is she doing getting a ride from that foreigner? Are they on a Chinese bike? Her hands are so close to his body. Are they lovers?

Dan and I wave to the frozen faces, big smiles on our faces. We have become used to the deer-in-the-headlights look we receive when we walk anywhere in public together. Not only is it rare to see a foreigner in this isolated town of 3 million inhabitants, but it's also rare to see a young man with a young woman talking so openly, so freely, as if they don't care what other people think.

Dan weaves between the standing people, skillfully dodging the open holes and sudden drops in the pavement. The cool air freezes our skin. I dig my face deeper into my scarf while Dan pushes harder to pedal the bike forward. With each corner we turn, my grip tightens around Dan's seat.

We leave the campus boundaries, entering the sterile neighborhood that has been our home for the past two months. To the right stands a five-story pile of coal that burns black smoke into the murky air. During the winter months, when the apartment complexes compete for heat, the dense smoke sticks in small particles between my teeth. The white tissues I blow my stuffed-up nose into turn gray and gritty. There is a continual film of grease and dust that sticks like taffy to my cheeks and forehead. No matter how many low-pressured showers I take, it cannot be washed off. Slowly, I would notice acne forming on my classmates' faces, and my own as well. Cleanliness is a perpetually hopeless process: we wash our dirty faces with dirty water.

Today the toilet paper venders are out, distributing their goods from the back of a truck. The hierarchy of the different kinds of toilet paper fascinates me. First there are the individually wrapped rolls with the cardboard in the center that are sold in packs of ten for fifty cents. Then there are the rolls that are not individually wrapped that still have the cardboard center sold for forty cents. Then the cardboard center is taken out for twenty cents. And at the very bottom for five cents, there is a huge stack of rough, newspaper-like tan sheets, tied together with a red string—unwrapped and exposed to the daily dust and pollution of the streets. I imagine the people who can't afford to pay fifteen more cents for a drastically improved luxury. Every day after relieving themselves they wipe their burning behinds with a coarse square of sandpaper that has been sitting outside, unwrapped, next to a coal-burning factory. I cannot imagine such poverty even when it is in front of me.

Past the toilet paper stand, I spot the familiar steam floating from a garbage can, warming a bamboo basket of meat-stuffed buns. I often eat these *baozi* if I sleep through my lunch break and I am late for class. They sell these bite-sized buns, thirty cents for six, in a small plastic bag with two splintery chopsticks.

Then we turn the corner and arrive at our building—a six-floor cement box with balconies with doors that do not open. Spider webs of cable dangle from the roof, connecting to all the windows and meeting at a green generator protruding from the second floor. Disorganized cables hanging loosely from Chinese buildings is so normal that it is almost a part of the architecture. Not that architecture is a practicing profession in China. Communism eliminated all buildings with style and replaced them with cement squares with rectangle windows. I often get lost in the city because all the buildings look the same.

I climb off Dan's bike and my foot slips on a frozen puddle on the pavement—human saliva and urine frozen together in a miniature hockey rink. I circle my right arm wildly in the air to keep myself from falling. We both laugh at my clumsiness as Dan locks his bike and we enter the dark, low-ceilinged front room.

The warmth relieves our bodies as our arms and legs relax, our facial muscles defrost. The maid from the front desk says: "Ying Shang-Fen, this woman is here to see you." She points at a woman dressed in a black coat lined with fake fur. The woman removes her black gloves, then pauses. She scrutinizes my face, my hand held out in a Westernized greeting. She tentatively takes my hand.

"You are Ying Shang-Fen?"

"Yes, I am."

"But you told me on the phone that you were American?"

Instantly, I realize who I am talking to. Last night I answered an ad seeking English teachers for 100 RMB an hour, about 12 U.S. dollars. I had convinced myself that I needed the extra money, but in actuality I was hoping the job would boost my dwindling self-esteem. The continual line of questioning from the local people—noodle shop venders, college students, internet café owners—on why a Chinese person spoke such poor Mandarin, combined with my placement level within the program were causing me much intellectual insecurity. I answered the ad, and in a perfect American accent explained: "I am a native speaker from the U.S., majoring in English at a U.S. university." When I hung up the phone, returning to my desk piled with Mandarin textbooks, dictionaries, and flashcards, I felt relieved. My Mandarin may be horrible, but at least I could speak English.

I return the woman's similarly confused look and answer in English, "I am American." I was born in America. I have spent my entire life growing up in America. This is the first time I have ever been to China." I switch back to speaking in Mandarin, "Can you not tell from my thick foreigner's accent that I am clearly not from China?" I can feel my pulse quickening—the pressure of the same conversation every day.

"But Americans have blond hair and blue eyes. You look just like one of us."

My Confucian politeness quickly fades. "Not all Americans have blonde hair and blue eyes. American people can have red hair, brown hair, blond hair, or black hair. The stereotypes that you are referring to, the typical blonde-haired, fair-skinned Caucasian, was created through the media—movies, TV shows, magazine pictures. You have probably rarely seen an American in person, but you assume that you have because of the images of white people that surround you on a daily basis. I am just as American as a person with blond hair, similar to the millions of Chinese people who live in America as well."

The woman laughs again. "But the students, they will not want to learn English from a Chinese person. It is not exciting for them. They will not trust you."

I switch back to my mother tongue, "But I can speak English perfectly regardless of what they may think." I begin to whine like a teenager insisting to her parents that she is no longer a child. The moment of confidence from just two seconds before transforms into a naked self-doubt. I shrink before this woman into a timid creature, pawing at her pants like a helpless kitten.

Another student enters the building—a cold rush of wind blows my hair into my face. The woman aggressively approaches the student, showing me the back of her long black coat. "Hello? Are you interested in making a lot of money as an English teacher?" She preys on this innocent boy, wanting his blood, his white, creamy skin. The student removes his hat and I realize that he is our program's only German student. I look upon him jealously—apparently the German boy speaks better English than I do because he is white.

I walk up the five flights of stairs to my room, so easily dismissed. I hate it that this narrow-minded woman, who has probably never left Harbin, who is less educated, less traveled, less intelligent than I, has the power to make me cry. Frustrated tears gather in the corners of my eyes, but I don't let them fall down my cheeks. I smear my eyes with the back of my hand, feeling the redness rush to my nose and eyelids. I hurry up the stairs, slamming the door to my room. Once inside, I begin to sob. Why am I so upset? It is just a stupid woman who has never been outside the country. She doesn't know any better. I straighten my back, pulling down on my shoulders, but the tears don't stop. My chest caves as I grapple for the next breath. She called me Chinese. Isn't this what I have always wanted—to be a member of the elite dragon club?

All my life I have been struggling with my muddled identity, questioning which ethnic group I belong to the most. But today I think maybe it is not an ethnic group I should be searching for. Maybe it is a place. Maybe it is a person or a group of people. All I know is that no matter where I go, I feel like a stranger—in my hometown, on my college campus, in a foreign land isolated by mountains and coldness. I stare outside my window into the empty, gray courtyard—laundry dangles, colorless, on plastic lines of string—drying vegetables hang like curtains across windowsills. I take a deep breath, expanding my lungs. Releasing the pressure, I exhale the contaminated air—the air of my misplaced youth, of my unfulfilled desires, of my dissatisfaction.

Chellis Ying is an MFA writing student at the University of San Francisco. After she graduated from Kenyon College in 2001, she lived overseas for two years in China, Guam, and Spain. Her work has appeared in The Best Travel Writing 2005. *She lives in San Francisco.*

፠ ፠ ፠

Clicking in Greece

Worry beads act as an ancient codex for
"be here now."

ris Evangelinos snatched the komboloi from
Peter's hand and put a match to it. The orange
and yellow beads—my gift to Peter less than a week
ago—were wrapped in flames. Aris waited a moment,
put his nose to the beads and sniffed. I scanned the beads'
edges. Plastic would melt, amber would burn; Peter's
komboloi did neither.

Aris was uncertain. Peter's mood improved immediately. We had bought Peter's strand of Greek "worry
beads" in Crete a week ago and ever since then, we'd
been worrying.

Aris lit another match. The flames lingered.

"Well," I said before he could light a third, "what are
they?"

The *komboloi* was not the standard olivewood or monochromatic plastic. Peter's beads looked like geologic tie-dye—hundreds of layers of red and orange with sepia swirls and bursts of sunsets. The beads, we had been told in the small shop where we had bought them, were some mixture of amber and stone from China.

"Plastic," said the owner of our hotel when he saw them. He pulled from a pocket his own *komboloi*—deep red, as if cut from a glass of claret sitting in the sun. "Amber," he said, "from the Komboloi Museum in Nafplion."

Over the past few hundred years, the Greeks have evolved worrying from a lowly pedestrian experiment to high art. Worrying became colorful, rhythmic, sensuous. And after that, who was worried? The *komboloi* all but cured anxiety. In many countries beads are associated with prayer, but on the streets of contemporary Greece, a *komboloi* supplies calm companionship and a certain chic.

Peter wanted one. He wanted an internal, rhythmic grasp of the whirling or slow, drip-dripping *komboloi* he heard everywhere in Greece. Why were all these people playing with beads? *Komboloi* ticked and twirled in the hands of restaurant patrons waiting for tables. The beads dropped slowly, one at a time, through the fingers, rapping softly but resoundingly on the bead below like secret code. There were rhythms for every mood, lengths for every hand, beads for every budget. They wrapped around young and old fingers alike, and Peter wanted to know why all these rhythms, combined, sounded like the collective pulse of Greece.

The *komboloi*, traditionally a male distraction, caught my attention, too. There was something appealing about an ancient, compact, aesthetic, low-tech antidote to Palm

Pilots, cell phones, and Internet access anywhere anytime in the split-second timing of the twenty-first century. Stroking beads sends an entirely different message to the brain than jabbing at keyboards; even rhythms unlock a portal to a place light years from the office. The *komboloi* is an ancient codex for "be here now." And one of the best places to decipher its mystery is at Aris Evangelinos' Komboloi Museum.

The Komboloi Museum is a candy store for the anxious. One wall is covered to the ceiling in strands of cabernet-red, amber-orange, and saffron-yellow beads. They are smooth to the touch and feel like poetry to the fingertips. Some are translucent, others built of so many layers that the eye loses its way before the center is discerned. The strands closer to the window glow in early morning or midday light.

The museum is located in Nafplion, a tree- and fortress-filled seaside town on the eastern edge of the Peloponnese. Here, Aris Evangelinos repairs older *komboloi* and sells contemporary versions of traditional designs. Hanging on the back wall are black and white photos of a *komboloi* workshop in Egypt, and the first Greek workshop to make the beads. Upstairs is a museum of rosaries and prayer beads Aris has collected during his travels over more than twenty years.

Unfortunately, we did not make a good first impression. We arrived with a *komboloi* of questionable quality; we were obviously too ignorant to be buyers of consequence. I retreated up a well-worn, narrow staircase to the museum. Here were four small rooms full of beads—Hindu and Buddhist, Moslem and Christian and Greek. Made from red and black coral, cedar and sandalwood, glass, Bakelite, snake's bone, or mother of pearl, some strands held as few as nineteen beads, others over one hundred. Most surfaces were smooth, but a few had intricately carved or etched designs. A single, rare strand of horn beads from Tibet hung next to three strands of black coral mixed with ivory, silver, and amber; and a length of Chinese beads carved from elephant bones. Amber was clearly the material of choice: there were more than a dozen strands of beads, crimson and rust, gold and flaxen, cherry and brick. Most pieces were dated between 1750 and 1950.

By the display of Greek *komboloi* was a typed sign, heavily edited, which in its original format stated: "The only country in the world that never uses a *komboloi* for religious purposes. We have taken this habit from the Turks (Moslems). We made it little bit different than originally was and it became like a toy in our hands helping us to calm and also to have something to concentrate and gather." Perplexed grammarians passing through had crossed out certain words and written in others. "The number of the beads is not specified. It depends on the size and the length related to the size of the hand. The total number of the beads has to be an odd one."

I spent over an hour studying the beads, the signs, and the editing. I also flipped through the book Aris had written and published about his lifetime with the *komboloi*—his passion for this unassuming strand of beads passed down to him from his grandfather, his trips through Egypt and Turkey searching for workshops that made quality beads.

"The eyes alone cannot decide which is the best and most beautiful," Aris's grandfather had told him. "The fingers and the ears must agree as well."

The most desirable beads, made from solid amber, are all but impossible to find. If you do find a strand, they will be old and very expensive.

Second best are beads made from *faturan*—amber filings combined with some sort of resin. This is where expertise comes in: the color of the bead, its weight and shape, which account for the critically important harmonious "click" of bead on bead. The edges must be considered—are they rounded or squared off? Is the amber translucent or opaque? And then, there is the all-important final bead, the "priest," and the tassel. What of the cord on which they are strung? Many of these choices are purely personal, but certain qualities are unarguably superior to others. It was clear Aris was a connoisseur of *komboloi*, and any slipshod, crass, shiny, metal elements or lengths of chain were not to be tolerated.

When I came back down, Peter and Aris were ensconced. They might as well have been sitting on cushions sipping dark, sweet coffee, so thick was the ancient mercantile camaraderie. Aris had been a rug merchant before devoting himself solely to *komboloi*, and his history and expertise showed through his uptown connoisseurship. It was Peter, the shop-a-phobic who breaks out in hives at the entrance to a mall, who surprised me. He truly wanted one of Aris' amber *komboloi*. But not too expensive.

"Do you have any contemporary *komboloi* as fine as the old ones upstairs?" I asked. "Or the *komboloi* that belonged to your grandfather?"

Aris looked up. After a hard scan of my eyes, he opened a drawer under his desk and pulled out a strand of heavy, red, solid amber beads.

"This belonged to my grandfather," he said. Peter

and I both knew better than to reach for it. *Komboloi* etiquette is clear: never touch unless you're invited to. Some believe that the *komboloi* takes on the aura of its owner, and it can wreak havoc with your inner rhythms if someone else clicks your beads.

"Is this the piece that launched your life's journey?" I asked. Finally Aris smiled.

He replaced his grandfather's *komboloi*. Then he reached down to a drawer hidden beneath the counter, withdrew a tangerine-colored *komboloi* and passed it to Peter. Slowly, Peter ran the beads through his fingers. He held them to his ear and listened as one bead clicked the next. He rubbed the beads lightly between his fingers and sniffed the air above them. Aris watched and waited and finally went back to work. Eventually Peter cleared his throat and asked if there might not be one more *komboloi* he might see. Aris scowled and sighed while Peter smiled and stroked the beads, and the whole process began all over again.

While Peter studied Aris's wares, Aris had another look at Peter's original *komboloi*. He ran a fingernail over the surface, studied the inside holes. What combination of resin and amber, plastic and stone might this be? But now, he was being stumped by an earnest student—and a potential client—which made the unresolved mystery less annoying. For Peter, the enigma only improved his feelings for his day-glo *komboloi*.

I studied the monochromatic candy-colored *komboloi* in the window. There was a deep red strand of nineteen transparent beads to which my eye kept returning. I looked at various shades of orange and yellow, but none equaled the warm nuggets of solid claret. For six dollars, worrying had never looked so appealing. I took it from the hook, allowed my fingers and ears their input, and a few minutes later, decided these were the beads for me.

Twenty minutes later, Aris was still pulling *komboloi* for Peter. He sighed loudly, opened another drawer and withdrew a strand of *faturan*. Twenty-one beads, both transparent and opaque, it radiated a deep warmth and, when rubbed lightly between the fingers, the faint warm-earth scent of amber. Peter smiled. Here, at last, was his amber *komboloi*.

On a flight a few weeks later, we hit bad turbulence. I watched a few rows ahead of me, as 25B's breakfast burrito hovered twelve inches above her tray table. The flight attendant lunged for the dish; the captain pushed for seatbelts; I fished for my *komboloi*.

In the seat next to me, an ophthalmologist stowed his Palm Pilot. He glanced at the strand of symmetrical, crimson beads that I held in my hands. The edges were flat, like burnished slices of a crystalline tube. I was squeezing the glowing nuggets through my fingers, moving one at a time along the coiled red cord.

"Turbulence like this is enough to give me religion, too," he said.

"Oh, I'm not religious. I'm nervous. These are Greek," I managed.

The smooth beads eased through my fingertips, edging toward a short length of cord and the next bead, arriving with a calming "click." The light in the beads or their soothing rhythm caught his two-year old daughter's attention, and instinctively, she reached for them.

His wife, arms clenched around the child, studied my technique. A tense minute passed, and another, but the air got no calmer. "Whatever they are," she said finally,

eyeing my nuggets of sunny claret, "could you work
them a little faster?"

Mija Riedel writes about travel and the arts. She has written for
The Washington Post, Los Angeles Times, Islands, *American*
Craft, Metalsmith, *and numerous other publications. Currently
she works as a field researcher for the Smithsonian Institution,
Archives of American Art. She grew up in New York and lives in
San Francisco.*

RUTH KAMNITZER

In the Dust of His Peacock's Feathers

On the road to Murugan, the author finds the deity
in the pilgrims as much as in the shrine.

*T*HE CHANT IS ENDLESS, ITS POWER ENORMOUS. IT
fills my ears, my blood, carries me forward in this
human wave that knows no containment. It is the India I
have always dreamed existed. And now it has found me.

"Palani? It is nothing interesting madam. Just a small
temple. They will just raise a flag at the top of the hill
and everyone will go home. Nothing for tourists to see.
Better you come Madurai, we have float festival, very
nice." During the last month of cycling around the
Indian state of Tamil Nadu, my friend Karen and I had
passed many pilgrims dressed in green, on their way to
see Murugan, they said, the errant son of Shiva, at his

129

hilltop temple at Palani. But the man in the Madurai
tourist office had just assured us, nothing to see. Well,
we decided, we would, of course, visit the temple when
we happened to pass through, but there was obviously
no reason to rush.

Then biking along one day, we ran into a human
wall that stretched for miles in either direction. These
weren't just the pilgrims in green. This was everyone,
and they were all going to Palani. And so now, of course,
were we.

Only in India can you bike into a town where you
know absolutely no one, and ten minutes later have
found a secure place to store all your belongings for the
next week and be sitting down to a full feast while entertaining the steady stream of visitors who have come
to pay their respects. In our case it was the owners of the
local gas company who made us feel so welcome, and
their hospitality was so effusive it seemed we'd never be
able to leave for the mountain of food amassing on our
plates. Eventually our hostess was satisfied that we had
eaten all we possibly could, photographs were taken,
hands pumped repeatedly in farewell, and addresses exchanged. We ceremonially removed our shoes, wiggled
our toes, and set off, with the thousands of others, for the
temple at Palani, just over a hundred kilometers away.

The black tar is scorching, and it doesn't take us long
to realize why everyone else is waiting out the heat of
the day at the side of the road. But Karen has already
burned the bottom of her feet almost beyond repair, and
excruciatingly painful blisters will plague her the entire
walk. Families beckon us from the shade of tamarind
trees, where they lie napping on their jute sacks, or eating lemon rice out of banana leaf packages. Others softly

sing the names of Murugan while fingering the beads that hang round their necks. We sit with them, and learn the story of Murugan.

Once upon a time Shiva, the great god responsible for the destruction and recreation of this world, was given a golden fruit. The fruit was not to be broken, but consumed in one bite. Being a chivalrous type of god, he gave it to his wife, Parvati, who in turn wanted to pass it on to their children. Shiva and Parvati have two sons—Ganesh, the popular elephant-headed god who adorns the gateways of so many temples, and Murugan. Not knowing to whom the fruit should be given, Shiva and Parvati announced a small contest: whichever son managed to go around the world first would win the golden fruit.

Murugan at once mounted his peacock and set off, determined to claim the prize. Ganesh however, being rather stout and not much one for speed, merely walked around his parents, saying, "You are my world." Needless to say, by the time Murugan returned home from his transglobal journey, the fruit was already in Ganesh's belly. Outraged that he had been tricked out of his prize in such a manner he fled to the hill at Palani, where the temple now stands. It was there that we were going to see him.

As soon as the tarmac cools we begin to walk again. There are truly thousands of pilgrims. It is an indescribable feeling to be part of something this large, this powerful, this timeless. Rich or poor we all walk together, all barefoot, all carrying only a single small bag slung over the shoulder or balanced on the head. The men wear lungis, a simple cloth tied around the waist, and the women saris, many of them red and gold. Every

color is a symbol in India, a way of pronouncing something about your identity, whether it is your marital
status, your region or a pledge you have made with a
god. Almost all the pilgrims wear a *mala*, a string of 108
beads, put on at the beginning of the journey to signify
the pledge of the *padi yatra* to make the journey barefoot.
Padi means foot, *yatra* means pilgrim. This *mala* will be
blessed by the temple priests.

We walk, on and on, until night falls, and we sleep,
with countless others, at the side of the road, in fields, in
the homes of villagers who have opened their doors to
us, or in the courtyards of temples. In the morning we
rise and walk again. Never before have I felt so strongly
that past and present are not connected by any line, any
string, but rather the past tumbles like a snowball down
a hill, an avalanche crashes violently into us, so that its
pieces are rearranged but essentially the same. History
doesn't repeat itself, it just wears different clothing.

As the only two foreigners, Karen and I are the object
of much curiosity.

"*Ingeporinga?*" they ask in Tamil. Where do you come
from?

"Canada *poringa*," we answer.

"Kerala?" (A state to the west of Tamil Nadu.)

"No, Canada."

"Karnataka?"

"No, Canada. USA, Canada," we explain, holding
our fists up to represent neighboring countries.

"USA. England," they answer, nodding slowly with
a look of vague understanding. Another group approaches. "*Ingeporinga?*" It begins again. We estimate
that we meet at least twenty people an hour, for at least
ten hours of the day (there are some quieter times in the

day). If they have all come in groups of twenty, in the four days the walk will take, we will have met, directly and indirectly, 16,000 people. The figure is astounding.

With each passing hour, our line gets wider, longer, stronger. A man walks by, balancing on his head a rooster on a red velvet cushion. It is a gift for Murugan. Another family leads their cow who wears a garland of yellow carnations. She will be blessed by the temple priests before returning home. Women balance brass pots on their heads containing water taken from their village wells and scented with flower petals. It too will be blessed at the temple. Many villagers carry *cavatis*, temple replicas carried on the shoulder. No one can adequately explain to us what they are, and we only see what they are used for when we reach the temple, but they are beautiful nonetheless. Tiny children walk, trotting along to keep up with their parents who can't be slowed in their enthusiasm. Occasionally they are whisked up and carried on the head to save time. I see a couple pushing two children on a bicycle. There are groups of children who tell us their parents will join them in a few days, and groups of adults who say they have left their village in the hands of their children.

Karen's blisters are very bad, and she grimaces in pain as they burst and the tender flesh is exposed to the stony gravel road. The pilgrims carry her along, one at each elbow, chanting endlessly to keep her mind off the pain. *Subrimanike...Aro garah...Muruganike...Aro garah . . . Palanike...Aro-garah...Aro-garah?...Aro-garah*. At first her voice is thin and reedy as she struggles against the pain, and then she gains power. She hobbles proudly, head erect, Murugan ahead. I admire her determination and faith.

Sometimes we are adopted by groups of twenty or more, entire villages. Often they are followed by hired pickup trucks, carrying extra supplies, food, cooks, and tired children. Those riding in the back will at times go barefoot, at times wear shoes, but will not wear the *mala*, a sign of the pledge of the *padi yatra*. We rest with them in the midday heat. Karen and I are fussed over in Tamil, constantly shifted to more advantageous locations in the shade of the truck, while the cooks prepare huge vats of vegetable curry and rice that we eat off banana leaves on the gravel. Then we crawl right under the truck, spread our tarpaulin sacks and sleep till the sun at last dips enough for the pavement to cool and then we walk again. Sometimes we are swept along with richer folk, and we eat with them in makeshift restaurants at the roadside, where *masala dosa*, *idly, utapam*, and other south Indian specialities are served to thousands. These restaurants are like factories, the waiters sweating with profusion as *dosas* fly with lightning speed, the pails of *dhal* soup emptied almost as quickly as they are filled. Everywhere we are greeted warmly. Always we feel we are among friends.

For four days, virtually twenty-four hours a day, we are surrounded by Indian people. We fall asleep to them fussing over us, exclaiming over our hairy arms, our strange skin, or admonishing us for not covering our heads completely. They pull up our sheet and tuck it in, so that we blend in more fully with the faceless sexless sleeping masses. For a few hours we escape our identity.

On the third night we sleep in a large communal camp. There are at least 3,000 of us in this field. Oversized speakers scream *bajans*, devotional songs, till past midnight. Miraculously, the noise, which even a week ago would have been unbearable, now does not even bother me in the slightest and I sleep soundly. At 3 A.M. everyone rises as if on cue, and four minutes later their sheets are folded away, saris smoothed down and they are off. Karen and I are left alone in the field, still rubbing the sleep out of our eyes. The road is quiet, the pilgrims walking steadily to try to make some time before the sun rises and turns the black tar into a hot griddle. By draping our scarves over our heads and shoulders and looking down when someone passes we are for a few hours at least, just two more pilgrims on their way to see Murugan.

As we near the temple, numerous paths melt together. The line grows longer, wider, and with each hour more certain. It has no beginning nor end, no definition, not a line but a vector that points from everywhere to Murugan. *Aro Dgarah...Aro-garah, subrimanike...Aro-garah?...Aro garah!* There must be ten, twenty, one hundred, two hundred thousand of us. No one knows.

On the third day the gypsies arrive by the eastern path. They have a vibrancy that stands out even here, looking exactly the way gypsies are supposed to look; the men with long dark curls escaping colorful bandanas and the women possessed of a mysterious beauty that belies their rags and dirt-smudged faces. Murugan is the errant son of Shiva and so too the god of those marginalized in Hindu society. Now these people of the road are on the road to Murugan and the energy is uncontrollable. They discover us and swarm like locusts and we are carried in their wake.

In the lead is a woman I imagine as the elephant matriarch. Her sari is worn like an afterthought, doing nothing to hide her huge breasts and ass that stick out a mile in either direction. Bangles cover her arms and heavy gold rings sparkle in her nose and ears. She seems about to topple as she limps, very quickly, down the road, her bandaged, bloody feet unable to keep up with her spirit. A beautiful young man, his gypsy eyes dark and smoky, his body lithe and soft, begins to beat a tambourine against his hip. The cry mounts, the songs begin. The woman explodes in dance down the road, and her poor bloodied feet have no choice but to follow. I have never seen an Indian woman dance with such ferocious abandon.

Eventually they stop off at a temple for a free meal, beg some money off us, and we part warmly, with much hand clasping and promises to meet again. I am sorry to see them go.

Coconut stalls now line the road. The machete thwacks as it hits the nut and slices away the fibrous shell until at last the sweet juice runs and the white flesh lies revealed. We drink three or four of these a day, endless sweet tea and innumerable glasses of water from questionable sources. Roadside clinics have now appeared, where doctors dispense free medicine and treat wounded feet, while nurses offer massages. My feet are now almost as bad as Karen's, and I double my appreciation of her stoicism. We hobble together, the lame leading the lame. *Aro...garah?...Aro-garah!*

People from Rameswaram on the southeastern tip of the subcontinent have begun to arrive. Some have spent seven days covering the 300 kilometers, and their pilgrim's bags are even dustier than ours. But no matter where we have come from, we are all going home, and greetings are as between siblings not strangers. And we too have innumerable friends among this crowd. There is a group of six friends in their early twenties. One of them has taken a vow of silence for the duration of the journey, and his friends take the opportunity to arrange his betrothal to me. He only smiles devilishly as the joke is renewed every time we pass each other, dates set, and invitations designed.

The reporters find us. Amazingly enough, among the tens of millions and all that we have seen, we are interesting to them. Ruth and Karen become Ruda and Gareem, laborers who have saved for four years to make this return visit to India. The battle between being honest and trying to make Indians understand that our reality isn't as glamorous as they sometimes believe, lost. Our picture appears the next day in four editions of south Indian newspapers, boosting our already elevated status to new heights.

On the last day of the walk, we meet up with a group of about forty from our village of origin, relatives of the gas company owners with whom we entrusted our bikes. Two of them we recognize. They have covered the 100 kilometers in forty-eight hours, stopping only for a few hours in the night. They have been on the look-out for us, and they greet us now like long-lost friends. Another relative lives five kilometers from the temple, and we are going there for dinner, unannounced but surely welcome.

When we arrive, a well-dressed woman in a beautiful sari opens the door and introductions begin as pilgrim bags pile high in the corner. It takes twenty minutes to trace the lineage back to a common point. While the poor woman is mobilizing the household to feed the masses, the phone rings—thirty-five more are expected within the hour. She is unperturbed. Due to their strategic location near such a holy site, she tells me they receive about a thousand guests a year. I try and picture my mother in the same position. Dinner is obviously going to take some time, so due to our honored status as foreign guests a child is dispatched to the market to buy us *dosas*, which we eat with the women in the kitchen.

Then, unexpectedly, we are on the road again.

It is quiet now, most of the people having settled down for the night. Those last five kilometers take almost two hours, with frequent stops to laugh and argue over who is in worse shape. We imagine the story we will tell, how we hobbled to Palani, arrived at the throne of the great god bent and broken.

The next morning I realize that everything we have seen so far, the days of walking, the chants, the devotion, is only the beginning. Things only get madder.

Pilgrims are arriving by the thousands, and the wide two-kilometer road that rings the temple is fully packed by 7 A.M. The most auspicious day to pay respect to the half-meter-high idol will be tomorrow. We step out of the sleeping area and into the crowds.

I am swept up, the senses pulled in every direction. My eyes glimpse, but don't comprehend, the songs, the fever of devotion, the women whirling madly. Cymbals, drums, anklets of bells, Murugan's name a thousand times, we are almost there and it can't be contained any longer. Huge processions go by, and we fall into their song, our feet still bare following them as we dance down the temple road. A group of about twenty drummers passes followed by the holders of the *cavatis*, presents for Murugan, and in the front the dancers, goaded into trance. Karen is caught and I watch as her hands begin to tremble, her steps become feverish. An old Indian lady sees her, too, and holds her hand in caution. She shifts from one foot to the other, like a nervous animal, straining to be let off the leash. She dances, her bloodied feet that made her grimace in pain a few moments earlier forgotten, and they fly as the Indian boys urge the drummers to faster, more dangerous rhythms. I am afraid. The old woman eases her back from the crowd, from the vortex. The procession keeps dancing and we fall back, Karen still trembling. The air is pungent with jasmine, incense, and humanity. The crowd becomes even more dense, and then we pass through the temple gates like a cork. Countless stairs lie ahead but the crowd does not pause. They have walked one, two, three hundred kilometers and the road has not ended yet. The strong don't aid the weak, they carry them. Murugan cannot wait. I see mothers grab their children, fly up the stairs two at a time, grandmothers virtually dragged by a nephew on either side, toddlers bouncing on their fathers' heads.

Yet we too climb, run on all fours. I see the faces around me and I think, how could so many people be wrong? For the first time in my life I seriously consider the possibility that God exists, not as a facet of ourselves but as a completely independent entity. And I am afraid, because if he does exist, if he is Murugan, he's not going to be very happy that I've remained skeptical for so long.

The temple is huge. We have reached the top of the stairs and stand in a huge courtyard, dotted with various places of worship that surround the main shrine. People are going crazy everywhere. I don't know where I am or what's coming next. There is shouting and the crowd parts for a man, naked but for the simplest cloth, being rolled across the filth of the courtyard floor. His hands are clasped above his head, his eyes closed and when the hands of the group pause in their turning of him he lies slumped in exhaustion. In the coming days we will see that it is a fairly popular custom to be rolled around the circumference of the temple, for both men and women. Watch out, we will say to each other, there's a roller coming.

A man walks uphill, hooks in his back pulling a wooden *cavati* on wheels. Another is even more grueling—he walks backwards, the hooks piercing his nipples, in his cart a young boy tied to a stick. Everywhere people are falling into trance, lashing at the bounds of their bodies. Women dance and thrash, intoxicated with this promise of freedom, in a manner I would never have expected conservative Indian women to act in public. The man beside me, carrying his child, falls into a heavy trance, suddenly lurching madly. The child doesn't even seem to notice. Others rush up and take the child from his arms as the drums begin, the chants start. In the temple courtyard a small space is cleared. The now familiar beat, that builds up so rhythmically, almost then completely breaks down. Two men, a cloth tied around their waists, chests bare, are goaded into trance. They face each other like wild animals whose instinct for preservation has been demented by a long captivity. One has his hands tied behind his back, his tongue forced out and he is so wild I fear he will bite it off. The other man is given a short spear, one end the spade of Murugan, the other a gleaming point. They are released, circle each other, stamping in agitation, and the man with the spear rushes and stabs it through the other's tongue. They jump together in glee, ecstasy, and insanity.

The next day we rise early. Today is the day, the full-est moon, the biggest karmic bonus. The temple road is packed, fired with expectation. We walk the two kilo-meters in a dense crowd.

Eventually we climb the stairs and enter the temple courtyard. There are three ways to see Murugan: you can shell out 1,000 rupees (about US$30) and be ushered in within half an hour for a relatively peaceful visit, you can pay 100 rupees and wait for up to three hours before you file in with the others, or you can forego the concept of time altogether and sit patiently with the masses in a line already thousands long. We choose the 100-rupee option—you don't want to be too cheap when it comes to God, he's probably mad enough at me as it is, but he would be greedy if he thinks I've got 1,000 rupees to spare. The ticket booth has been swallowed and is only identifiable as the dense lump within this larger lump of people. A helpful man, also going for the 100-rupee op-tion, offers to buy tickets for us. We each hand him the 100 rupees and an extra 20 to assure speedy passage. He emerges ten minutes later, unrecognizable in his degree of dishevelment. But he has the tickets.

By now we have Murugan fever almost as badly as everyone else. The 100-rupee line is already quite long and beginning to move, so Karen and I decide why not scale the four-meter-high, wire-mesh wall maintaining order and jump the queue a little. A couple of white girls, surely no one will mind. We scramble up the wire mesh and start down the other side. Men pound at our ankles, scream abuse, try and push us back over the

other side—head first. I see the possibility for mob violence and quickly retreat. We go back and stand in the
line, wait like everyone else. Murugan again.

Two hours later we shuffle into the main sanctuary. It
is so crowded my nose is pressed up against the shirt of
the man in front of me, and the air is a strange mixture
of sweat and incense. The temple attendants keep us
moving along at a steady pace, prodding when necessary. The inner sanctuary is dark, and the various statues
difficult to make out. There is a small figure on my left,
which sparkles a little more brightly than the others but
almost too late it registers that this is Murugan, the all-
powerful god I and a quarter million others have walked
hundreds of kilometers to see. All of five seconds in his
presence and it's over, we're back in the sunlight.

The festivities continue. Things are winding down now
after the cusp of the moon. Every day the many shrines
and courtyards on the hilltop reverberate with music as
troupes from different villages perform for Murugan.
Music that makes my heart bleed for its devotion, music
that makes me cry for the richness of their lives, their love
affair with God. Music that makes me wonder how I, in
my twenty-six years, could have failed to sense a presence
of such magnitude. Always they urge us to dance, and
we often do, sometimes self-conscious at the scene we are
creating, two white girls dancing to the music of so many
young boys, and not wanting to draw attention away from
the main event, sometimes feeling perfectly natural, as if
we too are offering up what we have.

It goes on and on. Every day we think we are going
to leave something else catches our attention. Finally, on
our last night I go to see a singer on the temple sleeping

area where we had spent our first night. The place is not as full now, but still there are hundreds of people, and much more garbage. It still smells like a toilet. The singer is an incredibly beautiful woman, her plumpness a sign of her good health. She plays a harmonium and is accompanied by a tabla player as she sings in Tamil.

But she doesn't just sing. She recites a poem, the story of a young girl in search of her destiny, and her voice moves so gently between narration and song that it seems the melody is born of the language. It moves, above the crying babies, the suckling infants, the smell of the urine and seems to infect everything with its song. Sitting there, I see that this is the Tamil's world, that behind everything you will find this ancient song. And I can't believe such beauty exists.

Ruth Kamnitzer always dreamed of exploring the world and spent most of her twenties doing so, with a predisposition towards bicycles and her own feet. She recently returned to university to work towards a career in environmental management and conservation. She currently lives in Edinburgh, Scotland.

DEBORAH J. SMITH

❧ ❧ ❧

A Tale of Two Churches

Was she forgiven, or what?

I SKIPPED THE PENANCE SERVICE FOR LENT. I DON'T count myself among the Unforgiven. I've painted myself into an impossible corner: I wouldn't confess to the priests I know because they know me too well. But I found out it's a disaster telling your sins to a stranger.

At Saint Peter's in Rome, there were lines for individual confession. I'd read an essay extolling the virtues of confession at St. Peter's. In a moment I can only credit to madness, I thought, "Why not?"

It was forever since I'd last gone to confession—but I had *not* committed murder, robbery, infidelity or child abuse in any fashion. With those off the playing field, everything seemed innocent enough. I grabbed my parcels and got in the line.

I never do things the easy way. Forgetting that Vatican

City is a hotbed of religious conservatives, I also forgot my best shot was the Japanese-speaking priest. I kept on looking for one who spoke English. I was doomed.

After "Bless Me Father" I said it was years since my last confession. The priest asked why I was away so long? (Note to priests: Want the penitent to return again? Try congratulating them on having the courage to be here in the first place.) He said he'd just go down the Ten Commandments and ask me about them.

Without trying to blaspheme, the Ten Commandments are rife with Sins for the Unsuspecting. I can't imagine Moses going down the mountain with them and not interrupting God a few times—wanting to know exactly what God meant by this one or that one in terms of daily Hebrew life. Suddenly, a noise broke into my Biblical daydream.

"Did you take God's name in vain?" the priest asked.

Jesus Christ! is the typical exclamation of Irish people (and me) when frustrated, surprised, or amazed. It's usually not said as a prayer.

"Did I say 'Jesus Christ!' when I wasn't praying? Of course, I'm Irish." My humor sailed right past him. This was the second commandment.

Questions continued—something about excessive drinking, which led me to recall a night in Washington, D.C. when my best friends, also well oiled, caught me before I fell down the subway stairs. That spoke of loyalty and compassion, but I was pressed further about the number, kind, and frequency of my spiritual failings. I was bothered by this questioning without context, with no consideration of my reasons or my life. How do I own the spiritual consequences of my decisions without someone judging me?

I wasn't planning on offering excuses anyway. I'm glad there are only ten commandments, not twenty or thirty.

We were knee-deep into "thou shalt not kill." I had an informed conscience and an American accent. Use your imagination to figure out the topic. The portrait of me now—flitting across my mind's eye—was a drunk who swore and beat her family. I thought suddenly: this skewed picture just isn't me.

In the cold light of this new perspective my personal, examined morals seemed less and less a part of the priest's business. So when he asked me point blank what I did about the particulars, I used a point-blank solution. Praying intently to God, I lied.

Lied.

Now I had crossed a new threshold for transgressions: a Third Dimension in Sin. What happens when you lie in confession?

Funny though, what a sense of humor God really has...two minutes later, the priest asked me if I'd ever lied.

Quickly I replied: "Yes, I did." Whoa!

"How many times?"

I stared at the wavy glass in the confessional and crossed my eyes. More lies now? No, no...wait, random numbers! I haven't kept track since forever, remember?

Now penance? Would I have to impale myself on a Swiss Guard's spear? Or could I negotiate for a root canal without anesthesia? That fellow who wrote about the spiritual boost he got from confession at Saint Peter's? I'm convinced he's a lunatic.

As entertaining as these thoughts were, my blood ran cold when I couldn't remember the Act of Contrition at the end. This is the truth: I can *always* remember the first line. My high school teacher, Father Jim Hartley, would say "Oh my God, I am heartily sorry...I'm Hartley, hey God, remember me?" as the class groaned at the pun. Thirty years later, I always got the first line, but after that? Nothing. I'd forgotten.

His voice wavering with frustration, the priest asked if I was sorry for my sins.

"Yes."

"Do you resolve not to do them again?"

"Yes." Oh please, oh please, oh please.... My hands were like ice. It was close to 90 degrees that day in Rome. I thought of sunshine outside.

"Say ten Hail Marys." The priest launched into Absolution; he wasn't looking to prolong this either.

Outside in the Basilica, I felt like I'd been a player in a video game. All I could do was dive through moral loopholes. Oddly, I wasn't feeling guilty.

Was I in denial? Was my life as terrible as it sounded? Most importantly, were my sins *really forgiven*, even if I'd lied and then (truthfully) admitted so? Every question had been formulated to catch me in sin, not help me see the love of God. I'm old enough to face my failings; but I swore to myself I wouldn't be caught in a setup like that one again.

I was off confession permanently. My penance, along with ten Hail Marys, came when I left my parcels behind in the box. I had to get back in line to retrieve them.

A year later, the good Sisters in Assisi asked if I'd like to go to their Penance Service for Ash Wednesday. I politely declined, mentioning I'd gone to confession at Saint Peter's. Had to give up *something* for Lent.

But at a nearby college during this Lenten season, when talk centered on the parable of the Prodigal Son, the matter took a different turn.

For those who aren't familiar with the parable, here's a quick version:

The Youngest son of a wealthy man grabs his share of the family fortune and heads out to see the world. This adventure fuels his wild living and loose women by the score—until his money runs out. Then Youngest son is forced to take an underrated service job slopping pigs for market. In the midst of work, the son realizes his father's servants have a better life than this. He quits and heads home to talk his way into becoming one of Dad's hired hands.

Meanwhile, the Eldest son is home doing his bit with Dad. The father has resigned himself to his Youngest being dead in a big-city gutter. So you can imagine how thrilled the father is one day, when he looks over the countryside to see Youngest son coming down the road towards home.

Dad gets more than excited—he throws a big bash to celebrate his son who was lost, but now found. This is all going swimmingly, especially for Youngest son, until the Eldest brother asks Dad why he never celebrated anything with him, even though he's done what the father wanted all these years? And Eldest son has the party details—one of the servants told all.

Dad's reply? All you had to do was ask, Sonny Boy. In the meantime, someone we thought was dead is alive. Good reason for a party if you ask me.

The college discussion started out trying to examine which character in the story each person could identify with. Soon it rapidly evolved into an examination of character portrayal in the parable. The entire interaction said lots about each contributor's individual orientation to people, a fact I quietly chose to keep to myself.

The priest in the discussion would like to have been the all-forgiving, compassionate father. But he just couldn't see himself really doing it. He also thought the Eldest brother picked the sleazy servant who was the House Tattler, so he'd get all the details of the homecoming party for his Younger brother.

One of the students insisted it wasn't this way, that the Eldest son bullied the servant into forking over the party details. Maybe, she insisted, it was the desperate act of hired help cornered by the boss. Hey, we've all been *there*.

Truth is, the Prodigal Son is an allegory of God's love for us; about love without limits and second chances, given in the most unlikely of circumstances. Some call this foolishness and cheap grace, but it says much about what unconditional love really will do.

Later, I thought about it more. I claim that I've given up confession. After one particularly nasty experience at the Vatican, of all places. Fried to within an inch of my life, I swore off confession, an endurance test for me at the best of times, for the rest of my days. Or, as my husband likes to say, until the next time....when the grass is green, the sun sets over the hill, and the moon is full...

In Italy with my young son this year, I found myself riding the bus at the day's end, down the hills past the green fields of Assisi toward the Basilica of Santa Maria degli Angeli. This Basilica was built over the Porziuncola, a tiny chapel where Saint Francis worshiped with the early friars and accepted Saint Clare as one of his own. The place where Saint Francis died is also nearby. I hadn't taken the time to see it on previous trips.

Entering the Basilica, I saw the lights and asked my son if he wanted to go to confession. He declined, indicating he goes when his Catholic school at home takes him there. I was off the hook; this forgiveness thing was behind me, too.

Even as light fades and the night approaches, the Porziuncola remains the central feature shining in the middle of the Basilica. I approached the entry and stood with the others who were there to pray, thinking of Francis and how different life must have been when all this was woodland and fields, a simple stone church with friars camping outside and everyone living in poverty. For Saint Francis, this was his home. I offered a prayer or two, and read the Latin inscription along the doorstep: "Here is Holy."

My son dragged me over to an audio guide and asked me to put in a euro. We shared earphones as we listened to the story of the church and watched the light change in the Basilica with the coming of the evening. The Catholic Church, said the audioguide, grants forgiveness of all one's sins as an indulgence to those who visit the Porziuncola to pray.

I was stunned. After the grandiose hair-splitting at the Vatican, here in the quiet simplicity of this chapel, my sins were simply forgiven? To my mind an even, decent trade—a rarity in life. Although that wasn't the reason for my visit, like the Youngest son in the parable, I wouldn't decline the offer either.

Call it foolishness or cheap grace if you like. As the sun slipped away and the moon rose over the hill town of

Assisi, I stumbled onto an earthier, more compassionate kind of Christianity. It didn't deny responsibility, good works or belief, but as I always knew, my life needn't be lived as a moral loophole. Rather than engineering faith, perhaps it was a second chance given from unconditional love.

Or maybe I am more like the Prodigal Son than I care to know.

Deborah J. Smith is a faculty member at Empire State College in Saratoga Springs, New York. A contributing writer for Tastes of Italia *magazine, her work also airs on NorthEast Public Radio. She will return again to Italy—four years of high school Latin won't go to waste—and remain Catholic for the foreseeable future.*

❧ ❧ ❧

Asia and Bust

The guidebooks should warn you:
Loneliness is the true danger of traveling solo.

I F THE HEAT WEREN'T SO SMOTHERING I WOULD HAVE climbed that tree and perched myself on its farthest reaching branch. *Dead Woman Climbing*, I would chant as I steadied my nerves for a neck-breaking swan dive into the shallow depths of the Mekong River; the locals watching with mild interest from their shanty cafés; the heavy air suffocating us all. I can't imagine that anyone would rush to my rescue if this plan of mine were to gain some momentum and actually unfold.

This kind of incarcerating heat slows life down to the dragging beat of the second hand on the clock above my head which reads 8:03, 7 1/2 hours off the real time of 3:30. I release a sigh of resignation which says, *I can't even count on the goddamn time.* This is too much to bear, all these seconds on my hands, which stretch and lag, creating the ideal circumstances to replay a time when traveling was actually fun. When I was trekking through the Himalayas with a handsome Israeli boy I just so happened to love, who taught me every version of the F-word imaginable, and even how to roll a joint and pick out a good plant, though most of the ones I passed on the Annapurna Circuit had been over-dried by the stringent sun. But the air is cool in Nepal, so it's a different kind of heat, and much preferable to the jungle lethargy I am feeling now. Here in Laos. Alone for the first time in several years.

Loneliness is the true danger of traveling solo; even more than getting my pockets picked because I don't have an extra set of eyes to guard me; or contracting malaria because I don't have an extra set of hands to rub the insect lotion on my back; or being kidnapped and held for ransom by Islamic rebels in the southern Philippines because they happen to target women who journey unaccompanied.

The only travel guides worth reading are the ones warning me that when loneliness decides to creep into my insides like a hookworm and take up residence among the entire spectrum of colorful parasitic flora I've consumed over the years, my will to continue on the bumpy dirt roads will take on the form of a terrible little ache. The fiery zeal I started my journey with will actually morph into misery. I didn't believe it was possible, not from the way I once scribbled "Asia or Bust" in the margin of a coffee table book about Japan. Not from the way I eagerly researched my destinations in bookstores, on the Web, and on microfiche machines searching for back issues of *Outdoors* and *Backpacking*. Not from the way I sought out those top-of-the-line travel gadgets like the motion alarm I once hung from a window latch in a plywood hovel in Jakarta that speared a siren off into the dead of night because a sudden rainstorm had agitated the windowpane. All of my neighbors screamed obscenities at me in Indonesian while they flailed their arms and their frightened children wailed. To think that all of this chaos ensued because two years ago the salesperson at the outdoors store saw that glint in my eyes and convinced me that one should never venture into untamed lands without the SoundPro 200 Motion Alarm with three different danger signals and a pulsating halogen lamp. "An indispensable accessory for the *solo* traveler," he flattered.

I accepted the compliment, vowing to devote at least the next 365 days to prove myself worthy of that exclusive travelers' club, the club in which the members carried their home on their backs for extensive periods of time as they traversed overland from country to country, their passports creased, torn, and nearly reaching their expiry dates. These travelers bathed when they could and rotated between three pairs of underwear, turning them inside out if necessary. They were dirty, unkempt people. Complete anathema to my Virgoan nature which demands cleanliness and order, yet strangely I could not wait to join their ranks.

The good travel guides should tell me to press on. To expect such dips in my spirit because they are as much a part of the experience of long-term travel as the serendipitous discoveries of hidden nooks that serve the tastiest lamb curry or the most fragrant *chai*. They should inform me that it's O.K. that the mosquitoes eat me alive, or that my stomach is always sour. It's O.K. that nasty reprimands itch to leap off the tip of my tongue as I am beseeched for money every time I walk down a filthy, rat-infested road.

The book should stipulate that loneliness, while vague, will certainly feel like a distinct burden—one with a physical mass and shape—sagged upon the spirit. A burden that could lighten with a phone call home to my mother, and dissipate altogether with the right travel companion. It's not at all alleviated by a voluntary act of seclusion; but that's where it's driven me, oddly enough. Straight through the gates of Hermitville.

The useful guidebooks should caution that some days I will not gather enough energy to roll out of bed, either because I am exhausted (fourteen hours on a bus in rural Asia assures little more than a splitting headache) or homesick (three Christmases ago I said I'd go home for good) or a bit friendless (sometimes I am unable to keep up the chain of travel companions, each person linking on just as the last falls away). Then the books should explain that these days are to be indulged and used for rest. Tending to my callused feet, stripping the grime from my hair, and most importantly, allowing my stimulus monitor to *flatline*, are all part of intrepid travel. After a while, the cackling chickens, the vrooming motorbikes, the locals arguing with each other about how much a bowl of Vietnamese *pho,* a bottle of BeerLao, or a dish of *pad thai should* cost will tornado through my enthusiasm and leave in its wake good memories with jagged edges. The guidebooks ought to reveal that travel experiences can be kept fluid and lush just by devoting a few days to MTV Asia, a few trashy magazines, or an internet café.

Because then even small discoveries would stay magical. Like the treehouse in Saigon that was lit in twinkling white lights, where I played billiards in a black spaghetti-strap dress with a handsome Kiwi man and drank something tall and minty cool. Like the small area of trees on the South Island of New Zealand whose branches reach out toward the sea instead of skyward because the unrelenting winds sculpted them that way (and not far from there: the southernmost McDonald's in the world). Like the backroom eatery I happened upon during a stroll through Kathmandu one evening with a girl I met while I was shopping for woolly sweaters.

We caught a faint whiff of the meaty stew and spicy milk tea from over a thick brick wall, even through the diesel exhaust that spun around us like vile cotton candy. As I tried to scoop the food into my mouth with my fingers, the cook's three young children sat across the table giggling. My efforts to eat the meal in the traditional way were admirable at best. Rice covered a six-inch margin around my plate and my t-shirt was flecked with curry. I smiled at the children whose red-clay-and-marigold-petal blessings from the morning were now mere smudges on their foreheads. I whispered to my companion, *Jeez, do you think they're laughing at us?* And she said, *Us? Darling, I'm not the one who will need a bath after this*. I thought, *This is a good day*.

Screw the guidebooks. Because unless one of them was written by a neurotic twenty-six-year-old who, nearing the end of a four-year trek through Asia, was forced to accept grief as her shadow in the final stretch of her journey, then those books will not have anything relevant to teach me. (Had I stuck to my original 365-day plan, perhaps I would not be in this precarious state of mind.) Unless in their sections on loneliness, there happened to be a sidebar of tips on mustering up dignity in holiday romances lasting four to six weeks. And unless the books caution that these particular heart-shaped barricades are the most unpleasant ones to maneuver since they're gooey with hope, attachment, fondness, and the like, then those books are not worth one thin dime.

If only a book could have warned me that if I pleaded, "I wish we had more time," a mere twelve hours after my sexy Israeli boyfriend and I arrived in Thailand from Kathmandu, he would say with firm resolve, "It's over." I could have heeded the warning and not have to drag myself, weighty with sadness and trailing behind me pieces of a once vibrant spirit, to the Bangkok train station for a ticket going in the most extreme direction away from him—north, to Laos—to prove that I wasn't completely devastated, not at all.

I stared blankly through the window of my sleeper compartment, summoning up the best memories of the last weeks in Nepal: prayer wheels spinning furiously, each rotation casting *Om Mani Padme Hum*—the Tibetan mantra of salvation—into the universe. Birds soaring at eye level once I reached 4,500 meters. Pockets full of Twix candy bars. Sore blisters on my toes. And eggs. Eggs! I've never eaten so many. As I ascended into the Annapurna peaks, the menus at the little huts along the trail pared down in proportion to the availability of ingredients. If I could get a complex, meaty curry at 800-1,500 meters, I could only get simple spinach omelets and lentil soups from elevations higher than that. I discovered not only that I liked eggs but that I liked them runny, oozing rivers of golden cholesterol onto my rice. And I never got tired of them. Not even after eighteen days on the trail.

But my favorite memory was not a blurry shape passing swiftly by my window; in fact, its edges could not be more seamless. Had I been content with such a sweet ending and cut my losses while my pride was still intact, I might have saved myself the torture of rejection. But then again how could I expect myself not to hope for more? During our final night together at the Tom & Jerry Bar in Kathmandu, I tried to muster up the courage to tell him that somewhere between the tenth Twix candy bar we shared and the fourth soaked bandage he removed from the third sore blister that erupted on my feet, I had toppled into love. (Even though I knew that such a transient creature would evaporate if it felt the slightest bit contained.) The inhibition was depressing. I woke in the middle of the night ready to profess my feelings, but instead found most of the bed empty. I panicked a little before I felt him breathing into my back, and realized that I had simply migrated toward his warmth. His 6'2" frame balanced precariously on a sliver at the edge of the mattress. "Do you have enough room?" I asked, and he answered, "I have all that I need."

It's now 3:34. I've got my head down on the rickety table where my noodle soup lunch was served three hours ago by a woman with a paring knife tucked into her sarong. She used it to cut the vegetables, wiping it down by gripping it in the crook of her long-sleeved arm and sliding it through. *Good God, has she ever sliced herself open doing that?*

I have no plans for the hours until I can respectfully

go to bed without appearing like a loser to the staff at my guesthouse. Foreigners do not turn in for the night at 3:30 in the afternoon, not in Luang Prabang. Not when there's a mountain smack dab in the center of the city that I can climb and watch the colors of the sunset peel away until it becomes night. Not when I can wander the small streets and poke my head into the paper-lantern workshops, lit with bright turquoise and magenta stars strung together by twine. Not when I could go to the Red Cross for a eucalyptus sauna to clear out the gunk in my lungs (Bangkok's little bon voyage *cadeau* for foreigners). I could even sit outside the Healthy & Fresh Bakery with chocolate macaroons and write my postcards or watch the ebb and flow of people on the streets. I can watch the local children in their navy blue uniforms and dingy white button-ups dilly-dally their way home; their freedom from the confines of the schoolhouse showing up as joy in their faces; their fingers cupped around their friends' ears like an amphitheater for secrets. I can watch the shiny-headed monks walk by in their mustard-colored robes, their hands in prayer position always, even as they return a stray soccer ball by kicking it over the school fence, or pass through a flurry of camera flashes set off by tourists. At least people-watching could be considered "doing something," (it could even be classified as "cultural" and thus *hardly* a waste of my time) and my attention would be diverted away from this awful misery.

It is entirely possible that dozens of other tourists might have the same idea, and I could be caught in a traffic jam halfway up Phousi mountain and miss the sunset completely. I cannot expect that the fat paper stars strung on twine will be lit in the workshop on the night

I hope to see them—maybe the electricity will cut out (again), or the craftsmen will simply prefer not to open shop that day; just as I cannot expect that the monks, steady in prayer, will appreciate being photographed.

Much of Southeast Asia believes that the camera steals part of the spirit. Conscientious travelers should leave the monks' spirits alone, having already violated their pristine lifestyle just by showing up with an MP3 player tucked into one of their many pockets. Advanced societies, with their sophisticated technology and materialistic aspirations, should not interfere with the normal development of less advanced societies; but tourists stow these ideas in their backpacks anyway, without considering how they might complicate the simple, pleasant lives of rural people. An internet connection can trigger a chain reaction that starts with wide-eyed wonderment and ends with the destruction of nature by corporations, a weakening of the family structure, and the evaporation of a strong spiritual identity in the scorching heat of greed. Right?

This breakdown of consequences may sound accurate with its business report rhetoric, but then again it is doubtful that someone who writes business reports on a 17-inch G4 Apple Powerbook and navigates their way to a charity luncheon at the Ritz using OnStar technology, ever met a little Laotian boy who carried his baby sister in a sling and sold sticks of Doublemint gum to keep them both in peanuts and plain noodle soup. And because these business people have never seen this little boy (or the thousands like him), they wouldn't know that his dirt-smudged face lit up not when I slipped him a few thousand kip (only two measly American dollars worth), but when I placed my earphones on his head and let him listen to the *Les Miserables* soundtrack. The emotion of the music produced a smiling face, and the novelty of the technology sparked a curious mind. He unplugged his ears and stared for a while at the spongy buds that streamed music. How could such fascination and delight be wrong? Who are we to stand on our soap boxes in the West, pointing our telescopes in the direction of the Third World, and somehow feel compelled to spout remedies for poverty? Before Westerners traveled through Southeast Asia or Latin America or most of the African continent, were the locals there actually destitute, or is poverty a concept that only exists in relation to our Cadillacs, Bose stereo systems, and Maytag dishwashers?

Nevertheless, the remote Karen hill tribe village in Northern Thailand sets up vending kiosks at 9 A.M. for the trekkers passing through; Bangkok, with its Manhattan-esque skyline, can hardly qualify as Third World any longer; Manila has the most beautiful (and indeed largest) shopping mall I have seen *anywhere* in the world; and Western developers in Bali sprout new lavish, 5-star resorts in the heart of poverty without a speck of guilt. Or at least I didn't feel any trace of it when I was lounging on Kuta Beach drinking coconut juice and the ocean breeze wafted fallen orchid blooms in my direction. The pitiable children walking barefoot in the blistering sand, the ones selling canned sodas and water were barely noticeable. My refreshments, complete with fresh fruit garnishes skewered by novelty toothpick swords, came from the bar.

While I don't know how much harm I've done with my preference for fresh pineapple juice cocktails over canned Pepsi, or how much rainforest destruction I've caused with my hiking boots, or how much damage I've inflicted with my never-ending stack of travelers' checks, I do know that no one directive will soothe the souls of those who have glimpsed on tourists signs of a "better" life. Even if they don't write it down in coffee table books like I did, they say it as a prayer: *America or bust.*

I lift my head off the card table intending to find a reliable internet café. I hope that someone from home is online so that I can have an IM heart-to-heart; explain to them that I focused all of my attention on one man during the last six weeks and wasn't able to keep up the chain of travel companions. And now the days are moving by painfully slow, and even the act of forcing myself out of bed is important enough to be registered on a to-do list, along with applying sunscreen, drinking plenty of water, and checking my e-mail. Surely some digitized persona will have even a pea-sized bit of sympathy for me.

Mary pops up on the screen after ten minutes. She's not my first choice for an IM heart-to-heart, or even my fifteenth, but at this point I'd yank a monk from his morning meditation, so Mary's not a bad choice really, considering she speaks English.

I met her two years ago in Hanoi, at a café near Hoan Kiem Lake. She was sweeping the crumbs from her breakfast baguette off her Lonely Planet guide.

"Your breakfast looks good. What is it?" I asked.

"Triangle cheese and bananas," she replied, spreading the plasticky wedge on her baguette with a heavy silver butter knife that she unwrapped from a square of brocade cloth.

"Triangle cheese?"

She stared at me perplexed. "You know, the Laughing Cow?"

"Oh, right. Elsie."

"The cow has a name? You silly Americans."

Ten weeks pregnant by a Vietnamese-Frenchman, she came to Vietnam alone so that her unborn child could soak up some of his Asian heritage. She intended not to bring him back to Vietnam after he was born. The idea was culture through osmosis. Along with the time-consuming tasks of developing a brain, lungs, limbs, and fine-tuning pertinent biological systems, the fetus also had to harvest as much of Vietnam as he could during that ten-day whirlwind tour, since he would only be returning to this "dirty land of beggars and triangle cheese" over his mother's dead body.

Mary carried her own silverware from home and would use the table chopsticks to hold her hair in a French twist. This made me cringe. Asian cultures are offended by any misuse of chopsticks. Like when people tuck them under their upper lip to imitate a walrus, or use them to point, or jab them upright into a bowl of steamed rice, which is a symbol of death (the chopsticks represent the incense sticks lit for the deceased in the Buddhist temples). I can't imagine how they would feel about foreigners using the utensils for vanity. Also, Mary sucked her thumb incessantly. She was thirty-two years old.

I wonder if she might find it a bit odd that I am suddenly available for an online chat, since I hadn't bothered to acknowledge her in this way before. We functioned for one another in Vietnam as warm bodies that ate together, shopped together, and stood guard when faced with having to pee in the bushes just to avoid entering the putrid WC. Since we had almost nothing in common, this was all accomplished in nearly complete silence.

Should I start with some general questions about her life and her child, just so the rant I really want to spew will be cushioned by this act of goodwill? Will she respond with sympathy and tell me to keep plugging through, since I've nearly reached the finish line anyway? Will she pluck the unoriginal, beat-down "This too shall pass," from her reservoir of comforting adages and hand it to me with a smiley-face emoticon tagged onto its tail like this: ☺ Bing!

> hi mary it's me leilani. how are you doing? how is your baby boy? jasper, right? he must be walking by now. catch me up on your life. i've got all day.

There are many rules for the visitors to Ho Chi Minh's Mausoleum; among them are covered feet and shoulders, no photography, and absolute silence. Ho Chi Minh's corpse, embalmed once a year in Russia, demands absolute stillness for the sake of solemnity. So when the only sound in the cold, marble room is the slurping of a thumb-sucker who happens to be my spontaneous travel companion, I expected the Honor Guards to escort both of us out immediately. But they were preoccupied with trying to catch people who slyly slipped their index fingers over the shutter buttons of their cameras, intending to snap flashless shots of the macabre display. The people back home would never believe the yellowish hue hovering over his waxy body. It looked like a decayed spirit. The voyeurs gaped in wonder at this nicotine-tinged phenomenon.

> mary, are you there? can you believe i'm still out on the road? i'm in laos now, and it's my last stop in asia. i'm a

little grimier than the last time you saw me. i feel like
that damned ho chih minh corpse. lifeless and ready to
move on. you were right when you said, if only they'd
bury the guy and let him rest in peace, his spirit might
just shed its dingy finish. i've decided that the business
of travel is heartbreaking with the irregular flux of
people, the loneliness, the poverty. i'm afraid that i've
traveled irresponsibly, mary. i didn't stray far enough
from the beaten path. i got lured in by shiny elephant
statues and heavy stone necklaces. i spent the majority
of my time eating and shopping when i should have
been building houses and planting crops. how can i
atone for the past 3-1/2 years of my life?

And now, sitting in front of the computer eagerly
anticipating a response from a thumb-sucking, chop-
stick-wearing, processed cheese-eating woman while the
power source groans in the background and the screen
flickers in five-second intervals as if it were trying hard
to fight off sleep, my mind briefly alights upon the word
atone and I wonder if it's actually part of my vocabulary,
because as far as I know I've never used it, so there is that
possibility that I sound...*high falutin'*. As the eyes of the
other travelers in the café cast upon me, a few fugitive
tears roll down my face, and I become convinced that the
heat rising off my body is not embarrassment or frustration, but my own corroding spirit. I feel for the first
time what it must be like to be kindred with a deceased
Vietnamese Communist Party Founder.

❧ ❧ ❧

Upon returning to America after a four-year stint in Asia, Leilani Marie Labong promptly forgot her backpacking survival skills and slipped back into her habits of royalty. She currently resides in San Francisco, where she avoids public restrooms at all costs, insists on drinking Pellegrino daily, and works as the research editor at a local lifestyle magazine, 7x7.

KELLY SOBCZAK

⁊ ⁊ ⁊

Fruity Pleasures

For one brief day she was a sensual,
alluring woman wrapped up in mangoes.

*T*HE OLD MAN LOUNGING ON THE SIDEWALK SLOWLY nodded his head and mumbled "*tamam*" (meaning "good" in Arabic) when he saw me. Other men heartedly called out "Sudanese" and waved their arms in approval, while passing women met their eyes with mine and gently smiled. Walking through the streets of the eastern Sudanese town of Kassala, I was creating quite a stir in my traditional Sudanese outfit.

As I struggled with the the billowing fabric, I felt like a royal fool. I never intended to wear the damn thing when I spied it in the shop, I just wanted to look at it. After having admired for the past week the colorful cloth that a Sudanese woman wears wrapped around herself, called a "top," I wanted to check one out up close.

The vast array of blinding colors and patterns was overwhelming. But as I meandered through the town's market, I was immediately drawn to the plump, juicy-looking mangoes that virtually danced on a vivid blue-and aqua-colored wrap. Slowly I ran my fingers over the soft fabric as I envisioned myself walking tall and proud, as Sudanese women appear to me. They looked feminine, sexy, and exotic, and after now wearing the same grotty t-shirt and army-green pants for the past five days, I desperately needed a pick-me-up. So when the male shop owner wanted to swathe me in the mangoes, I figured why not. The only problem was he didn't know how.

By now neighboring shopkeepers and curious male passersby had stopped to watch this white woman trying to maneuver the mounds of mangoes. The shop owner had since given up, and so we all stood there, stupidly staring at each other and not knowing what to do. Boldly, a man from the bemused crowd stepped forward. Plucking the fabric from my fingers, he clumsily proceeded to envelop me in it, while the others cheered on and called out instructions. He proudly stood back to admire his work, but within an instant, the mangoes rolled down my body and the fabric lay limp on the sidewalk.

Relatively few women were on the streets, but soon enough an elderly woman in a traffic-stopping red-and-yellow wrap walked by. Not giving up on me, the men called out for assistance, but with a scowl on her face, she continued on, not even glancing in our direction. Soon enough a girl no older than fourteen came by. Like many young women, she wore only a long skirt and shapeless blouse, with a simple scarf around her head.

But she knew how to tie a Sudanese top, and with her fingers moving deftly over and around my body, she instantly enshrouded me in the fabric. With one last tug, she nodded and walked away. There was no time to ask how she did it.

After paying the shop owner the 3,000 dinars ($12) for the wrap, I went to take it off, much to the protests of the crowd. I needed to go back to the hotel and didn't want to walk through the streets enwrapped in my mango top. While I try to respect customs and traditions by wearing modest clothing that covers my arms and legs, I am not a big fan of adopting the local look. I often think back to the Japanese tourist I saw running all over Yemen decked out in a traditional red-and-white Arab headcloth, even though he wore an Adidas t-shirt and a pair of Levi's as well. But here in Sudan, they seemed to like—no, love—seeing me in a Sudanese top, so I opted to leave it on as I returned to the hotel, where the plan was to pack it away. I did quickly lift the veil to take off my beige baseball cap underneath, though. No reason for me to look even more like a fool, I figured.

During the ten-minute walk towards the hotel, dozens of men called out to me. "They like me, they really like me," I thought, as I suddenly stood a tad taller and added a slight wiggle to my walk. And for those ten minutes, I was a sexy and mysterious woman. Even if my sport sandals did kind of ruin the look.

Sauntering by the sidewalk stand where I had enjoyed a tea earlier that day, I decided to stop and visit with Habiba, my new friend who serves up tea every morning to the neighboring merchants and anyone else who passes. Upon seeing me sporting my new look, she gleefully clapped her hands and declared me to be Sudanese.

Soon enough, the same nearby shopkeepers who had surrounded me earlier that morning when I had my tea, flocked around and showered me with praise. Hearing that I am unmarried, they proclaimed now that I was a Sudanese woman, I was to marry a Sudanese man. They even had someone in mind, but seeing that he had only a few remaining bottom teeth as a result of years of chewing snuff, I graciously declined. A girl has got to have some standards, even if she is thirty-two years old and still single.

And so for the rest of the day I strolled—no, glided— through the town market while dressed in my Sudanese top. Men clapped and called out to me, but who could blame them? For that brief day I was a sensual, alluring woman wrapped up in mangoes.

Kelly Sobczak traded in her job at the French Government Tourist Office and her mice-infested New York City apartment for an eighteen-month solo trip around the world (well, halfway around). And she hasn't looked back since.

FRAN PALUMBO

Highland Remedy

A world-weary traveler restores her spirit
on a detour to Scotland.

T HE SCENERY MIRRORS MY OWN INTERIOR LANDSCAPE: gray, drizzly, melancholy. Even though it's rained every day since I arrived a week ago, I find it difficult to dislike this place. Light mist coats the austere, rolling terrain, giving it the soft, delicate appearance of a giant pastel. Throughout the day, the sun pokes through occasionally and an ivory northern light illuminates a distant hill or a crumbling stone wall as if the entrance to Camelot lies ahead. Zooming northeast on Route A9 from Inverness to Wick, I shift the gears of the red subcompact rental car, left-handed, as if I've been driving on the other side of the road my entire bloody life. What better place to hide away from the world than the Scottish Highlands?

Following three turbulent months in India, I decided on an impromptu detour to Scotland on the way back to San Francisco. My mind was still whirling from the too recent past of sweltering heat, despicable filth, abject poverty, utter chaos, and claustrophobic hordes of people. My stomach was still churning from the parasite that had maliciously hitched a ride in my bowels. A perhaps irreconcilable rift with my best friend, who accused me of not being grateful enough for her hospitality in India, had rendered me bereft. Plus, I was still suffering from a painful failed romance that ended badly prior to my departure for Asia. It seemed as though everybody within the small solar system of my life wanted something from me. I had exceeded my tolerance level for fellow human beings. My entire body and soul reverberated with a Garboesque "I want to be alone!"

Now, cruising through the coastal towns of Dornoch, Brora, and Dunbeath, I stop methodically to quickly snap photos or visit castle ruins noted by a miniature red star on my map. There are dozens of these freckly red stars and I am determined to see the site representing each one. This preoccupies me and helps me to quiet the demon voices chattering in my head. The voices in my abdomen, however, are not so easily subdued. They let out a grotesque whine. I need to eat.

It's been a long day of driving and I plan on stopping in Wick, a town that looks like the largest one around judging from the bold typeface on the map. Upon arriving, though, I find it a dreary place except for a few historic stone buildings and a couple of geriatric-looking three-star hotels. I motor straight through, even though it's early evening and I just want to settle down with a hearty meal and comfy room.

Continuing north, the route becomes less traveled and eventually ends at Duncansby Head, the north-easternmost corner of the Scottish mainland where the harbor village of John o'Groats squats humbly in its midst. This windswept piece of Scotland is empty and flat, nothing but land, sky, and water punctuated by a stiff seaborne breeze. From here you can catch a ferry in the summer to the Orkney Islands, but other than that, it barely deserves a dot on the map. There's no homey brick B&Bs, no discernable center of town. Across the road from each other are two rectangular fifties-style motels, about half a kilometer from the water where only a few boats are docked. A caravan park sits oddly off to the right with several large vehicles parked randomly like perverse modern-day monoliths. Worse yet, there isn't a restaurant in sight. This feels like the loneliest place on earth.

I look at the map, and the next town appears to be far away. The type is too small. It might not even have a place to stay. I reluctantly check into the Seaview Motel and drop my suitcase in the room. One tiny window looks out onto the deserted road, and a lumpy double bed covered by a chenille bedspread patterned in pink, green, and white sits against the wall in the middle of the room. Hanging over the bed there's a tacky, faded print of a cherub holding a fishing pole. John o'Groats is not the charming place I'd hoped to hunker down in for a good dinner and a night's rest.

Directed by the motel desk clerk to a place a kilometer back that might still be serving dinner, I wearily head off in the car again. At least it hasn't rained in a few hours. Peeking through dark, pregnant clouds the summer sun glows stubbornly, descending toward the ground in a slow, languid motion. I am so far north it won't get dark until around 11 P.M.

Arriving at a modest building that looks like it might have been a small church in a previous incarnation, I walk in and head to the counter to order some food. In thick chalk letters, a blackboard menu overhead offers burgers, sandwiches, and soup. The room is spartan and honest like a Quaker meeting room; the odor and hiss of fried food from the kitchen hangs in the air. I order the fish and chips, make a mental note to eat healthy tomorrow, and take a seat where the cheerful husband-and-wife owners direct me among the few tables scattered on the hardwood floor. The only other customer—an elfish, white-haired man in dark, baggy trousers and a windbreaker—who looks to be in his seventies, smiles shyly at me from the next table.

"Aye." He nods in my direction. I nod back.

"You're not from around here, are ye?"

"No," I confess. "From California. Just here traveling." Damn. I was hoping to blend in with the locals so no one would bother me. But at least I can understand him. Most of the Scots I've talked to, although only briefly, sound as if their tongues are always getting in the way of what they are trying to say.

"So, are ye plannin' to take the ferry to the Orkneys?"

"Well, no, I hadn't really thought about it. I'm just driving. Didn't think there was much to see there."

"Well, y'ought to consider it. Last year I was here and took the ferry on o'er and spent the day. It was lovely."

He launches into a guidebook-like monologue about the birdwatching and ancient sites—something called the Ring of Brodgar. I am given directions and details on the ferry schedule and how to get to the attractions. Even though I know I won't go, I feign interest and make conversation as though I really want all this information. In fact, I don't even want to talk to him. I want to eat in silence, want to listen to all the activity going on in my head. This friendly chitchat is wearing me out, but he's such a nice, pleasant man that I talk to him anyway. He's alone. He's probably lonely.

A huge platter of fish and chips is placed in front of me and I can't shove the brown chunks into my mouth fast enough. After a few minutes, as if not wanting to interrupt my eating, the old man rises from his table and, with a slight bow and twinkle in his eye, shakes my hand and tells me he enjoyed talking with me.

It's getting late and I want to get back to the motel, take a walk down to the water and catch the sunset, so I devour the rest of the meal and head up to the counter to pay. The owner waves away the bills I hold out.

"It's paid for," he tells me. I am confused.

"The ol' man paid for you when he left."

Amazed that a stranger would pay for my dinner then leave without any acknowledgement of his kindness, I smile and think, "How sweet." No one has ever done this before in any of my travels, and I am incredibly touched. All of these months, after feeling as though every single person I encountered was a living, breathing "give-me" machine, I meet one person in a remote corner of the world who gives just for the sake of giving, wanting nothing in return, not even a "thank you." This small gesture is, ironically, larger than he will ever know. I have an inexplicable urge to find the old man, a desperate need to thank him. I don't even know his name.

Sure enough, way up ahead on the side of the road, I spot his dark silhouette shuffling along, hands in his pockets. "Would you like a ride?" I ask, pulling up beside him. His face lights up in a broad smile and he eagerly accepts the offer. He is short and agile and has a perky, turned-up nose. For a moment I think that maybe I've encountered a leprechaun, but then realize I'm in the wrong country for such occurrences, even if they were possible. I drive back to my motel, park the car, and we stroll side by side toward the water, to the coastline of Pentland Firth, which separates the mainland from the Orkneys.

His name is Walter. He's from Newcastle, a city just below the Scottish border, and is staying in the caravan park. As if reading my mind, he comments matter-of-factly, "My wife, she died a few years back," and his face becomes as wistful and lonely as the Highland landscape itself. For a moment, I have another silly thought: I wish I was seventy so that Walter and I could tour around Scotland in his mobile home for the rest of our lives. He touches my arm and points to something a few hundred meters away.

An old Victorian hotel I hadn't noticed before sits way off in the shadows looking haunted near the shoreline. "It's been closed for many years," Walter tells me. He travels often to John o'Groats, and as I look around I begin to understand why. The sun dangles low in the sky as if trying to prolong its inevitable kiss with the horizon. Wide, dramatic stalks of light radiate through billowy clouds, providing an ethereal backdrop for a distant house sitting squarely on a desolate plain. The house looks how I feel: forlorn and alone, but illuminated. Standing there together we are an unlikely pair, yet are kindred spirits, drawn to the healing power that blows in from the rigid, ancient waters.

Mesmerized, we watch the sun as it gradually extinguishes itself into the edge of the world. Sometimes the best conversations occur with strangers, without words. Here, with Walter, my faith in humanity might just be restored.

Born on Columbus Day, Fran Palumbo has journeyed around the world indulging in a lifelong compulsion to explore. Recently unshackled from her day job, she aspires to visit the rest of the places in the world she has not yet been and to pursue a career in freelance writing.

LEAH KOHLENBERG

෯෯ ෯෯ ෯෯

The Tao of Simon

With the help of a wry Armenian,
the author begins to see that "life is beautiful."

"LEAH, THIS IS HAND JOB, NO?"
I MUST QUALIFY HERE THAT SIMON AGHABALYAN,
MY DRIVER AND GUIDE HERE IN ARMENIA, ASKS THIS QUESTION
WITH INNOCENT IMPUNITY—HE IS HOLDING A HAND-CRAFTED
METAL COFFEE URN AND IS MERELY TESTING HIS NEWLY LEARNED
ENGLISH VOCABULARY. BUT WHEN BRIAN AND I, THE ONLY
AMERICANS AT THIS DINNER TABLE FULL OF ARMENIAN JOURNAL-
ISTS, SIMULTANEOUSLY CHOKE ON OUR COFFEE, SIMON KNOWS
HE IS ONTO SOMETHING GOOD.

"WHAT MEANS THIS, NAIRA?" HE NUDGES NAIRA
KHACHIKYAN, OUR TRANSLATOR, WHO HERSELF IS BENT OVER
DOUBLE, TEARS RUNNING DOWN HER CHEEKS, WHEN I WHIS-
PER THE...AHEM...MEDICAL TERM IN HER EAR. "I MAKE JOKE?
WHAT I SAY?"

No one laughs harder or longer than Simon himself when I finally manage to produce the universally understood hand gesture for...well, you-know-what. ("Oh Brian," huffed Brian's wife, Donna, when we told her this story later. "You let *Leah* tell him?")

Simon, after all, loves to pun, and he's a master of them in two languages: Armenian and Russian. Now he can officially add a third to his belt, which he does with abandon. "Hand jobs," as he readily points out, are everywhere.

They call us the *shad lav collectiva*—which means *very good team* in Armenian.

There are many perks to the consulting work I do in this country, but none more paramount than my association with Simon and Naira. Twice in the past year, we've bundled ourselves into Simon's rambling Russian Lada and traversed the width and breadth of Armenia offering journalism courses to reporters in the smaller cities.

Simon is thirty-four, and officially employed as the head mechanic for the department of interior affairs (aka the police), a job that last paid him a salary more than a decade ago. About the only thing his government position is good for now is to get him out of paying the exorbitant, random "fines" police officers indiscriminately charge drivers, waving them down to the side of the road, as a method of supplementing their own meager paychecks. So Simon works as an itinerant driver for the Pro-Media program and other non-government organizations, consistently retooling the twenty-year-old engine to keep it running. The car speedometer had turned over four times—that's kilometers, not miles, but still a heck of a lot of ground covered. Once, I asked him why we were driving so slowly along a (for Armenia) well-paved highway.

"Car is tired," he said, affectionately patting the gear shift. "Like my brother, I know him. So I resting him."

Naira, in comparison to Simon's steady, mountainous affability, sparks and flutters with the buoyancy of a rosy brown robin. At forty-one, she is an experienced English teacher at Yerevan State University, but as this pays about $60 per month, she also looks for extra assignments as a translator. Her large brown eyes flash with humor, her voice has a musical, soothing ring, and her skin glows like a woman half her age.

She is full of secret recipes and tips on how to preserve a feminine appearance. "Lick your lips as often as you brush your hair," she advises, "and they will be rosy and not get those age spots. Oh yes, and add a little honey," here she stops to lift her eyebrows in a conspiratorial way, "which is a good moisturizer and will make you taste delicious for kissing."

We are always happy to see each other, if for no other reason than it means the three of us will be employed for the month. I must confess that for me, my Armenia trips don't properly start until I stumble off the plane in Yerevan, Armenia's capital city, at the ungodly hour of 2 or 4 a.m., and see Simon through the plate-glass window outside baggage claim, grinning, pointing to his waving hand and mouthing "hand job."

"What means the word 'insatiable,' Leah?"

It's Simon again, with his ever expanding vocabulary. "Where on earth did you pick up that word?" I ask, and he pulls out a cassette tape.

"Name of song is 'My love for you is insatiable,'" he says. "Singer is Darren Hayes. You know him?"

When I shake my head no, he adds approvingly, "He has very good voice, very high. Sings like woman."

Simon is pleased with this new word, and as is his wont practices it on everyone.

"Anna, my love for you is insatiable," he says to the pretty office manager at Pro-Media, who laughs and waves him off. "Peter," he says to the Pro-Media office director, "I learned new words: my love for you is insatiable." He merely chuckles at Peter's surprised expression.

Back in the U.S., I'm a romantic cynic and I scoff at the over-simplistic lyrics of bad pop music. Yeah, right. Love doesn't last. People kill each other, kill their own children. In Africa half the population is dying of AIDS. In Armenia, rampant unemployment for over a decade has left decaying houses and infrastructure, frail old people, single mothers, and angry young men with no chance for earning a living. I could go on and on.

But Simon's only musical accompaniment on our trips is an odd, variegated collection of cheesy pop songs on cheap pirated tapes with Russian labels, and he plays them endlessly during our four- or five-hour road trips. I stretch out on the back seat, submit to Elton John, Boyz II Men, and Julio Iglesias, and watch out the car window as golden light plays off snow-capped mountains and the roadside fruit stands draped with necklaces of apples, pears, pomegranates, and persimmons.

Despite myself, I feel my heart begin to swell with a new hopeful possibility and my body to relax. I begin to wonder, langorously, whether my baby will come back, whether you can jump-start my heart, what in the world would I do without you. My eyes get misty as I contem-

plate the deeper implications of Britney Spears's trilling
that she's "not a girl/(but not yet a woman)." Naira and
I sing along with some of the songs, such as:

> Wise men say
> Only fools run free
> But I (pause) can't (pause) help (dramatic pause)
> falling in looooooove with thee

"*Vonces,* Leah?" (*How are you?*) asks Simon, peering
back in his rear view mirror.

"My love for Armenia is insatiable, Simon," I reply.

"Armenia, where dreams come true," adds Naira,
with both genuine feeling and just a touch of irony.

"You are right," says Simon, nodding his head gravely,
and employing another of his favorite phrases, "Life is
beautiful."

As the *shad lav collectiva*, our triumvirate has divided
our duties on the road nicely: Simon drives, I teach, and
Naira translates.

The translation is not as straightforward as it sounds.
My students are traditionally the hardest group of people
to teach: adults, many of them much older than me, who
have been practicing their brand of journalism for many
years. And it is Armenian culture, I'm assured, that allows
for the inevitable cacophony of contradicting voices that
resounds in every classroom I've ever taught in here.

I initially found the constant arguments intimidating
and rude, but Naira laughs and shrugs it off. "Armenians
want to learn, but they don't know how," she says. "You
must find the way in."

So Naira softens my tone when I get irritated, her
voice ringing with musical consistency in the classroom.

attention that makes people want to know about his
life and share theirs with him. I myself have been to his
house to celebrate his wedding and subsequent birth of
his son. We once stopped a class in the southern town of
Goris during the week his wife, Marina, was expecting
to go into labor when Simon's phone rang. All twelve
people leaned toward him eagerly as he answered it.

"It's petrol man," he said apologetically, with sheep-
ish-but-pleased grin on his face.

Over a bottle of vodka, Simon and whomever-it-is-
that-he-has-just-met bond. This is when interesting
things happen: we've gone fishing, rabbit hunting,
munched *horavatz* (a fragrant Armenian style of barbe-
cue cooked on stakes over outdoor fires, then wrapped
in a paper thin bread called *lavash*) in front of centuries-
old ruins, dined in restaurants full of Persian truckers
surrounded by spectacular wooded hillsides. Once, the
owner of a hotel where we were the only guests brought
in an entire Armenian band in for the evening, and
made us dance—along with the cook and waitress and
two local passersby—until 4 A.M. All inevitably accompanied by vodka.

Simon assiduously cultivates these people that he
meets on the road, and whenever we are back in the
area, we look them up at least for a meal, if not some
elaborate adventure. When we are in the north, he gets
calls from the friends he made the week before, when
we were in the south. We give them rides into Yerevan,
and when they arrive he takes them out on the town.

"Oooh, Marina very angry with me," he admitted
to me one Sunday about a fight he'd had with his new
wife. He'd apparently spent a particularly long night at
a strip joint with the assistant manager of a television

station from the southern town of Kappan. "I come home very quiet, at 5 or 6 A.M., but when I open the door, she awake." He shakes his fist in the air and mimics the look she gave him, and can't help but crack a smile. "She shout."

"When you have good friends, Leah," he'll tell me often, "life is beautiful."

My second week in the country, Peter informs me that the Pro-Media program has run out of funds and this will most likely be my last trip to Armenia. This will be the last gig for the *shad lav collectiva*.

This is a sobering thought, not only for me but more seriously for Simon and Naira, who work itinerantly when I come here. We fret about our various difficulties on the road: me about the uncertain future of my consulting business; Naira about her philandering husband; Simon about the end, as he calls it, of his "freedom" and worry about how he will support Marina and his infant son, Levan.

One night, when Naira has gone to bed and it's just Simon and me splitting a bottle of mulberry vodka, I say, "Sometimes, Simon, life is not beautiful, true?"

Simon throws back his head to take a shot, looks at me seriously, and says "You are right." And reading the question in my eyes, he continues: "If life was always beautiful, we would not know what beauty was," he says. "So sometimes, it's O.K. if life is not so beautiful."

He fills his glass again, lifts it, and said: "Don't be afraid, Leah. I wish you everything. I wish Naira everything. I wish myself everything."

And we drink to that.

Postscript: A year later, I received the following e-mail from Naira:

Dear Leah,
    A terrible thing has happened. Simon crashed his car and was killed—while driving to the airport to pick up an expert. Sometimes life is not beautiful.
                                                —Naira

♪♪ ♪♪ ♪♪

Leah Kohlenberg is a journalist, international media trainer, writing teacher, and painter who has lived, worked, and traveled in the former Soviet Union and Asia, including the Caucasas, Hong Kong, and Mongolia. She has worked for TIME *magazine and ABCNEWS.com and has written for the* Asian Wall Street Journal, *Salon.com, MSNBC.com, the* Far Eastern Economic Review, *and the* Seattle Weekly, *among others. These days she's based in Seattle where she writes, teaches, splashes a lot of paint around, and is learning to draw the figure.*

❧ ❧ ❧

Where Boys Grow Up To Be Girls

In Samoa, the author encounters the ubiquitous
fa'afafine—men who live "in the way of a woman."

Not long before the plane from Hawai'i to Samoa departs, the airport ladies' room is crowded. A dark-haired woman in a flowered blouse checks her makeup in the mirror. She's a beefy gal, with a tattooed armband and impressive biceps, which isn't unusual—Samoans tend to be big-boned. But as she deftly plucks a few hairs from her cheeks, I realize that "she" is a "he."

Startled, I trade glances with another woman in the mirror, who smiles knowingly. The she-male catches our interaction and does a little exaggerated primping for our benefit, and all the girls at the sinks giggle.

Five hours later, arriving in Pago Pago, American Samoa, I see more transvestites—not obvious drag queens, but men done up in everyday women's dress. When my cousin's nephew, Joe, picks me up, I ask him about them. (My cousin is married to a Samoan, which gives me a closer glimpse of Samoan extended-family life than most "*palangi*," or white people, get.) Joe uneasily explains that the transvestites are called "*fa'afafine*," meaning "in the way of a woman," and are simply an accepted fact in Samoan society.

With their similar traditional dress, it's sometimes hard to tell Samoan men and women apart—especially when some women have big biceps encircled with tattooed armbands and some men have long, luxurious black hair. Samoans descend from people who were strong enough to paddle from island to island to survive, quick enough to escape rival tribes, and who fed on the starchy breadfruit and taro roots that grow everywhere on the islands. They're like tropical flowers—big, bright, and meaty, with a humid, amorphous sexuality.

Joe says that *fa'afafine* are treated as women and play the same roles in Samoan culture as "genetic" women—caretakers, teachers, Bible-school leaders. A long-standing myth about transvestites in the Polynesian islands has been that when families have too many boys and too few girls to do all the women's work, they appoint a younger boy to "be a girl." But Joe says that isn't quite right, or at least not anymore: No one appoints *fa'afafine*, they just grow up that way. They usually aren't discouraged—nor are they considered homosexual, a taboo in Samoan culture. "We can have *fa'afafine* singing in the church choir, and the preacher will turn around and preach how ungodly it is to be gay," Joe explains.

But how can they **not** be gay? Whom do they sleep with? Judging from Joe's expression, I've asked too many questions. "Well, when boys are young and first experimenting..." he falters, then says, "You need to see Dr. Sele."

We drive to a boxy, modern school, and Joe introduces me to Dr. Vena Sele, dean of student services at American Samoa Community College. Dr. Sele is an imposing woman, conservatively dressed in a flowing pantsuit, with painted fingernails and delicate gold jewelry. She is every inch a middle-aged, churchgoing lady—except that biologically, she's a man. And so is her pretty secretary.

"*Fa'afafine* are ladies," she says pointedly. "We're well-educated and highly respected."

Dr. Sele is justifiably defensive of Samoa's sexual reputation: The country has been misunderstood by anthropologists ever since Margaret Mead wrote about the supposed promiscuity on the islands in 1928. The few today who have studied *fa'afafine* say the only way to understand them is to leave aside cultural notions of what it means to be gay or even male and female. Samoa is a community-oriented society, with more focus on extended families and villages than individuals, says Jeannette Mageo, an anthropologist at Washington State University. So a person's gender is based more on his or her role in the society than on actual anatomy. "As long as you're playing the female role socially, and in sex, then you are as good as a woman," she says. So, if a Samoan man has sex with a *fa'afafine*, it's considered a heterosexual relationship.

One of the reasons *fa'afafine* have flourished, Mageo says, is that they're valued as entertainers. Before

Christian missionaries arrived in Samoa circa 1830, men would hold ceremonies and give speeches while women performed Polynesian dancing and comedy shows for visitors. "As the night progressed, there would be a lot of dirty dancing and sexual joking," Mageo says. Once on the scene, missionaries ordered the women to cover their breasts and drove them from the stage. Transvestites subsequently replaced the women as the main entertainers, free to make sexual jokes in the Christian atmosphere of repression.

Today *fa'afafine* are, like women, treated with courtly respect—except that men are more likely to banter and make bawdy jokes with them. And, for the most part, they're accepted as long as they dress modestly. But while they aren't discriminated against for being effeminate, Dr. Sele says, they do face the same glass ceilings at work and in villages as women. *Fa'afafine* who want to be business executives usually have to dress as men at work. Dr. Sele is one of the few *fa'afafine* who has reached a high position while living as a woman, a feat she attributes to her Ph.D. "My education counters any criticism," she says. "To be a *fa'afafine*, you have to be educated—it's our weapon."

The next day, I take a puddle-jumper over to Samoa— an independent country sixty miles from American Samoa, consisting of two islands. Samoa has a distinctly less American atmosphere than Pago Pago, with fewer cars and more palm-thatched huts, fishermen, and nut-brown kids playing in the waves. Here, *fa'afafine* gravitate toward the main city of Apia.

I make my way to Apia's oldest hotel, Aggie Grey's, which has long put on *fiafia*, or evening dance and fire festivals. I end up sipping mai tais under an umbrella by the pool with Tania Toomalatai. Tania, now fifty-five, started dancing at Aggie's when she was seven and became a star. One of her claims to fame is that when Marlon Brando visited decades ago, he didn't realize pretty Tania was a *fa'afafine*. "He was surprised," she says with a sly wink.

Tania, wearing a tight tank top, capri pants, and heels, is considered the "mother" of Apia's *fa'afafine*, who are more flamboyant and open about sex than those in the villages. In a soft, smooth voice, she explains that "the difference between our *fa'afafine* and your gays is that gay men make love to each other." *Fa'afafine*, on the other hand, have sex only with straight men—usually young ones. "In my time, a man's first sexual experience was with a *fa'afafine*," Tania says. Samoan girls tend to have few partners early in life, so boys "practice" with *fa'afafine*. "That does not make Samoan guys gay—they see *fa'afafine* as women," says Tania. In other words, most of the macho, muscular men in Samoa—the rugby players and the tattooed taro farmers—have had sexual experiences with other men, whom they consider to be women.

Fa'afafine seem to provide a sort of sexual relief valve to an otherwise repressed culture. "We know how to sat-isfy men better than women do," Tania says. She explains that *fa'afafine* mimic male/female sex by tucking their penises between their legs; they also engage in oral sex, but rarely anal sex. And men continue to see *fa'afafine* on the side even after they're married. "It's still cheating, but it's more cheating to be with another woman—that's when the wives really get ferocious," says Tania. "Being with a *fa'afafine* is like a joke to the wife."

The waiter comes by, says "excuse me" to Tania, and then laughs. She explains that the way he said "excuse me" doubles in Samoan for "suck me." *Fa'afafine* are known for their sexual double entendres, and waiters know they can banter back. As we leave, Tania points out a young man in a baseball cap.

"That's one of mine," she says proudly. "I practically changed his Pampers."

That evening, I visit a small club called Sel's Seabreeze Café and chat with Tara and Kayla, both twenty-nine, who perform in the floor show. Tara wears an exuberantly ruffled green dress and ropes of Polynesian shell necklaces; Kayla, who has the build of a bruising rugby player, is sweet and shy and doesn't speak English very well. After a glass or two of wine, they reveal that *fa'afafine* aren't always quite as accepted as others have led me to believe. "Some families will give them beatings and warn them not to wear dresses anymore, but they can't change," says Tara. Nor are their romantic relationships always easy. "Straight men are always going to leave us for relationships with women," says Tara, sighing. "*Fa'afafine* can't bear children. We laugh it off, but it's really heartbreaking."

Taaloga, the club's owner, says that some *fa'afafine* end up in Apia after being kicked out of their homes. Her brother is a *fa'afafine*, and the club has taken in another who had been drifting. Everyone in this motley family performs, and when the lights dim, they give a dancing tour of the Polynesian islands, complete with grass skirts, headdresses, and coconut-shell bras.

After the show, I talk with two other *fa'afafine* who are dressed casually in jeans, tight t-shirts, and subtle make-up. Unlike Tara and Kayla, they never wear dresses; they consider them "too femme." *Fa'afafine* run the gamut from exaggerated femininity, like Tania, to these young, faintly feminine hipsters. Another extreme is Patty, a friend of Tania's, who looks like a stout, short-haired, fifty-five-year-old man—except that she wears a little flower behind one ear. What they all have in common is that no matter how they dress, they play the role of being female. After dinner, they do the dishes.

Still, their masculine sides sometimes come out. The next day, I see it in full force when I visit the playing fields—expanses of cool, thick grass above Apia, with views of both the bright-blue sea and the jagged volcanic peaks above. On the field, you can see why the locals sometimes call *fa'afafine* "50/50s," since they cheerfully show their masculine brawn. A big, buff *fa'afafine* will whack a baseball out of the park while her friends cheer her on. In the outfield, another will charge after a ball, then deliver a girlie "yoo-hoo" wave after she's caught it.

After the heat of the game, I go to Mango's, a restaurant overlooking coconut trees and the distant beach, for a beer. There, *fa'afafine* are more masculine than the "girls" at Seabreeze. The owner, Ken Moala, is a well-educated, articulate *fa'afafine* who dresses like a man. Peter Taurasese, a flight attendant, is a *fa'afafine* who has gone so far as to sport the traditional Samoan male's *tatau*, or tattoo, an intricate design that stretches from the knees to the midriff and is applied during a month-long span of ceremonies that typically prove a man's "machoness." "It's my male warrior side," she says. "I like to hunt—I just like to hunt men on the sea wall!"

The sea wall that surrounds the port at Apia is where the town's *fa'afafine* and other night crawlers traditionally meet up for a cheap drink before going to a bar, or hook up for a quick tryst after the clubs let out. Across from the sea wall is Seana's, another bar with a *fa'afafine* floor show. I'm sitting at a table with Tania and her friends. Men spin her onto the dance floor, and they dance with other *fa'afafine* interchangeably with real girls. They flirt more with *fa'afafine*, though, pretending to peek up their skirts.

As men ask Tania to dance, I notice one of them has the traditional knees-to-midriff tattoo. I joke to Tania that I'd like to see his whole tattoo. Little do I realize that she'll later arrange for him to show up at my hotel at 2 A.M.! (The hotel manager discreetly tells me, "Madame, we have a strict policy against that sort of thing.") *Fa'afafine*, explains anthropologist Jeannette Mageo, often act as go-betweens for shy women and the men they're after. Tania was simply trying to show me a little Samoan hospitality.

The next day—before I can get into any more trouble—I leave Apia for Savai'i, a more traditional Samoan island, to see how village *fa'afafine* are different from the big-city girls. Savai'i is an hour—and a century—away by boat, a volcanic island with a profusion of gardens, Samoan huts, and colorful oval houses. I go to the village where Talavai Leaoa, thirty-four, a *fa'afafine* teacher, lives and find her parents' open-air house, where pigs graze in the front yard. Inside, her mother weaves straw mats on the floor. No one speaks much English; when I saw the name "Talavai," her niece starts giggling. "My auntie," she says, laughing at the joke of her uncle being "female."

Talavai wanders in, wearing her school uniform: a *lavalava*, the traditional cotton print-cloth skirt, and a white shirt that any man might wear. Gentle and intelligent, she has short hair and a quiet femininity. Most village *fa'afafine*, says Talavai, have to live more conservatively than those in Apia. "Every village has rules to control the people," she says.

Talavai takes me to visit Hacy, a *fa'afafine* farmer who also takes care of her mother. We sit in the shade near Hacy's jungle hut, eating fresh pineapple. Hacy, fifty, dressed in a dirty t-shirt with dyed-blonde hair, rolls her own cigarettes and has the weather-beaten look of someone who's seen hard times. "There are people in Savai'i who have never seen a *fa'afafine* dressed in ladies' clothing," she says.

Hacy says she isn't sure when she became a *fa'afafine*. As a child, her father beat her, and when she was ten, she was out feeding pigs when her brother-in-law raped her. "I didn't know I was a *fa'afafine* yet, but maybe he could sense it," she says. "He grabbed me and pulled down his pants," she says. Talavai, too, was "initiated" by older boys.

Now, Hacy and Talavai laugh freely about sex. "The girls get jealous of us," says Talavai. "*Fa'afafine* are free to have sex, but the girls are protected by their families." Hacy says, "Some girls will tell *fa'afafine*, 'Take my husband for a few nights! Maybe it will improve things.'"

"We have a lot of skills," nods Talavai with a little smile. "And methods."

The next day, I return from Savai'i—reluctant to leave the paradise of banyan trees and ocean blowholes—to attend the annual "Miz Samoa" drag pageant in Pago Pago, where a church hall is packed with 800 people. I'm sitting between last year's Miz Samoa, Tiare, and the priests of the parish. There's a long runway with a backdrop mural of the Virgin Mary. Contestants come out wearing white angel costumes, then start shimmying to techno choral music. They compete in casual wear, evening wear, Samoan wear, and the favorite, the swimsuit competition. The crowd claps politely for a red leotard, boos a *lavalava*, and roars for a 5'11" queen who strips down to a bikini. The priests next to me are chuckling. When I ask about *fa'afafine*, they get serious. "They are respectable people with talent," one says. "They are fund-raising for the parish."

Tiare, in her silk gown and crown, is enjoying the final evening of her reign. She has a boyfriend and tells younger *fa'afafine* that they don't have to sleep with every man who comes along. "We don't want society to think that we just troll the night to give blow jobs," she says.

Tonight, *fa'afafine* strut their stuff before an adoring pageant crowd. Tomorrow, they'll go back to their schools and workplaces, surrounded by the sounds of gentle, teasing laughter.

Laura Fraser is a journalist, writing teacher, Italophile, and the author of the travel memoir, An Italian Affair, *and* Losing It, *an exposé of the diet industry. Her work has appeared in many national publications and she lives in San Francisco.*

❧ ❧ ❧

The Naked Brew

The author gets the skinny on the ancient
Japanese tea ceremony.

*T*HE OLD WOMAN STARED AT MY BREASTS. SHE
laughed heartily and spoke Japanese to five giggling
ladies. Although she herself had limp melons, thick ankles,
and legs bent into a fat horseshoe, she had an advantage
over my skinny youth. She was wearing clothes. I was clad
in only underwear and dinky split-toed socks.

For the past couple of months the old woman's
daughter, Hideko, had been giving me tea ceremony
lessons in exchange for English instruction. As this was
our last class before my return to Canada, Hideko had
invited four of her other students to join us for a ceremony, complete with kimonos.

There was a tidy pile of kimono undergarments on the
table, however the old woman seemed to have forgotten

her intention to dress me. Blushing-anxious for her to remember, I was beginning to feel like a defecating platypus
or a copulating cockroach on the Nature Channel.

"What's she saying?" I asked Hideko who had her
fingers over the shame of her laughing teeth and lips.

"That you have nice breasts," she answered, still smiling. "She likes your pink—what do you call them?"

"Nipples?" I offered.

"Yes, nipples."

Although comforted they didn't think I was hideous,
I was perplexed by this talk. I thought a tea ceremony
teacher would be dignified, that her demeanor would
match the lofty philosophy of her art.

Tea ceremony, or *chanoyu,* is a ritualistic way of serving tea that reflects the fundamental principles of Zen
Buddhism: purity, harmony, respect, and tranquility.

Although the literal translation of *chanoyu* is simply
hot water for tea, it is a practice that combines painting,
food preparation, interior design, gardening, flower ar-
ranging, and performance.

In 800, C. E. Lu Yu, a Chinese scholar steeped in Zen
Buddhism, wrote the first definitive book about tea. In it
he codified methods of cultivation, production, and ritualistic consumption. Monks, who used tea as a means of
staying awake during meditation, introduced Japan to the
beverage and to Lu Yu's style of service. But as tea gained
in popularity, much of the original Zen concept attached
to it was lost. Aristocrats began to hold tea tournaments,
in which participants placed bets on where various brews
had been grown and geishi began to specialize in the
ceremony.

Between the fourteenth and the sixteenth centuries
three Zen priests restored tea to its original sacred place.

Sen-no Rikkyu, the most notable of them, refined the tea ceremony's rigid etiquette and his great-grandsons founded the two largest schools of tea. Today the tea ceremony continues to be popular in Japan and even high schools have clubs devoted to it.

Practitioners seek to discover Buddha's teachings in the simple gesture of filling a bowl with tea. Although I'd suspected there wouldn't be enough time for me to reach enlightenment, I'd hoped my study would at least give me a deeper understanding of Japanese philosophy. At any rate that's what I'd hoped for until the end of my first lesson, when I found myself more full of rice cakes and surprise than new knowledge.

Hideko had said, "I am looking for a boyfriend. I want foreigner boyfriend. Please introduce me." Feeling both surprised and offended, I told her politely I didn't know anyone suitable. I was surprised because she was being undignified and I was offended because I felt she wanted to use a foreign hunk for her cultural kicks. In short, her request for a boyfriend and her mother's inspection of my nipples bothered me for similar reasons.

The giggles eventually died down and the old woman began to dress me, to replace one form of discomfort with another. None of my own Western fashion torture had prepared me for the vise grip of the kimono—not my heels too high for running or my skirts too snug for sitting. The old woman bound my body so tightly I was forced to take shallow breaths and tiny doll steps. So tightly that I wondered how I would swallow even three and a half sips of tea.

Seemingly unaffected by their kimonos, Hideko and her other students pitter-pattered around the room, tidying and preparing for the ceremony. After helping out for a few minutes, the old woman went downstairs to watch television with her husband.

Although Hideko had soft lines on her face, she still lived with her parents, as virtually all unmarried Japanese women do. She often talked about wanting to find a husband and didn't agree with me that she was better off staying with her mum and dad. Hideko worked full time, paid no rent, and ate her mother's cooking. She owned a car, went on holidays abroad, and had a sprawling bedroom divided into areas for sleeping, entertaining, and *chanoyu*.

Her tearoom was set apart from the rest of her space with a sliding door. Inside the color was a soothing beige-on-beige. Uncluttered, there was no furniture—only a simple scroll on the wall and a brazier built into the floor. The rest of the floor was covered with tatami, sweet and clean smelling reed mats.

With the tearoom tidy and the utensils in place, we were ready to begin. Normally only one ceremony is performed on any given occasion, but as most of us were students, eager to practice the etiquette of both roles, we planned to have multiple informal ceremonies—taking turns serving and being served. The etiquette for formal and informal ceremonies is more or less the same, however a formal ceremony involves a meal and lasts for approximately four hours.

We took our places on the tatami, our legs tucked underneath us, our backs straight and our hands resting in our laps. Then we bowed to Hideko, the first host, and watched her bring in the trays of sweets and powdered tea. As I was the guest of honor, Hideko prepared my drink first. Using a long-handled wooden spoon, she put one and a half scoops of tea into the bowl. She added boiling water and frothed up the mixture using a bamboo whisk. She put the bowl on the floor and I slid towards it.

I picked up the bowl with my right hand and repositioned it by a few inches. Then I moved back to my original place and once again repositioned it slightly, this time so that it was close to my left knee. I was attempting to follow the many rules Hideko had taught me—rules that may seem cumbersome, but were designed to achieve an economy of movement.

After excusing myself for drinking first, I picked up the bowl with my right hand and rested it in my left palm. I turned it around, put it to my lips using both hands and drank. The tea tasted bitter—a perfect contrast to the gummy rice cakes filled with sugary bean paste.

I wiped the edge of the bowl with my fingers and then wiped them on my paper napkin. I turned the bowl, placed it on the floor and put my elbows on my thighs. I picked up the bowl with both hands and for the next few minutes examined it, admiring the craftsmanship. When my turn was finished, Hideko prepared tea for the other women and then closed our first ceremony by simply announcing its end.

As the second host, I carried in the trays of tea and cakes, careful to step into the room with my right foot and careful to never step on a line in the tatami. The long-handled spoon and the lacquer tea caddy were already clean, but I nonetheless used my silk cloth, my *fukusa*, to wipe them again, to purify them. *Fukusa* folds and movements are complicated and I had been practicing them for weeks, mostly on the subway while other commuters smiled, amused to see a foreigner intent on learning *chanoyu*.

After Hideko drank the tea I prepared, I washed the bowl with a white cotton cloth and made tea for her four other students. Then I closed the ceremony and took my place as a guest until my legs were numb from kneeling.

Finally it was time to hobble to Hideko's car, to perch in my seat and try not to crush the bow of my *obi,* my kimono sash. Why are we going to a French restaurant, I wondered. To me, Japanese food seemed more fitting after *chanoyu.*

It continued to seem more fitting until some point between the escargot and the chocolate, when I suddenly remembered a white Canadian friend speculating on the nature of Asian pubic hair. I realized then that the old woman had stared at my nipples, that Hideko wanted a foreign boyfriend, and that I studied tea for the same reason. All humans, Japanese and Canadian alike, are camera-wielding anthropologists, cultural difference diggers, exotic thrill seekers.

As a white North American I had been used to doing the probing, used to seeing myself as the cultural norm, as nothing to warrant study. Finding myself under the microscope for the first time, I discovered the vulnerability of that position and that my subjects have their own subjectivity. Their lips are on my teacup and we can learn a lot by sharing.

"Hideko sensei," I said, over the tinkle of Japanese and the clink of cutlery. "I think I do know a Canadian man you might like."

❧   ❧   ❧

Andrew Miller has lived in Japan, Korea, Spain, France, England, and Mexico. Her work, including fiction and poetry, can be found in various anthologies.

ॐ ॐ ॐ

Sister Thomasina

Who ever thought the most fearsome creature
in Ethiopia would be a nun?

S OMEHOW SHE WILL FIND A WAY TO GET HER HANDS
on this story. Using her rather unsettling ability to root
out each and every one of my mutinous thoughts, she will
sense my villainy even as I write, half a world away. The
infallible grapevine of Roman Catholic nuns will sleuth out
and dutifully report my treachery. My betrayal. In the next
instant, Sister Thomasina, Mother Superior, will holler out
the kitchen door of the mission house, ordering the driver
to fire up the Land Cruiser. Then out of the lush green hills
of southern Ethiopia's Great Rift Valley she will ride, with
nagging memories of me, this troublesome and disobedi-
ent American, a stubborn thorn in her side, plaguing her
afresh. "Faster! Faster!" she will command, as they slip and
slide around steep muddy switchbacks and careen around

canyon-sized potholes in the red dirt road. Her pale gray veil will flap insolently in the warm wind. She'll clutch her rosary beads tightly in a plump fist, murmuring a vengeful prayer. Oh, there is no doubt about it. Sister Thomasina will find a way to get her hands on my story, my greatest and most affronting of sins, and she will not fail in her efforts to track me down.

I am going to Hell.

"What do you mean you can't be out after dark?" my friend Ruth asks in disbelief. We sit across from each other at a wobbly little table at one of the local pastry shops. A mere three weeks I have been in Ethiopia and a startling realization is just beginning to sink in.

"I'm not *allowed* to," I answer, still stunned myself.

"Who on earth told you that?"

"Sister Thomasina!" I throw my hands in the air to emphasize the complete absurdity of the situation.

"You *must* be joking."

"Nope."

"You're not a nun, for Chrissakes," Ruth points out the obvious. "She shouldn't expect you to act like one!"

"I know," I groan, frustrated and bewildered.

"You're not even Catholic!"

"I *know!*" I slurp at my mango and pineapple juice, swatting at flies and feeling defeated. How on earth could I have managed to travel all the way to Ethiopia only to find myself cloistered like, well, a nun?

Ruth is British and, same as me, a volunteer come to teach English in Dilla, a small town halfway between Ethiopia's capital, Addis Ababa, and the Kenyan border. Any white folks here are mostly European or Australian backpackers passing through on their way to Kenya who might stay a night or two if they feel like dawdling over mango and pineapple juice in the beautiful green hills where coffee was born.

Sitting together at the pastry shop, I suddenly find that I envy Ruth and her freedom. She hasn't traveled to the other side of the world only to lose it. Ruth teaches at Dilla College, not at the mission school on the Sister's compound. But more importantly, Ruth lives in town in her own private house. She does not live inside the Catholic compound's gates. She does not live with eight Roman Catholic nuns. She does not live under Sister Thomasina's thumb.

No, Ruth can sleep in past six o'clock on a Saturday morning without a worried nun or two tapping sweetly but insistently on her bedroom window to call her to breakfast. Ruth can marvel at a field full of fireflies and not be scolded when she arrives two minutes late for dinner because she'd never seen fireflies before that dark, moonless Dilla night. Ruth can get sick to her stomach after too much spicy *doro wat* without having it blamed on "going about too much." Ruth can even spend a few days on holiday in Addis without Sister Thomasina calling her mother at home in the States to let her know what her troublesome, headstrong daughter is insisting upon this time. ("Sara wants to do some traveling?" my mother confirms over the crackling static of a bad overseas connection. "That's *wonderful*!" Sister Thomasina believes she may have found the source of the problem and throws her hands in the air to emphasize the complete absurdity of the situation.) No, Ruth isn't made to feel like a misbehaving child. Nor has she been forced to the confounding and outrageous realization that a stern mother superior is monitoring her every move.

"Did Amy have this problem?" I ask Ruth about the last American woman to volunteer at the Mission. "Or am I just crazy?" Crazy. Somehow I might manage to cope with the daily hallucinogenic malaria pills, the lonely and seemingly insurmountable language barrier, a telephone that doesn't work when it rains, overwhelming bouts of homesickness, and a thousand other challenges, but the Mother Superior? I could not cope with Sister Thomasina.

"Oh yeah," Ruth assures me. "Amy felt the same way. But she only had to put up with it for six weeks. You're here for six months!"

After Ruth and I finish our mango and pineapple juice, we say goodbye and I take my time wandering back to the compound. It is late afternoon and the intense heat of the dry season uncovers new freckles on my pink sweaty cheeks. My short hair is covered with a colorful scarf (for which the sisters regularly tease me, cheerfully praising my progress as a nun), but the top of my head still feels burning hot. My sandaled feet drag and gather more dust. Evening is not far off and I must return to the compound before dusk settles in order to be on time for dinner.

As I walk, children stop their play long enough to shout, "*Ciao*, Sara!" and wave. I wave back and ask, "*Dehna nachu?*" "*Dehna!*" they reply and giggle at the white lady's Amharic. Perhaps one of them who knows me from church or school on the compound will take my hand and walk with me for a while before turning back to join her playmates.

After a while, I turn off the main road and continue down the path to the compound. I enter through the unlocked gates. Under a canopy of cool and beautifully green trees, I pass the brick church, the kindergarten, and a small orchard full of guavas and avocados before pushing open the rusty gate that leads to my little house.

I do love my little house. It is surrounded by endless twisting knots of leafy green grapevines and enormous drying racks covered with freshly picked coffee beans. My little house has bright green doors, maroon tiled floors, hot and cold running water, and a framed picture of the Pope hanging in the sitting room. Together he and I correct essays and write letters home. From my bedroom window I can see the kindergartners at play in their bright purple uniforms and hear their cheerful shouts. I watch groups of local women pound roasted coffee beans with giant wooden pestles. I keep my windows and flowered yellow curtains wide open to catch breezes and exchange smiles.

Before going inside, I stop to gather my morning's laundry from the line. In the hot Ethiopian sun and unforgiving dryness of the season, my t-shirts and skirts stiffen like cardboard in no time. Too shy to string my colorful bras and panties up within view of the nuns, I drape them around my unused kitchen, out of sight of the Pope as well. Taking in an armload of freshly clean sun-dried clothes is immensely satisfying. Every scrap of my clothing, sheets, and towels I wash by hand. I scrub. I rinse. I wring and I watch the water turn brown with the dirt of Ethiopia. I plunge my pruny hands back into the cool water and scrub some more. I empty the buckets and begin again.

From my little outdoor laundry porch, I can look up into the bluest and widest and wildest of skies and just make out the tiny black specks of birds soaring impossibly high above me. They mesmerize me. For a moment, I forget how a controlling and unreasonable Sister Thomasina literally frustrates me to tears. I forget that I may never see Dilla at night. I forget myself in this sky. And my hands have never been so clean.

Dilla also has the most beautiful sunsets I've ever seen. I try not to remind myself that I may only see that magnificent orange sun set behind the compound walls. One particularly lovely orange and pink evening, I climbed up one of the fences and perched atop the gate for a better view. A white woman sitting atop a fence in Dilla, however, is a bit of a spectacle and so I soon became self-conscious and climbed back down. So much for unobstructed sunsets.

When I finally go inside, I discover there is no electricity, a regular evening occurrence in our part of the country. I dump my clothes on the extra bed and fumble about for matches in the thickening darkness. I know that in a little while as my favorite nun, Sister Rebecca, and I set the table for dinner, she will take the opportunity to test my Amharic.

"*Anchi biet, mabrat alle?*" she will ask. Is there light at your house?

"*Ie, mabrat yellem.*" I will answer. No, there is no light.

"*Shama alle?*" Do you have candles?

"*Ow; shama alle.*"

"*Gobez,* Sara!" She always congratulates me on my progress. Sister Rebecca is a young Ethiopian nun with a wicked sense of humor and a keen sense of irony. Earlier, when setting out silverware, we will go through a similar routine about soup and spoons.

For now, I will spend the last few minutes before I grab my flashlight and head to the Sister's house for dinner continuing the latest letter home to my family. The stack of my students' grammar exercises can wait until tomorrow. Having found the matches, I light the two candles on my desk, take out my letter and sit quietly for a moment. I peer out my window to the night sky above. When the lights go out in Dilla, without a moon there is complete darkness. I have never seen such stars.

The next morning, Sister Rebecca and I have just finished washing the last of the breakfast dishes when I remember Ruth's invitation to a coffee ceremony being held at her house with our Ethiopian friends, Tesfaye and Tadese. I certainly plan on going, but I know I need to ask Sister Thomasina's permission before Ruth comes to fetch me later this afternoon. I also know that I have already used up all of my usual excuses this week for pushing past the compound gates and walking the sun-baked, dirt footpaths into town. Smiling at the ex-otic look of Ethiopia's colorful stamps, I have already mailed my usual stack of letters home at the *posta biet*. I have exchanged pleasantries and currency with the excessively polite bank manager. I have even purchased enough candles and powdered drink mix to last until the rainy season. Another made-up invitation to tea with a student's family might look suspicious and the tower of toilet paper rolls stacked in my bathroom is getting ri-diculous. And even though Sister Thomasina is running out of her own excuses to keep me within reach, she will undoubtedly frown on such a frivolous outing.

But I need friends. I need Ruth, Tesfaye, and Tadese to rescue me from behind the mission gates and spirit me away to the lively and colorful world that is Dilla—a world we have grown to love and admire and one that

Sister Thomasina rarely visits. I need to pick my way through the maze of the marketplace and try to hammer out a bargain with my feeble Amharic. I need to buy my own mangos and bananas. I need to go exploring with my friends among the hills of green trees and abandoned coffee plantations, searching for monkeys and ancient rock carvings. Without these things I surely would not survive this madness so far from home. I would crack in my loneliness. And so I steel myself for another confrontation with Sister Thomasina.

Beautiful early morning sunlight streams yellow through the kitchen windows. Pink-cheeked cordon bleus and hornbills sing contentedly into the cool, bright sky. Outside small groups of my students walk slowly toward our classroom, hugging English grammar books to their chests, laughing and whispering. The swing sets are full of energetic kindergartners with their little legs pumping furiously, back and forth, back and forth. But now I do not see them and smile. I am distracted. I am preparing for battle.

Sister Thomasina enters the kitchen with her dirty coffee cup and places it in the empty sink. I must tell her about coffee at Ruth's before heading off to my first class. I take a deep breath and charge forward but her name is slow and painful off my tongue. "Sister Thomasina..." Each of the six syllables is a hateful chore; a necessary evil suffered for an afternoon of freedom. I am certain the time it takes me simply to pass her name between my lips is enough for her to muster up every last ounce of irritation and disapproval at her disposal to counter my request. "Sister Thomasina..." She has surely chosen each long syllable of that name solely for this purpose, to torture me and every person in her dominion. "I've been invited to Ruth's for coffee this afternoon, Sister Thomasina..."

Turning, she faces me, her eyes daring me to continue with this insolent nonsense. One eyebrow imperiously cocked, it's as though she's challenging me to question her authority. Surely there are reasons for her rules and curfews and Lord knows she will not have some impudent girl declare mutiny on her watch. Then her whole operation would sink into the dark deep. Wayward young American women are kidnapped after dark by clever Eritrean rebels and traded back to their rich nation for potfuls of dollars. Any twit could understand the risk involved.

"Sister Thomasina...?"

Her disapproving stare is wickedly powerful. In this never-ending moment the birds have stopped singing into the cool morning sky and the sun has lost its yellow. I cannot remember a time when a stern and hypercritical Roman Catholic nun did not dictate my daily schedule. Sister Thomasina undoubtedly cannot remember a time when an arrogant American with no respect for authority did not disrupt hers. But here I am. That thorn in her side. I have come to Dilla and, in this place, we meet.

"*Si*," she responds at last. Her piercing eyes test my resolve.

"It's O.K., right?"

There is a long pause. I stare unseeing into the kitchen sink and scold my heart for beating faster. She cannot lock me up behind her gates, Eritrean rebels or no Eritrean rebels. I will not allow it. The pause stretches longer still. Neither one of us can ignore the other. In the end, Sister Thomasina knows this. And I, with every stolen and insubordinate step in Africa, most certainly do.

For better or worse, I have happened inside her queendom by way of a small fleet of half-empty airplanes, three continents, and more than a little courage. It is a place never in my bluest and widest and wildest of dreams did I imagine I'd come. This holy queendom is warm and green and indescribably beautiful and her fences are high and her gates well guarded. We will drive one another crazy. And then one day, I will return home.

"Sister Thomasina, it is O.K., right?"

Her eyes drop to the dirty coffee cup in the sink. "*Si.* O.K."

"*Grazie*, Sister Thomasina."

And we almost smile.

Sara Bathum hails from the Pacific Northwest. She has a B.A. in Theatre and Women Studies from the University of Washington in Seattle and a M.A. in Performance Studies from New York University. This is her first published story.

☙ ☙ ☙

Wild Olives

A traveler learns a lesson deep in the Moroccan desert.

ABDASALAM POUNDED HIS HAND ON THE DASHBOARD with the thick beat of the Arabian music, waking me from my uneasy slumber. The light of the rising sun filtered through the dust so that the sky appeared to be covered in gauze, its single golden eye staring at us above the veil of the Moroccan desert. I looked at the man behind the wheel. He was about fifty, with peppery hair, a broom mustache, and long lashes shading tired eyes. He sang along with the music, "Aaah! Eeehhhah! Ahh! Ahh! Heyahh!" Then he turned to me, completely ignoring the road, and ordered me to sing, "*Chantez! Chantez!*"

Coming out of my daze, I started chanting, "Hey! Hey! Hey!" as I slapped my hand on the dash in rhythm.

Suddenly, Abdasalam stopped pounding. "*Je suis fatigué,* Jennica." Faaaa-teee-gay. He said each syllable

212

as though he were holding it up to the light like a gem. Abdasalam had been driving non-stop for three days, singing to keep himself awake. With travelers' spontaneity, my boyfriend Mike and I had accepted a ride with him the day before, hoping to make it from a remote ferry station in Melilla to the busy city of Fez, more than eight hours away. Now we were in the middle of the desert in Africa with a half-asleep, half-delirious stranger as our driver. We had no road map, no compass, and no assurance of our future—only the memory of why we had decided to join Abdasalam in the first place.

Our journey with Abdasalam had begun under the dazzling sunshine of southern Spain. Mike and I had approached the booth of the ferry station ticket vendor in Almería ready to buy passage to Morocco. The vendor told us that the ferry that left that day went to a small town, Melilla, and it would arrive around midnight. Transportation and accommodation would be hard to find at that time.

"But," said the vendor, "I know the man behind you, and he lives in Fez. Maybe he can give you a ride from Melilla."

I turned to see a man who had the relaxed, indifferent stance of a camel. The vendor didn't wait for our response, but called out to the man. They spoke in Arabic, their tongues flicking gracefully around the hard rocks of the language. Was some kind of deal being made? I peered more deeply into the dark booth of the ticket vendor. He was young, with black hair slicked back in the machismo-meets-beauty-products way of Spanish men. He looked ordinary enough to be trusted, but in this bright light, I couldn't quite see into his eyes.

"You can trust this man," the vendor said. "He will give you a ride to Fez."

A dry hot wind blew and paused, blew and paused. Mike looked at me, and I could tell by the way his blue eyes caught the sun and held it there that he wanted to take this ride. But I was wary of a man who would drive two strangers eight hours through the desert.

I thought back to earlier that morning. We had been riding in a bus to Almería through a naked landscape. Suddenly a grove of olive trees appeared on a hill. Sinewy branches stretched all directions, and slender leaves hung from every stem. Without a farm in sight, it appeared these trees had been abandoned. They were so exposed to the elements, yet they were more beautiful for being unprotected. Like me, a young woman on her first trip around Europe without her family, they were wild and free.

I returned Mike's fiery look. "Let's go with him," I said.

His name was Abdasalam, and he spoke to us in French, my high-school foreign language of choice. He was an imports merchant who drove back and forth between Fez and Paris once a month. He had a wife in France, a wife in Morocco, and three girlfriends. He said this with such glee that I laughed, imagining the women spaced evenly along the route between Paris and Fez.

After the ferry ride, we met Abdasalam at his truck. By the time we passed through customs and started driving, it was well past midnight. The headlights of the truck illuminated only a little of the road so that Morocco unrolled like a carpet before us as we drove. Sometimes we'd pass through a sleeping village with abandoned dirt streets and ribby cats slinking along buildings. A café would glow florescent in the distance, and we'd approach to find it filled with men sitting in loose circles, smoking and pouring steaming tea into delicate cups.

I tried to keep my eyes open, to be vigilant about our route, to never totally disarm my trust. But as the night dragged on, the flutter of moths in our headlights and the drone of the engine fused with my dreams.

When I awoke to the sunrise and Abdasalam's pounding on the dashboard, we had been driving about five hours.

"We will stop at my friend's house," said Abdasalam. Feeling tender and exposed from my sleep, my stomach lurched with doubt as I thought of spending time hidden away in some stranger's house. Abdasalam had been kind and unthreatening, but still I could not fully believe in such great generosity. Stories of kidnapping schemes blossomed dark flowers in my mind.

We drove into a small town and parked in front of a house that was plain and blocky as a sixties office building. My heart beat faster and faster with each step toward the door.

A small man with a shriveled smiling face and warm sparkling eyes greeted us, "*Al salaam a'alaykum!*" From behind him, a woman, gentle as a turtle dove, stepped out and beckoned us to come inside. Their home was cool and tranquil, decorated in hues of blue and green. Graceful designs on tiles covered the walls. Immediately, my fears vanished and my heart calmed.

Soon, I could think only of sleep. I asked if there was a place where we could lie down. The woman led us into another room lined with a pillow-covered bench. I barely remember her returning with a blanket and covering me.

When we awoke a few hours later, I sat up and looked around the room. Where were we? In some family's home, somewhere in Morocco. And we were safe.

Just then the woman entered the room, as though she had been waiting for us. She held her hand to her mouth. Yes, we nodded, we were hungry.

She led Mike and I into another room and pulled out chairs for us at a dining table. The men came in, but did not sit down. They had already eaten. Abdasalam asked if we felt better and then told us to eat, "*Mangez! Mangez!*" The woman set down dishes of scrambled eggs with tomatoes, cucumber salad, bread, butter, and jam. Abdasalam and our hosts watched as we filled our plates, and then asked how we liked each item as we ate. Finally we sat back in our chairs, but the husband set a bowl of dark, wrinkled olives soaking in oil in front of us.

"These are from his farm," said Abdasalam. "He owns many olive fields all over the countryside."

The husband beamed and leaned down toward us. "*Bismillah,*" he said. Thanks to God.

I picked up an olive out of the thick oil and placed it on my tongue. Then I looked into the warm face of the husband and realized I had been wrong about the olive trees on the hill in Spain. They were not wild and free, but had grown strong and beautiful from years of care by a farmer who trusted they would produce fruit. Abdasalam's willingness to drive total strangers across the desert, and this family's dependence on the land and graciousness to two foreigners made my struggle to overcome my fears seem insignificant. Perhaps it is the farmer's trust in the tree, and the tree's trust in the farmer, that allows the fruit to grow. Perhaps it is one human's trust in another that allows us to move past the unknown.

As I pushed the olive to the roof of my mouth, its skin broke and the fruit crumbled. It tasted like the rich, healthy soil of my own family's Nebraska garden.

Since she left Nebraska ten years ago, Jennica Peterson has traveled to thirty countries, worked in three national parks, and moved eighteen times. Currently she is an editorial intern at VIA magazine and is working toward a full-time career in writing and editing. She lives in Oakland, California with her husband, Mike.

KARI J. BODNARCHUK

❧ ❧ ❧

Outback Overview

In the hinterlands of Australia, the mail doesn't
arrive in high water—but it gets there eventually.

𝒜 RUSTY OLD REFRIGERATOR LAY ON ITS BACK IN THE
Australian desert. It was the only sign of human
life in the burnt orange landscape, at least as far as I could
see, and I could see a good few miles. Matthew lifted the
door of the fridge and dropped in a canvas sack full of
mail.

"It'll stay dry in here," he said and secured the door
in place.

It'll *stay* dry? We were surrounded by parched desert in the 120-degree heat of an El Niño summer. The
air was so dry, my lungs felt like crêpe paper. Unless it
spontaneously combusted, which wouldn't have surprised me at all, I figured that sack ought to be well
protected inside the rusting hulk of metal. But, as I was

quickly discovering, nothing is as it appears in the desert. That fridge was the communal mailbox at a remote cattle station, which turned out to be nearby but hidden from view by the desert bush and rolling terrain. And Matthew, who was wearing a flight suit, was the local mailman: In the Outback, the job description includes "pilot."

Matthew and I climbed back into his four-seat, twin-engine plane and accelerated down the runway—nothing more than a several-hundred-foot dirt clearing. The plane lifted off and as we rose above the red earth and the refrigerator, the station finally came into view: a handful of wooden buildings surrounded by hundreds of cattle, with a "backyard" that seemed to stretch to the horizon. Since we would have to touch down again a few minutes later, Matthew angled the plane off at 1,000 feet. From this altitude, I could see the texture and patterns of the desert landscape—the dips and bumps, the swirls of multi-colored dirt, and the wind-blown marks that rippled across its surface.

As a pilot for Augusta Airways, Matthew had been covering this route for five years. Each weekend, he crossed more than half the continent and four deserts on "the world's longest mail run." It was a 1,600-mile plane trip that took him to cattle stations and mining towns sprinkled across the Outback. His little Aero Commander soared over areas that were completely inaccessible by car. Towns, cattle stations, and communities along the mail route were so remote it could take a week to reach them by 4WD. By plane, it took Matthew just two eight-hour days to make twenty-eight deliveries.

I first found out about this trip from an ad in an Australian magazine, which said there was room for up to three paying passengers on the mail run each week. After two months traveling through Australia by foot, boat, bus, and car, I felt this would be a great chance to get off the main roads and find out what really lay "out back of beyond," in the country's Red Center. I was also curious to see who lived out there—and why. I had heard that up to 85 percent of all Australians live within earshot of ocean waves, so I imagined it must take a hearty soul to survive the great interior. Mulka, a cattle station en route, held the distinction of being "the driest inhabited place on earth," according to the *Guinness Book of World Records*, averaging four inches of rain annually. Surely the people living there would be a little loopy—I knew I would be.

What I didn't realize until I arrived for the trip—the only passenger that weekend—was that it was a unique time to visit the area. As Matthew and I boarded the plane the first morning in Port Augusta, a city in South Australia, he told me about the rain. Typically, the deserts of central Australia don't get much precipitation, but it had been an unusual season. Sections of the Tirari, Sturt Stony, Strzelecki, and Simpson deserts had flooded, and Lake Eyre, which hadn't seen water since Europeans arrived in 1770, was half full. Australians had been driving thousands of miles just to see it.

"The earth here is sandy with rock or clay underneath, so when it rains the water doesn't soak into the ground," Matthew explained. "It just sits on top of the land and eventually evaporates. So we can't make all the stops, because the airstrips are too muddy."

No mail for another week? I thought about how at home, I wait impatiently for 4:30 P.M. EVERY DAY, WHEN MY POSTAL WORKER MAKES HER DELIVERY, AND HOW I CHECK my e-mail a good dozen times a day. As if Matthew knew what I was thinking, he said, "These people don't mind. Some haven't seen rain for six or seven years, so not getting their mail is the least of their worries."

Matthew ran through his safety check and then wiped down the dew-covered windscreen with the cuff of his sleeve. I was strapped into the seat next to him, feeling anxious and excited, and completely dumbfounded by all the dials and switches surrounding me. But mostly, I was awed. Matthew was exactly who I pictured when I thought of hotshot pilots. With his Ray-Bans, leather jacket, and clean-cut, schoolboy appearance, he looked the part. But his soft-spoken tone and down-to-earth demeanor brought him back from the realm of the gods. To him, I'm sure I must have looked the part of the globetrotting backpacker, with my thick hiking boots, overstuffed bag, and fake brand-name clothes, which had definitely seen better days.

At 8:30 A.M., Matthew radioed Melbourne Air Traffic Control to let them know our plane—"Alpha Charlie Zulu"—was air-bound and due into a town called Leigh Creek at 9:20 A.M. We soared over the rust-colored earth and patchy scrub, while the sun glowed on wet roads below us. A morning haze crept through nearby mountain valleys and hung veil-like over a section of the South Flinders Ranges. Below us, I could see Wilpena Pound, a natural amphitheater that rested in the middle of the mountain range and looked like a giant cereal bowl from the air. Its dramatically sloped cliffs leaned outward, leaving an interior of red gum trees, native pines, and spinefex—plants with tall, stiff blades of grass that radiate outward like needles on a porcupine's back.

To the east of the Flinders Ranges, pockets of rain

formed little puddles on the bronzed earth, and a chain of trees snaked across the landscape. This was definitely not the type of desert scene I had expected. I pictured smoothly textured sand dunes devoid of water or vegetation. Instead, there were bushes and scrub grass, winding creeks, and plenty of inviting, though not thirst-quenching, salt lakes.

"It'll bloody kill ya if ya drink it," one Aussie said of the water in Lake Eyre South, which had five times more salt than ocean water.

I had never seen a dry salt lake before and was amazed at how much color they added to the landscape. One of them, Lake Torrens, had white- and rust-colored swirls across its middle, and white streaks along its rippled edge, making it look like a sea wave had washed up and dried there. My nose was getting sore from being pressed up against the rattling window, but I couldn't draw myself away from these otherworldly views.

At 9:20 A.M. sharp, we touched down at Leigh Creek and loaded canvas mailbags into the belly of the plane. Leigh Creek was the so-called last stop of civilization before the real rugged Outback. People heading onto unpaved, 4WD roads like the Birdsville, Strzelecki, and Oodnadatta tracks loaded up on supplies here—car batteries, spare tires, jugs of sunscreen, and Tim Tams (a type of Australian cookie), not to mention plenty of gas and water (at least two to three gallons of water, per person, per day was recommended in the desert).

We took off from Leigh Creek an hour later and headed north toward Moolawatana, a small sheep station that sits just south of the "dog fence." This fence is the longest in the world and runs 3,293 miles, clear across three Australian states. It's about six feet high and was built to keep dingoes—a type of wild dog—away from sheep farms in South Australia.

Matthew decided it was too wet to land at Moolawatana, so we headed north to Merty Merty, where the runway was like most landing strips in the Outback: simply a dirt and grass field. But that day, it was a soggy field and we slid along a patch of orange, muddy soil as we landed, with me gripping the sides of my seat and visions of a fiery crash running through my head. *Who will find our bodies out here?* I wondered, while trying to remind myself that Matthew does this landing every week. Eventually, the plane slid to a crooked but relatively gentle stop near Merty Merty's mailbox: a big metal drum on a wooden stand.

Next we headed north, toward Cooper Creek, one of central Australia's main watering holes. At a small bend in the creek near Innamincka cattle station, Matthew pointed out the Dig Tree, a well-known Australian landmark. It was here that Aussie pioneers Robert O'Hara Burke and William Wills perished while leading an expedition to link north and south Australia. The explorers set off from Melbourne in 1860 and followed their compasses several thousand miles north to the Gulf of Carpentaria, reaching its shores sometime in 1861. They returned to Innamincka to meet the rest of their expedition party, but as the legend goes, Burke and Wills arrived two hours (some say a day) after the others left.

What they found was a message on the side of a coolibah tree saying, "Dig" with an arrow pointing down. Buried here, they unearthed a stash of provisions, which they survived on for several weeks. Eventually, their supplies dwindled, forcing them to scavenge for food.

But they didn't know how to prepare bush grub like the native Aborigines and slowly poisoned themselves to death. Now, the gnarled Dig Tree stands on the banks of the Cooper Creek, as a monument to these Australian adventurers.

The idea of pure, authentic exploration seemed thrilling and appealing, but I couldn't imagine spending months walking through an unknown desert with a few dozen camels and an army of men (and maybe women) who were all looking to me to guide them and keep them alive.

As I was thinking about what makes people true, hardcore explorers, Matthew rolled the plane onto its side for a closer look at the Dig Tree, and then we flew into the middle of the most vibrant, Disney-like landscape. In Channel Country, as it was called, hundreds of tiny creeks spliced out across the landscape like tree branches and the earth was dotted with bushes the color of clover.

We rolled across sand and scrub as we landed at Mungeranie, a cattle station that was home to South Australia's first pub, a very important distinction judging by the huge sign that was posted there, in the middle of absolutely nowhere. Just after we landed, a man with a long beard and two young girls pulled up in a pickup. The truck kicked up a long trail of bull dust—finely textured red sand—that took a good ten minutes to settle and completely coated us in the process. We delivered a package—an eleventh birthday present—to one of the girls and watched her tear it open. The parcel contained a pair of red socks with black horses on them. She giggled and waved them around, obviously thrilled. She then told us how she had had a birthday party with twenty kids, and when I asked where the heck she found all those kids, she started pointing in different directions.

"Eighty kilometers that way there are two kids, at 120 kilometers there's one, at 140 there's five, and at 40 kilometers in that direction there are three..." she said, listing off all those who came to her party. She was trying on her new socks as our plane pulled away.

Around noon, we crossed into Queensland, Australia's most northeastern state, and set down for lunch in Birdsville. It was a typical, dusty Outback town where kids road their bikes up the middle of the street, local stockmen dipped into the pub for a midday drink, and tourists rolled through in their 4WDs. I went for a walk around town to stretch my legs, but soon discovered that the black flies were maddening. Hundreds of them swarmed around me and finally forced me into the Birdsville Hotel, where I found the Outback's most famous pub. I joined Matthew at the bar and as I scanned the menu, I quickly realized the humor was as dry as the air out there. We were sitting in the blistering heat, about six hundred miles from the ocean, where the mail only comes once a week—at most—and yet the appetizers on offer were "hot soup of the day" and "fried calamari with a spicy plum sauce." Not only that, the entrees were just about the most mouthwatering options I had seen on any Australian menu: scotch fillet with the sauce of the day, chicken breast pan-fried and caramelized in a honey and soy sauce, and kangaroo with a red currant and port glaze.

As I waited for a simple tomato and cheese sandwich, Matthew told me the town was settled in 1882 and now has a population of 70, "when everyone's at home." But when the two-day Birdsville horse races take place each September, the population can swell to 4,000.

"Not everyone watches the races," said the bartender. "A lot of people just come for a major piss-up. But all the money goes to the Royal Flying Doctor Service. They're the only doctors who can reach us out here, so it's a choice cause to drink for."

I ordered a pint of Victoria Bitter to support the cause, while Matthew told me another odd fact about Queensland: "They refuse to switch to daylight savings," he said in mild exasperation. "And you should hear the nutty reasons—'afraid it'll fade the curtains,' they say. Or, 'It'll throw off the cows for milking.' Crazy!" I liked the sound of their free-thinking spirit, but didn't want to stir anything up, so I kept quiet.

The last stop of the day was Boulia, located on the western banks of the Bourke River and surrounded by white grassy fields. It was one of the Outback's largest towns (population 250) and home to the Min Min Lights—odd, blinking lights that reportedly follow people as they drive through the desert at night. Ron, a friendly, weathered local who ran the post office in town, said he'd seen the lights, and that the phenomenon had been recorded in Aboriginal stories for generations. A big flashing sign at one end of town paid tribute to these desert twinkles.

We unloaded the mail at a brick post office and made our way to the Australian Hotel—an all-in-one, 3-star hotel/restaurant/pub/dance hall/hangout, where we would spend the night. In the bar, locals sucked on bottles of VB, played pool, and listened to songs like "Rock Around Sue" and "Copacabana."

We were scheduled to make fifteen stops en route to Port Augusta the next day, and only four were inaccessible due to flooding. The flight time between landings

was anywhere from six to twenty minutes, so we rarely
climbed above 1,000 feet. At Sandringham, a cattle station
twenty minutes south of Boulia, we met Shirley Shrader,
who ran the 1,700-square-kilometer station with her
husband and raised their two kids in this coral-colored
sandbox. Shirley would drive five hours in a day just to
take her kids to a dance in Boulia. It was a tough life with
kids, she said, but they managed.

We folded ourselves into the plane, waved g'day to
Shirley, and trampled grass patches along the runway as
we took off again. From 1,200 feet above the Simpson
Desert, just south of Sandringham, the trees looked like
mini broccoli heads and the land was a series of sand
hills with yellow, mauve, and orange swirly patterns.

I was relieved to hear we weren't stopping in water-
logged Durrie, after reading that, "when in flood, the
land around the homestead becomes infested in snakes,
being the highest piece of land." I hated snakes. It turned
out that Matthew the hotshot pilot hated snakes, too, so
he was just as relieved. He pointed the plane due south
and gave the engine a little boost.

Jane Smith, a seventy-five-year-old Bedourie resident
who was known by everyone as Mrs. Smith, had made it
her job to collect the mail each week for the town's thirty
residents. Sure as heat rises, Mrs. Smith was standing on
the runway when we arrived. With hands on her hips
and not a bead of sweat on her forehead (I was melting
by this point), Mrs. Smith waited for Matthew to unload
the plane and talked about the last big desert rain, back
in '91.

"Set heaps of records," she said. "I thought we'd get
stuck here forever." By the way she said this, I couldn't
tell if she welcomed or abhorred that idea, but I sensed

it was the former. No one I had met yet had had a bad word to say about the Outback. No one had dissed the heat, the dust, the flies or the long drives. And no one had clung to our legs, pleading to be taken oceanside.

Even in record-breaking-hot Mulka, life seemed bearable. When we landed there, Trevor and Jane, the station managers, came out to meet us. In their Levis, Blundstone boots, and Gap-style shirts, they looked too trendy to be living in this no-man's land. And, as it turned out, they weren't loopy—even after years out there. As we leaned against the parked plane, rearranging our footprints on the dusty red earth, I asked them how they survived, mentally, in this remote, barren oven.

"I reckon some people couldn't manage it, but it's bloody excellent out here," Trevor said. "No place like it. There's heaps of space, plenty of room to breathe, and no one gets in your way. And the heat's alright—you just get used to it, I guess."

I told them I grew up in a rural New England town, where the cows roamed free, public buses didn't exist, and the closest supermarket was a twenty-minute drive—and that felt remote. But once I discovered the city, there was no going back except, maybe, for visits. Now when I'm home, I live with 500,000 people in a city where cows are found on ice cream containers, public buses seem to outnumber pedestrians, and there are five different supermarkets within a ten-minute walk. Therefore, I was quite certain the Outback's lack of people and intense physical isolation would make me batty.

Jane mentioned that without her satellite phone, she would probably feel the same way. But they keep in close touch with friends and relatives by phone, and occasionally hop a lift with Matthew to Port Augusta, or drive more than one thousand miles to Melbourne whenever the mood struck, which wasn't too often—six times a year, at most. And once in a great while, friends come to visit, bringing them good company and, under Jane's insistence, plenty of good books. In fact, it turned out we were bringing a box of Jane's old books back to Port Augusta to be donated to schools and libraries.

"They don't need these things anymore and there's nowhere to put them out here," said Matthew. "There's no rubbish pickup, so if something isn't driven out of the Outback by truck or plane, it just gets burned."

Or, like the refrigerator at Clifton Hills, it just sprawls on its back in the blistering sun and rusts away. We were forced to skip the last two stops because of muddy surfaces and flooding. "Maybe next week," Matthew said, matter-of-factly. "Or the week after." There's no overnight delivery in the Outback, and the mail doesn't arrive in high water. But it gets there, eventually.

Kari J. Bodnarchuk is a Boston-based freelance writer, who earned a gold award in the 2004 Lowell Thomas Travel Journalism Competition for a story on Rwanda. She is author of Rwanda: Country Torn Apart *and* Kurdistan: Region Under Siege, *and has contributed to such publications as* Outside, Sports Illustrated, Islands, *and* The Boston Globe, *as well as* LIFE: The Greatest Adventures of All Time, *and* Her Fork in the Road: Women Celebrate Food and Travel.

VICTORIA SHAW

❧ ❧ ❧

Desert Cure

A sick traveler finds succor among the
giant sand dunes of Namibia.

I AM LYING IN BED, SWEAT POURING FROM MY FACE.
My stomach at peace for the moment, I know soon it
will become restless again and I will be perched over the
toilet vomiting.

Two days ago I drove seven hours from the north to
get to Swakopmund on the Namibian coast and I have
been sick ever since. I have been in Namibia for six
weeks now, most of my time spent on a quest to glimpse
even one of the few remaining cheetahs in the wild.
This is my first trip to Africa. This is my first trip alone.
Everything up until now has gone incredibly well. I
have been on an adventure far beyond any stretch of my
imagination or expectations. I keep reminding myself
of this as I continue to throw up. I have only allowed

myself three days here in Swakopmond. I have come to see the giant sand dunes of the oldest desert in the world. This is day two and at this rate my chances of getting out in the desert are looking pretty slim.

When I awoke yesterday I was feeling better so I ventured into town for some bottled water, having lost any trace of liquid that once inhabited my body. Walking through the town with its picturesque tree-lined streets and colonial architecture, it is hard to believe that I am in the same country I was last week. In the north, where I spent most of my time, the earth is parched and barren and due to over-farming, there is massive bush encroachment with thorns that can tear you to shreds. Here in this quaint German town I look out my hotel window at an expanse of green earth, and then, the Atlantic Ocean.

But that short excursion into town yesterday has reduced me to a shivering mass as the chills and the turning of my stomach again consume me. I am dehydrated, weak, dizzy. I want to go home. I've been gone a long time. I want a hug; I want someone to fuss over me.

Maybe it's stupidity, maybe I'm delirious, probably it's just that I'm stubborn but no matter how bad I feel or how much I want to leave I have to see the dunes...I'm too close now.

I have figured out that I have about thirty minutes after throwing up before the churning in my stomach will return again; I timed it. I'll be ready next time. Soon my head is once again dangling over the toilet bowl. With a zombie-like walk I exit the bathroom and fall onto the bed, the phone barely within my reach. With a shaky voice and trembling hands I call the front desk and arrange for a guide to take me to the desert tomorrow afternoon.

I awake the next morning feeling somewhat groggy and blurry. I lay staring at the ceiling, O.K., how bad do I feel? I wait.

Twenty minutes, a half-hour, dare I move? Twenty more minutes, my stomach although very sore seems to be more stable...for the moment. I take a chance and sit up. I wait. Fifteen minutes go by and no urge to upchuck, I decide to push further. I sit up, my legs quivering hanging limp and rubbery over the side of the bed. I keep telling myself what will forever become my travel mantra, "baby steps." Eventually I am actually standing. My body after three days of constant vomiting is in shock. I sway back and forth and debate whether to try to take a step and I wait for the nausea to hit once again...it doesn't. I am excited at this re-alization; too bad my body isn't in sync. I'm like a newborn calf, I'm trying so hard to stand up that I twist myself in a knot and fall on my face! My mind is willing; my body is not the least bit interested.

I slowly make my way into the bathroom. Everything is spinning and very bright. I have six hours to get ready. I will need them all.

I don't really remember much of the next several hours, I know I have been moving very slowly and on several occasions have found myself just standing in one spot, not really sure why or for how long. Somehow I have man-aged to get dressed. I have a vague sense that I must have combed my hair and brushed my teeth at some point. It is time to summon forth all that is within me and make my way down the three flights of stairs to the lobby to meet my guide. I hope that I don't have my clothes on inside out. "Baby steps."

Somehow I make it to the lobby. A tall blond man in the cliché khaki shirt and shorts and hiking boots that all guides in Africa seem to wear, greets me with a thick south African accent and a broad smile, which upon closer scrutiny fades quickly. Do I look that bad?

Before he can question my ability to function, I grab his hand and with all the energy I can muster, I shake it vigorously. Perhaps too vigorously, as now his look is one more of fear than concern. Ah, another crazy American.

We walk from the darkened lobby out into the Namibian sunlight, the brightness after being confined to my room, is like being hit over the head with a board. I am still reeling from the light when my guide announces, "Off to the dunes."

We are riding in what must be the first Land Rover ever built; it has nothing even resembling shock absorbers. I can feel even the tiniest pebble in the road; a kind of "Princess and the Pea" goes mobile. Every once in a while the guide says something and then looks at me with a smile awaiting a reply.

I hope he won't be too offended if I throw up on him.

We turn off the main road; all of a sudden we are surrounded by the desert. Spread out as far as the eye can see are gigantic mountains of reddish brown sand stretching into infinity. I have totally forgotten about my stomach.

It is mid-afternoon and the sun is shifting, the dunes sparkle and the breeze blows the sand which hovers like a mist just above the surface of the desert.

The Rover stops and we get out. I don't know how long we have walked or how far. I have all the energy in the world right now. It is like there is a healing force emanating from the ancient sands beneath my feet. As we walk we come to a place were there are fossilized elephant tracks from another time when desert elephants roamed here. Several more times we return to the Rover and drive farther into the dunes. Everything looks the same to me—I can't make out any kind of landmark at all, but somehow my guide knows exactly where we are. This absolutely amazes me. By now I have sand in my eyes, nose, ears, and hair, not to mention that I am walking in boots that are now filled with the stuff.

The desert transfixes me. I stand and stare in amazement at its vastness and tranquility. I feel small, humble.

As we head back to the hotel, I watch the sun slowly sink into the Atlantic Ocean, the horizon transformed into liquid fire dancing on the water.

I climb the stairs to my room and look around the place where only hours before I was sick and weak, feeling now more alive than I ever have before, healed somehow by the desert dunes.

Victoria Shaw is a documentary and travel photographer and filmmaker who lives in Seattle. For the past ten years she has served as the director of a children's art and cultural exchange project that has taken her around the world to meet many wonderful children and teachers and learn about their cultures. Namibia and its deserts have a special place in her heart and she returns there as often as possible to recharge.

LUCY MCCAULEY

❧ ❧ ❧

The Beauty Contest

A competition among indigenous women
raises questions for a visitor to Bolivia.

THREE AYMARA WOMEN SWISH INTO THE ROW IN
front of me, their full skirts floating about them like
technicolor meringues—peacock blue, magenta, emerald
green. They unfold pieces of cloth, spread them over the
dusty concrete seats of this outdoor amphitheater high in
the Andes, in La Paz, Bolivia.

We are here to watch the "Miss *Cholita Paceña*"
pageant, an event sponsored by city hall. *Paceña* means
"a woman from La Paz"; the word *cholita* designates
the woman as an indigenous Aymara. Of the hundred
or so people here, about three-quarters are Aymara.
All around me, couples and families picnic from food
they've brought bundled in rectangles of handwoven
cloth. Babies squirm in the arms of their mothers; chil-

dren run up the amphitheater steps, taking them two at a time.

The three *cholitas* in front of me laugh out loud, their dark bowler hats bobbing over round, brown faces. They suck tangerines, talk with their mouths full of orange fruit, display teeth outlined with gold. Speaking their native tongue, musical with its syncopated clicking sounds, their faces grow animated, opening like flowers in full bloom.

I am in Bolivia for several months, writing a case study for an American university about La Paz's municipal government. Sometimes at night I watch the *cholitas* of this city. In those hours when it is too late to eat and too early for bed, I wander the streets behind the Plaza de San Francisco. I know that if any part of La Paz is dangerous after dark, it is there. But I cannot resist those streets at night, alive with gaslit corridors where *cholitas* sell coca leaves and dried herbs and unwrapped chocolate bars stacked high like bricks. The vendors smile toothless gums at passersby fondling the goods at their tables. Well past midnight, the women patiently refold every alpaca sweater they have hung to display, repack their herbs and sweets into bright, striped cloths that they carry on their backs out of that street, just as they carried them in that morning.

You wouldn't guess by looking at them, but those mild-mannered women and their sprawling outdoor markets comprise a powerful financial force, generating almost $200 million each year in La Paz's "informal economy." And yet, despite that statistical index of success, the reality of Aymaran lives tell a different story: that financial gain doesn't always translate into social or even economic power.

City hall administrators and the municipal police wield a great deal of power over these markets. They levy fines, collect rents on stalls and taxes on goods sold. And for the most part, the indigenous people continue to live separately from the more citified Latinos of mixed blood or Spanish descent. Most Aymara homes rest high in the city's outskirts, poor neighborhoods built into the incline of the bowl of La Paz, where trash dots the hillsides like confetti. La Paz is a city where, in a paradoxical twist, the poor look down on the rich.

Central La Paz rests in a valley of about 10,000 feet above sea level, formed by glacial erosion. The altitude and mountainous landscape mean the entire city hurts from problems with water, sewage, and transportation. But the neighborhoods at the rim of the city suffer most. Getting drinkable water and plumbing out there is nearly impossible. And travel to and from the upper rims is a difficult traverse of dirt roads that are continually eroding. In the rainy season, dozens of houses are simply washed away.

In the amphitheater, the late afternoon sky turns pink and gray, and the moon comes out. It is "holding water," an upturned slice of melon, a single star shining beneath as if it has just spilled out. The snow-capped triangle of Mount Illimani towers in the distance. A full hour has passed since the scheduled starting time of the pageant, and no one has yet appeared on stage. The people around me wait and so do I, by now having become used to the Latinos' flexible conception of time.

Finally, a master of ceremonies takes the stage. He speaks Spanish and repeats each sentence in Aymara. "This is the *only* official *Cholita Paceña* contest," he announces, with perfect seriousness. "All others are fake." I can't imagine what he means by that, unless perhaps there have been recent pageants that weren't part of this city-sponsored festival. Several performances follow, including three separate Andean music groups, one after another, playing pan pipes and tiny stringed *charangas* made from the backs of armadillos. But still not a single contestant appears onstage.

Watching the indigenous people around me, I think of the ancient Tiwanakans, from whom today's Bolivian Aymara are descended. I have visited Tiwanaku, a vast, windswept landscape on the Bolivian high plain, empty except for some scattered ruins of the longest-lived empire in the Andes. Tiwanakan armies defeated all rivals and ruled its neighboring kingdoms for about a thousand years. The people, accomplished engineers, devised a reflecting-pool observatory that mirrored the night sky, the outlines of which can still be seen among the ruins. Their talents for tilling the earth led them to create a rich agricultural network that dominated the continent.

Those are facts at Tiwanaku that archaeologists can explain. But some things scholars can't account for, like the large monoliths with squared-off heads that stand on the site. They weigh many tons. No one knows how the Tiwanakans maneuvered them there. The Spanish, however, when they arrived in the sixteenth century, puzzled little over such mysteries. They smashed the monoliths in search of gold, finding none.

I marvel at the strange twists in history that led Aymara like the three women in front of me to hold the lowest positions in modern Bolivian society. Conquest by Spaniards bred a serf mentality that the Aymara still haven't been able to shake, leaving them with few skills and seemingly little motivation to act. Until the 1952 Bolivian Revolution, the indigenous people were serfs to descendants of Spanish colonials who owned most of the land. Today, although the Aymara own land themselves, they can barely raise enough food to live on the unforgiving *altiplano*—high plain—that they farm; droughts, floods, and frost conspire at different seasons of the year to ruin their crops. Sometimes these Aymaran families—probably some of those who sit around me here in the amphitheater today—head to the city in hope of finding work. Too often they end up in the adobe shantytowns perched precariously on the rim of La Paz.

Onstage, two hours after the MC first appeared, the contestants at last parade out, twenty-three women in voluminous skirts with multiple petticoats. They wave their bowler hats, smile and bow. The full skirts and the bowlers mimic those of Spanish peasant women in the eighteenth century. Spain's King Carlos III insisted on that style for indigenous women, during those years when Spain nearly drained Bolivia's silver mines—an attempt to make the indians appear less different from themselves. Even the way that *cholitas* part their hair—straight down the middle—is a result of a decree from the Spanish Viceroy Toledo.

I am thinking of the Spanish, and how these *cholitas* continue to wear styles that conquerors imposed on them, when I notice several men arguing onstage. Finally one approaches the microphone and tells us that the judges cannot decide who exemplifies the "best qualities" of a *Cholita Paceña*. Although they've already

picked several sets of finalists—narrowing the competition to three women—the judges have asked the *cholitas*
no questions. From what I can tell, the only "event" had
been the parade on stage. It's becoming clear that we
in the audience won't know what the judging criteria
are—and neither will the contestants.

I think how in this city, where these women hold so
much economic might, their dignity is still so easily com-
promised. How they are often belittled by city administrators, with whom I've seen the *cholitas* haggle about
rents on their market kiosks. And by police officers
whom I've seen pacing among the stalls, "regulating"
the markets high-handedly. And now here today, they
are paraded onstage in a city-sponsored event to choose
a queen among them.

But I've often wondered, since my arrival in La Paz,
if rather than passivity the Aymara's apparent retreat is
simply self-preservation. After all, they've lived through
many periods of unrest, including the disorder of countless coups d'etat and literally hundreds of changes of
government since Bolivia's independence from Spain in
1825. And they carry with them the tacit undercurrent of
fear that characterizes indigenous people who have been
conquered.

Yet I know too that the Aymara have a fighting spirit:
Bolivia's coal miners, mostly indigenous, have fought
bloody battles to preserve their unions. And I've heard
that, during the people's Revolution of 1952, *cholitas*
approached soldiers on the streets and grabbed rifles
from their hands. The revolt, instigated by the miners'
union and carried out with popular support, unseated
a military junta that had seized power after a left-wing
president had been elected.

The MC has appeared onstage again: He announces that the winner will be selected after the three finalists dance the *Cuenca*—the national folkdance—with three judges. Handkerchiefs are brought out, which each person will twirl in the air as part of the dance. The next scene is of three male judges, white-skinned descendants of Spanish lords—stepping in time to accordion music blaring from a cassette player—and three *cholitas* who skip forward and back, bowler hats sliding from their heads.

I watch the dance, and I think again of the contrast between the Aymara's social situation and that of their Tiwanakan forbears. What happened to those ancient tribes remains a mystery: Tiwanaku's fields, after being cultivated for more than 2,000 years, were suddenly abandoned around 1200 a.d., and their empire collapsed. But villagers who live near the ruins today say they sometimes see strange lights in the night sky, small spheres that orbit above the plain where the Tiwanakans once ruled. They believe that creatures from another universe had something to do with the Tiwanakans' disappearance. Or perhaps that even the Tiwanakans themselves had been visitors from another dimension in time and space.

In one way, at least, the Tiwanakans were indeed aliens—so far were they, in terms of power, from the Aymara of the crumbling villages around La Paz, and of the markets so firmly beneath the thumb of city bureaucrats.

I can't make myself sit to watch the rest of the dance, or wait to see which of these three women will be crowned according to whatever arcane criteria the judges have chosen. As I see it, there's no contest here. Like the three *cholitas* in front of me, all of these women possess a beauty that is uniquely theirs: round, open faces; sturdy bodies that move with the rhythms of the earth, as if deeply rooted here; loveliness that harmonizes perfectly with the natural world around them, with the elegance of the night sky above us tonight and its upturned moon. And timeless as the majestic Mount Illimani that looms over the city, watchful and abiding.

I leave my seat, slip up the aisle and out to the street, the circusy music of the *Cuenca* fading behind me.

Lucy McCauley is the editor of this collection as well as three other Travelers' Tales anthologies. Her full biography appears at the back of this book.

KIERSTEN ASCHAUER

❦ ❦ ❦

Open-Road Therapy

Journeying in Indonesia to mend her heart,
the author meets many kindred spirits.

*T*HE SANDAL CRACKED AGAINST THE WALL, REBOUNDED
into a lamp and knocked the clock off the bedside
table. The drone that followed was too loud to be silence.
It was a grating pulsation that circled my empty suitcase,
my cloudy head, my salt-burned cheeks.

I sat surrounded by bobby pins, furrow-paged books,
rolls of film, and loose Ibuprofen. My knuckles went
white around the passport clenched in my hand. Body
crumpled, I sobbed.

Just an hour earlier I'd been packing; boogying
around my parent's guest room to a Fatboy Slim CD and
eating Twizzlers. Into my backpack went the no-wrin-
kle dresses and mosquito repellent. In went the laptop
computer and story assignments from various editors.

In went the sexy little nightie and garter belts, carefully hidden in the pocket of my Gore-Tex rain jacket to save embarrassment when going through customs. Sitting on the edge of my bed with my Thailand travel guide, I fantasized about a romantic Bangkok weekend with Mike before heading back to our home in Chiang Mai. It was going to be a surprise.

We'd just spent some time in the United States to see our families and make some American money before heading back to our $100-a-month teak house and fifty-cent meals prepared by the best vegetarian chef in town: our life in paradise. I'd stayed an extra month to finish up my freelance projects. He'd rushed back to spend a week in the mountains of Chiang Dao before the next semester started at the British Council, where he taught.

The CD had just forwarded to track two when the phone rang.

"Hello?"

"Hi, it's me," he said blankly.

"Hey, baby. Only a few hours 'til I leave and I have a surprise...."

"Um...I can't do it anymore."

"What, honey?"

"I...I can't do it. The relationship. It's over. I can't do it."

"B...but, I...I don't...WHAT?" I whispered. I thought my heart would pound out of my chest. The pain was jarring.

"I'm sorry to do it to you this way but it's dead in me. It's just dead."

"What...what are you talking about? *What are you saying?*"

There were a lot of other words that followed. Screams, questions, obscenities, gasps. WHAT DO YOU MEAN? and HOW COULD YOU? and WHO DO YOU THINK YOU ARE? and WHAT DID I EVER DO TO DESERVE THIS? I'd only been loving and caring and would have died for you, you son of a bitch, you son of a bitch, you son of a goddamn bitch.

I hung up the phone, dazed. Five years, down the drain in a thirty-minute phone call. I had no home. No job. Very little money. And a heart that felt as though it had been carved out with a butter knife.

I stayed in bed for two days. I fasted for seven and meditated, even though it was hard. I tried to visualize some sort of direction, hypothesize a future. But all I saw when I closed my eyes was a boundless, white passage, like some amateur perspectives class sketch where the trees lining a triangular path get smaller and smaller but never seem to end.

All I saw was an open road.

It was 5 A.M. one nondescript morning when I fired up my laptop and began writing story pitches. A couple weeks later, with plenty of freelance contracts secured, I re-packed my backpack and booked myself a flight to Bali.

"I'm going so that I can get my life back together. To remember what it's like to talk in the 'I' instead of the 'we.' Maybe even to restore my faith in humanity."

Those are just a few of the dramatic, stock answers I gave to all those people who asked: "Why go traveling alone right now? Why shove your already compact, boxed-up life into a backpack at a time when you need support and love...when you've had the rug pulled out from under you?"

"And what are my alternatives?" I wanted to know. Camping out on friends' couches or staying in the guest room at my parents' house? Not me. New job in a new city with a 401K and a cubical to decorate with Pez dispensers and Dilbert cartoons? Not yet. Back to Thailand? Not a chance.

No, I wasn't ready to lay down new roots. I needed to chill out where I wasn't known as part of the "we" that was no longer. I wanted to meet people and experience things through the eyes of Kiersten, not KierstenandMike.

But they still wanted to know: "Are you sure this is a good idea?"

Peering out the airplane window as we soared over the beautifully rugged topography of Indonesia, it sure seemed like a damn good idea. From the front porch of my first bungalow in Ubud, Bali—the one overlooking the lush garden and within view of a staff of soft-spoken, sexy Balinese young men in sarongs—it seemed wickedly brilliant.

From the little café overlooking the grays and greens of Gunung Agung volcano, as I sipped muddy Balinese coffee and watched the mist roll in, it seemed better than "a good idea." It appeared I'd found the perfect place for life repairs.

I didn't really want to like Alli. She was one of those women who could pull her unwashed hair back in a sloppy bun, throw on a ratty t-shirt and army shorts and still emerge from her $2 a night bungalow as if ready to strut down a runway, a la traveler chic. It might have been fun to find at least a few character faults, things that would help balance out her physical flawlessness.

But alas, she was sweet and funny, though she'd been through hell.

It was a pair of platform shoes that brought Alli and me together. I'd been in Southeast Asia long enough to know better but hadn't abandoned my inclination to wear inappropriately stylish footwear. She, in her clunky Steve Maddens, had also declined the typical Teva syndrome.

"I like your shoes," we said at the same time, while poking around a small shop in Ubud during my second week on Bali. After a string of "Where did you get thems?" and "Oh, you're from Americas?" and "How long you been heres?" we finally decided to move our conversation to the café across the street. An hour later, as we downed our second round of *arak* (rice wine), she admitted why she'd come to Bali.

"I went through some hairy shit," she said with a shrug. "Just like everyone else in the world, I guess. But there was a point where I saw myself dwelling on it way too much. I knew I had to leave...," she paused and exhaled her cigarette smoke, "so that one day I could go back and start again."

But her story wasn't like everyone else's in the world. It was horrific. Her boyfriend had committed suicide during a particularly rocky period in their four years together. She'd been the one to find him, in a bloody mess on the bathroom floor. She'd blamed herself.

Like me, she'd spent subsequent weeks watching too much television, curled up on the couch with a stiff drink. I shamefully admitted that concerning myself with Raquel's plot to wreck Haley and Mateo's marriage on *All My Children* had been my only focus for two weeks—she only laughed and filled me in on Alan Quartermaine's drug rehabilitation plight on *General Hospital*.

"Here's to the Quartermaines," I said, raising my glass.

"Screw the Quartermaines," she replied with a *clink*.

We spent the next couple of days, Alli's last two in Bali before she headed to Sumatra, hiking through rice paddies, finding cheap vegetarian *warungs* and getting massages. We made a pact not to mention the "hims," so discussed books, obnoxious tourist syndrome, our distain of suburban houses with lawn ornaments and what kind of dog we'd get when—if—we finally settled down one day. She filled me in on the ins and outs of Oregon life, where she'd spent the last few years, and I waxed rhapsodic about my various New England abodes.

We didn't pretend that we were somehow exempt from travel-as-escape syndrome. We fully admitted that it allowed us to dodge the realities of a life left behind. But we also celebrated our abilities to use it therapeutically; to have sensory experiences we might not have appreciated before the "bad times."

The day of her departure, I arrived at her guest house to discover she'd taken an early shuttle to the airport. "Here's to a new chapter and a healthy heart" read the note she left for me.

Alli was one of the few women I spent time with in my four months on Bali. There was also Simona, who escaped her aggressive boyfriend at the Denpasar airport by grabbing her ticket off the counter after he'd already checked his bags on a flight back to Italy. And there was Joy, an elegant, silver-haired woman who celebrated the arrival of her divorce papers by booking an around-the-world trip—something "the bastard" never would have let her do. Sandra's fiancé at least had the decency to break off their engagement a few months before the wedding, right before he threw all her belongings out on the lawn in some 1980s movie scene.

Meeting men was much easier, of course, and they weren't without their own stories of heartbreak. Jay spent time in counseling after saying good-bye to his ten-year partner. Gary admitted he'd never quite get over his wife's infidelity, to which he'd been witness. Charles seemed to wince every time a brunette walked by, as if his ex was incarnate in all dark-haired women.

And there were plenty of others, men and women who'd hit the road in a period of limbo that had nothing to do with relationships or lack thereof. While on my way to the eastern beach town of Amed, I happened upon a group of recovering alcoholics and drug addicts, whose travel stories were rife with words like "prison," "stampede," and "malaria." One middle-aged couple I met on a bus ride alluded to financial troubles in their home country serious enough to prevent their return for several years. I met quite a few others who were between careers, wondering how the hell they'd make the transition from computer programmer to handicrafts dealer or executive to semi-retired traveler.

All these people empowered me. "You know, you don't have to undergo huge, life-altering transformations *right now*," they seemed to say. So I began to relax, not worry so much about "healing" or "moving on." I began to appreciate just sitting quietly, watching a sunset or a huge, bee-like insect with dangling legs the size of index fingers. Sharing a Sprite with a tiny Balinese girl with no shoes became as substantial an experience to me as the fact that I hadn't thought of my ex in weeks. Attending a temple ceremony was as important as my ability to date again. Every new occurrence seemed worthy of contemplation, while preoccupation with my past relationship and uncertain future quietly faded.

I didn't claim I'd found inner peace. And I knew I wasn't in paradise. The newspapers were daily reminders of the violence around me—a grounding contrast to the emotional unrest I was enduring. The price of rice had doubled while salaries stayed the same. The rupiah was still four times lower than its normal exchange rate. People were hungry and tensions were high.

All this put my "boyfriend problems" in perspective; made me humble and grateful. And perhaps prepared me for Ed.

I hadn't even made it to Bali yet when I was asked on my first date. I was still on the airplane, hovering somewhere over Malaysia or Singapore. I did not accept this dinner proposal, but by the time I made it to baggage claim in Denpasar, I'd pretty much decided to eat the words I'd only mumbled right before I left. "I hope I never meet another man again as long as I live." It just seemed so irrational and dramatic by then.

During my first five or six weeks on the island, I went on some mediocre dates, had some quasi-romantic courtings with passersby from England or Australia and was asked to be one American's "first" extramarital affair. I hadn't been seduced, or even that sexually interested in any of them, but was glad to get the chance to brush up on dating tactics I thought might have been too far gone after five years with one man. I also began to more closely shave my legs, don undergarments more Calvin Klein-y than backpacker-y, and periodically check to make sure I didn't smell too tropical—sure signs I was reawakening from long-relationship comfort zone.

Of course, the night I met Ed, all these things were amiss. I'd spent the day on deadline, in front of a computer. I sauntered out to dinner on Jalan Dewi Sita's Tutmak Café in morning make-up and with disheveled hair. My eyes were bloodshot; legs stubbly. I was a wreck.

I watched him scope out the scene and stall a bit to make sure I was alone before he chose the table next to mine. He asked if my food was good, if I was alone, and if he could join me so quickly I didn't have time to swallow my tofu. I just nodded and pointed to the seat across from me.

I immediately liked him, especially the syncopation of his London-and-Edinburgh accent and the choreography of his hair, which flopped in a question mark shape in front of his forehead. I was intrigued by the fact he was an art gallery owner, marketing dynamo, and spinach quiche lover. I appreciated how he truly seemed to listen to what I was saying and waited until I was surely finished before pausing to formulate an eloquent response.

Then something happened that made my heart race. While making a point about something or other, he leaned toward the table, weight on his hands. His broad shoulders, glaring clavicle, and prominent jugular—the objects of my longtime fetish—were alarmingly apparent to me. I found myself fighting the temptation to reach across the table and touch him. For the first time since the demise of my relationship, I had a *real* intimate urge and it felt good.

Still, however, the notion that this charming man could be remotely attracted to me was dubious.

"Well, maybe I'll see you around..." I began amateurely as we parted ways that evening. But he was quick, clearly so much better at this stuff, and cut me off with a "Want to get together tomorrow?"

"I'd love to," I said.

The next evening was much smoother, more relaxed, with ample amounts of rainy breeze and tropical drinks. I was a bit more enjoyable to be around (and definitely smelled better) and he was even sexier than the evening before. Over a three-hour dinner, our conversations became more personal, addressing the demise of our recent relationships and stories of people we'd loved and lost. We spoke of politics, travel, the power of the written word, and creative online marketing. We clicked.

Later that night, as we strolled straight past my hotel on our way to unspoken nowhere, it became apparent the evening wasn't over.

"Can I get your opinion on some silver?" he asked, suggesting he wanted me to come to his homestay and see the jewelry he'd picked up for his latest business venture. It was a cheesy, obvious line, one I'd chide him for later as I lay in his arms, but I just bit my lip to keep from grinning and answered, "Of course."

Minutes later, we stood on his porch, fingers clasped. Our first kiss—so different from that into which I'd folded myself for the past five years—was slow, melodic, and wonderfully unfamiliar. And each that followed was increasingly impassioned, severe, and dizzying. The next forty hours were equally as extraordinary. We didn't eat. We barely slept. Each touch and long silence more intense than the previous.

The billowing mosquito netting, rainy breezes, and slowly twirling fan were all part of an artistically choreographed tropical romance, the way we'd both wanted it.

"Where were you when I first got here, when we could have spent two weeks together and really gotten to know each other...to know *this?*" He asked this question at one point, but I knew deep down that neither of us cared how long it lasted or bothered to truly ponder the "us" possibilities. We simply basked in the comfort of this simple, quiet intimacy. He held me and ran his fingers through my hair until the ticking clock reminded us that it was time for him to leave for the airport.

"It's just so nice to know I can feel something again," I told him, my head on his chest. "It's so nice to know I'm *capable*..."

"...of connecting again," he finished.

I smiled, kissed his fingers, but didn't answer. He stroked my cheek. We lay together until the last possible moment. "I'll never forget those eyes," he said, finally.

As I watched this gorgeous, talented, passionate man get into a taxi, it occurred to me that I wouldn't be returning home to tell friends "he was the one who got away." I wouldn't even think about the "what ifs" as I strolled out for my afternoon coffee twenty minutes later. Instead, my story of Ed, just like my experiences with Alli and my trips to Mount Agung and the silver villages in Celuk would be torn into colorful strands and woven into a larger cloth of my life.

All these tales and experiences would show me that this journey wasn't about "getting over" anything. It wasn't about needing to affirm my faith in people again. It wasn't about "tapping deep emotions" or "taking risks" or—heaven forbid—"finding my new self." It was about having experiences that simply mirrored the ups and downs of life. Plain and simple.

For me, this journey just reaffirmed that the rest of my life would always be that narrowing, tree-lined sketch of an open road. And I was in no rush to find the end.

Kiersten Aschauer is the former editor of a Connecticut weekly newspaper and features editor for an online publication called the New Haven Mag. *Her work has also appeared in Accommodating Asia Travel guides, the* Boston Globe, Better Health Magazine, Dance Express Magazine, *and* Massage Magazine, *among others.*

ℐℬ℩ ℐℬ℩ ℐℬ℩

The Stones Also Are the River

A hike in Spain's mountains yields truths
about blisters—and grace.

$\mathcal{J}$ AM WALKING WITH MY FRIEND JUTTA IN THE *SIERRA* of the Alpujarras, south of Granada and the Sierra Nevada. Starting out from the village of Ogivar, we wind our way up through the steep streets of white houses and come out into clear country—high, falling ridges in the distance, and before us falling fields of olive and almond groves and vegetable plots. Passing the last of the houses, where a few men work repairing a water channel, we follow a dirt road around the base of a hill in the clear morning air. I look down with pleasure at my six-months-old pair of strong boots, now broken in, waterproof, high-topped; they cost a fortune, but they're worth it.

I am prone to spraining my ankles at the slightest opportunity, but what really made me decide to buy the boots was my first trip with Jutta when I wore what I thought were adequate boots, bought only the year before. That day we had walked with ten other people six hours up a rocky arroyo and into another part of the coastal sierra, then back down the same granite-strewn river course again, having somehow strayed from the track we were looking for. I climbed painfully up and over beautiful pink granite boulders, across the sharp, ungiving rock and beneath the clutching, pricking vines of wild rose, breathing in the scent of pine, then eucalyptus and trying to look around me instead of constantly at my feet. The last two hours were agony. I had a blister on my left sole the size of a large sand dollar. The boots were too short and too wide and my feet swam around in them while simultaneously my toes turned purple. They were fine for one hour but not six. When we got to the road the others had to leave me there and walk the last few miles into the village where we'd left our cars. I sat there smoking a cigarette, drinking the last of my water, and nursing my feet until they came back for me. That's it, I thought. If I'm going to walk in the sierra, I need good boots.

Jutta is practicing routes and trails for a job she's just gotten with a German travel agency that arranges hiking trips for tourists. The trails have been walked and written up by others before—she has pamphlets and books in German and English—but they aren't always that clear, and some landmarks inevitably change over the years. Today it is just the two of us and we like it that way. No one having to prove something. If she isn't certain about the trail, poring over her maps and papers, we try a likely fork and if it seems wrong, come back and go the other way. Sometimes we talk, usually we don't. We walk, breathe in that pure air, and gaze around us. Soon part of the path turns down to the river gorge, the river itself not visible from above, just the thicker concentration of dark green—eucalyptus and walnut trees, flowering shrubs, and river reeds.

The river, fed by springs and snow melt from the Sierra Nevada, is bigger than one would imagine from the dry land above. It rushes over rocks—an immediately refreshing sight. "Ah!" we say. "Time to eat!" We each choose a boulder to sit on, open our backpacks and pull out fruit, wine, water. We chew and sip wine and watch the river, which seems to wash my troubled mood away with it down, down to the distant sea, not visible from this spot tucked among the slopes.

Sitting there in the quiet company of my friend, I think, the river is only itself. It follows its way and doesn't bruise itself on those stones. I had been feeling bruised these past weeks. An emptiness that hurt, a void that seemed to open in my center and speak. The feeling would come suddenly, at odd times such as when I was washing the dishes or reading the paper. I would awaken from a nap inside the void. Alone. I felt so alone. I had lost my love. I had lost him forever. The signs he had been looking for I never deciphered, or if I had—I never knew—I'd not known how to display them. I felt adrift, floating through the days, my heart in exile, unable to return, ever, to a paradise I told myself I had only imagined. But telling myself didn't help. Some stubbornness would not allow me to listen. The empty, hollow feeling would dissipate but form again when I was not expecting it.

I sit in the blue air. A few white clouds make shadows on the earth and river as they pass over. It doesn't matter, I think. We flow, our lives are a flowing, from the source back to the source. Even the stones are flowing, back to what they were, only to be formed again, later, much later, some other way. "The stones also are the river," I say aloud.

"What?"

"It's from a poem."

"Look," Jutta says. She points to a violet growing in the crevice of a boulder near her. I walk over and touch its delicate head and pointed fingers. So stubborn. So amazing. The beauty of being alive, of being *here*.

I feel suddenly how good it is, how miraculous, to be able to drive out of my home village to almost anywhere up or down the coast and walk into the sierra. No matter what tangled knots I get myself into, what emotions from the past live in me like dormant viruses, periodically coming to life again to give me fevers and cramps, all I have to do is come to the sierra and walk and watch and feel how I am part of all around me. This is my paradise. This is why I'm here. My heart is not in exile. I am home. I forget—fixated on something I think I need, "suffering over my suffering," and going in circles—who and where I am.

I've been going through a kind of initiation, I think, learning how to discriminate and see how things fit, so that I perceive the world outside myself, and in relation to myself, more subtly. I am learning to be more sensitive to the reality of the other—instead of tromping through life in boots that do not fit and give me blisters.

As we walk again, up over another ridge, we pass ancient circular threshing floors paved with flagstones that explain the mysterious, narrow, leveled fields along the

slopes that now grow only grass. I imagine the time when
wheat grew here. I see the green wheat high and waving
in the breeze. I see the people winnowing the ripe wheat
on the threshing floors. The small *cortijos* dotted about
the area would have been alive with whole families during the harvest and threshing. We walk on, climbing
then dropping down again to the river. Eventually we
come to an abandoned hamlet and its enormous, empty
church. We sit on the parapet that overlooks the river
and valley. I look at the river and think of the stones,
the violet, and of the lives people made here. These lives
have changed now. There is more work in the village
itself. Visitors come from afar to walk in the sierra or to
stay in small hotels and relax. There are artisan shops.
People make pottery, run restaurants and bars. The olive
and almond groves and vegetable plots closer in are still
worked, and there are signs of passing goat herds, but
the wheat fields return to the sierra.

I feel myself flowing with and amongst the day and
all it holds, and I am happy, wanting for nothing. And I
know I have not lost my love—not now, not ever. When
we pass each other in the street, or come upon one another
in a bar, the force field of the one hits the other one. I see
him brace for the hit. He sees me. We are practicing—for
over four years now—how not to bruise one another or
be bruised. The force of the one attracts that of the other
almost too powerfully. We practice delicacy, walking in
the deep mysteries of who we are. I feel that sense of loss
and need leaving me. There must be some meaning in
all this. Or there is no meaning; it is how we are, how
it is. We practice grace. When one cannot know or understand, there remains the possibility of—the necessity
for—grace.

৵ঽ ৵ঽ ৵ঽ

*Sharon Balentine has lived in Frigiliana, Spain since 1995, after
more than thirty years in Austin, Texas. Her poetry has appeared
in* Aileron, Borderlands: Texas Poetry Review, Stone Drum,
Skylark, *and* West Wind Review, *as well as two chapbooks of
poetry (*Isis *and* Spellbound*). Several prose pieces, including an
excerpt from her first book, appeared in* Women in the Wild, *and*
A Woman's Path: Women's Best Spiritual Travel Writing, *and
she has published short stories in* The Missouri Review, Green's
Magazine *(Canada)*, The Tulane Review, Rosebud, Pangolin
Papers, *and* StoryQuarterly, where this story first appeared.

AMANDA COFFIN

※ ※ ※

An Utterly
Unremarkable Cave

A traveler finds her childhood faith transformed
among a luminous group of priests.

*T*HERE IS A SMALL CAVE ON THE SIDE OF MOUNT SILPIUS,
which rises above Antakya, Turkey. Antakya is in
the Hatay province, an odd appendix of land that dangles
southward into Syria. As caves go, this one is utterly
unremarkable. It has no stalagmites, stalactites, subter-
ranean rivers, or bats. It's the size of a two-car garage
with abundant headroom. Predictably, water drips from
the ceiling. Two temperamental motion-sensing lamps
cast a faltering glow upon its green-streaked walls. Men
have made a few changes—I won't call them improve-
ments—over the past twenty centuries: There are some
tipsy fragments of a white mosaic floor from the fourth

century. The First Crusaders built a façade across the
cave's mouth when they passed through in 1098, and
it's been restored since. Capuchin monks introduced a
simple white stone altar. Someone molded a hideous
statue of a saint from gray cement. I'm not sure who's
to blame for this, but there it stands in a niche behind
the altar. Just outside the cave is a shady, green terrace
affording an expansive view of Antakya. Steps curve
down the mountainside to a dirt road, which in turn
wraps gently down the slope. At its junction with the
main road, a faded, rusty sign points up the hill. It reads
"Senpiyer Kilisesi"—St. Peter's Church.

Antakya was Antioch in its earlier days. One of
Alexander the Great's generals founded the city around
300 b.c. It became such a melting pot that Libanios, a
second-century rhetoritician, boasted, "Indeed, if a man
had the idea of traveling all over the earth with a concern not to see how the cities looked but to learn their
individual ways, Antioch would fulfill his purpose and
save him journeying. If he sits in our marketplace, he
will sample every city; there will be so many people from
each place with whom he can talk."

Indeed, the first five centuries Anno Domini must
have been a riot. The Antakya Archaeological Museum
houses one of the richest collections of Roman mosaics in
the world, dating from the second to the fifth centuries.
They give a good idea of what the polytheists were up to:
Soulful Neptune gazes out from his teeming sea. Zeus,
in the form of an eagle, rapes Ganymede, who looks
rather oddly complacent given the circumstances. A
satyr struggles to prop up a totally inebriated Dionysus.
In another panel, wine flask in hand, Dionysus lunges
toward a nymph. (Antioch's citizens were renowned

for their decadence and self-indulgence; the god of the grape got a lot of floor space.)

On the monotheistic side of things, there was a thriving Jewish population that integrated fully into the community. According to most Christian timelines, Paul showed up in Antioch in a.d. 40, six years after his famed conversion on the road to Damascus. Antioch would be his home base for three missionary journeys. Peter arrived in 47. Antioch was the site of Peter's and Paul's dispute about whether or not converts could enter their new faith without first adhering to Judaic law. Paul, with his astute sense of marketing, noted that adult men might find the circumcision requirement onerous. It was becoming clear here that the newcomers were parting ways with Judaism, and it was in Antioch that the term "Christian" came into being. The new Christians retreated to the mountainside cave to listen to Jesus's most highly-favored apostle. No one disputes that articulate, fervent, peripatetic Paul deserves the credit for spreading the new faith so widely, but Peter had a different credential: he was a first-hand witness. I imagine them bickering in an Antioch kitchen at night, having reached some theological impasse. Peter could well have said, "Fine, Paul, you fell from your horse, hit your head and saw the light of day, but I had dinner with the man." It's hard to trump that.

I left my Antakya hotel early on a Sunday morning in September. The cave is only three kilometers outside the city, and the streets were quiet, so I walked. I climbed the steps leading to the terrace; a still-sleepy Turk was pouring tea in the ticket booth. He collected my fee and took two glasses of tea to a picnic table, where he sat down to help his son with schoolwork. I had the cave-church to myself, but without stained glass windows, vaulted ceilings, or frescoes, there just isn't much to look at. It was cool inside, though, and the sound of the dripping water was soothing, so I found a dry patch of mosaic floor and sat down. The cave's plainness suddenly seemed perfect. When Peter was here in "the first Christian cathedral" (as the Antakya tourist information grandly puts it), the faith hadn't yet become adorned. It hadn't had time to calcify into dogma. Peter spoke in this cave less than twenty years after Christ's crucifixion. Had any type of liturgy even taken form yet, or were the gatherings an informal story hour with the apostle? Bring your own bread and wine.

In a different St. Peter's Church in rural, upstate New York, a priest told our First Communion class—the town's three other Catholic children and me—that our Protestant schoolmates would not be joining us in paradise. No, only Catholics will pass through St. Peter's gates into Heaven. A mere two thousand years had turned a fresh, passionate faith into a religion more exclusive and rule-bound than the Augusta National Golf Club. In my opinion, neither God nor golf has benefited from this trend. I found the little cave far more evocative and serene than any brick-and-mortar church. More than an hour slipped by as I sat alone on its floor, musing.

How lucky I was, I thought, to have had the place to myself for that time. As I walked out, a group of men strolled across the terrace. It was a party of middle-aged Europeans, looking like standard-issue tourists in their cotton shirts, sensible shoes, and canvas knapsacks. I wondered how far they'd come, and what they would think of this hole in the ground. They entered the cave. I waited. They didn't come out. I admired Antakya from the terrace for several minutes, not wanting to rush my departure. Still, the men remained in the cave. Were they all daydreaming as I had been, and if not, what on earth were they looking at? My curiosity got the best of me: I wandered over and looked around the doorway in the façade.

The hole in the ground was transformed. Two tall, white candles illuminated the altar; a gold chalice in the center reflected their flames. The empty knapsacks lay around the cave's perimeter. The twenty-four men—I did a quick count—were making final adjustments to their white priests' vestments, tying sashes at their waists, draping stoles around their necks. Embroidered icons at the ends of the stoles gave the only splashes of color—a red sheaf of wheat here, a green cross there. Twenty-two of the priests formed two curving lines to either side of the altar. There was just enough space. The remaining two took their places behind it. Then, in a language that I could only identify as Slavic, they proceeded to say Mass. I pressed myself against the cave's back wall, wondering if the priests would object to my presence. Two of them made eye contact with me and nodded warmly; I relaxed a bit. When they spoke in unison, their deep voices were almost palpable, bouncing off the rock. The cave pulsed when they sang. They weren't saying this Mass for a congregation. They were doing it for themselves, and they were clearly losing themselves in the process. Time had seemed distorted when I was alone in the cave, but that was nothing. Flickering candles, gold chalice, white satin, liturgical song—the disorientation was now total, forming a flimsy bridge between the infant church and the modern one. I tottered on that bridge for an hour, feeling uneasy at either end but, at the moment, in awe of both. One of the priests jolted me into the present—he approached me and asked if I speak English. I nodded.

"And you are Catholic?" he asked.

"Not now, not any more..." I stuttered.

He invited me to receive Communion. That day, for the first time in my life, I did want to receive Communion. I wanted it desperately, but the contemporary Catholic Church forbids the sacrament to those who don't live in a state of grace. A schism of twenty centuries had only a couple of seconds to play itself out: I thanked the priest and shook my head, "I can't." I asked him where he and the others had come from. "Poland," he replied.

Grief, regret, and confusion swirled. How bizarre that I should be standing in a Turkish cave with Polish priests, crying over a Communion that I felt I couldn't receive. Stranger still was the fact that I'd even wanted to. Should I have ignored the modern church's rules and trusted that the cave's original priest would have welcomed me, sins and all, to Communion? In which century's church were we standing, these priests and I? Not that it mattered—I had just passed up what felt like a once-in-a-lifetime opportunity. The Mass ended. The minibus driver took a group photograph of the priests, standing in a semicircle before the altar. The vestments came off, the candles went out. The chalice and plate disappeared into a knapsack. The priests followed their driver out of the cave. I walked back down the side of Mt. Silpius to modern Antakya, and the utterly unremarkable cave was empty again.

As I look back, I should have accepted the priest's invitation. I felt less confined in the small cave than I ever had within the ornate structure of rules that comprises the modern Church. I'd always felt I could only accept or reject that structure in its entirety. The cave's history reminded me how dynamic religions are. The cave itself, and the appearance of the twenty-four priests within it, reminded me that my spirit hadn't altogether died. I wanted to share in the Communion to affirm that I'd been, however tangentially, a part of that wondrous confluence.

I have a photograph of the mosaic Neptune on my wall now. He's an exquisite god, gazing into the distance with deep, sad eyes, almost as if he fears for the future of his oceans. In light of their current state, it's a pity we stopped worshipping him, really. I imagine that a number of Antioch's residents in those early centuries paid homage to Neptune and trekked up the hillside to the cave, as well, seeing no inconsistency between the two expressions of reverence. It's a fine model, I've decided. Libanios was right. One can learn a lot in Antakya.

Amanda Coffin grew up in coastal Maine. After receiving a degree in Linguistics from Wellesley College, she drifted into a technology career that kept her amused for twenty years. She currently resides in Turkey.

♬♬ ♬♬ ♬♬

The Little Dog That Could

What was that sound in the night?

S A NEW PEACE CORPS VOLUNTEER IN A VILLAGE IN Mali, West Africa, I was prepared for any calamity that could come my way. I was fully, mentally prepared for snakes, scorpions, malaria, motorcycle accidents, and countless parasitic intestinal guests. Bring it on, I was ready! All of these, plus a number of other unanticipated challenges, were hurled my way in two years of living in the village of Kangaba. Yes, I was fresh out of college, and ready for my AFRICAN ADVENTURE. I liked to think of it in all caps, just like in *A Prayer for Owen Meany.* That way, it was sure to be significant.

About three months into my service, I had adjusted to eating millet (you know it more affectionately as "birdseed") every night, squatting over a pit toilet with the cockroaches, eating goat innards with my hands out of the community bowl with my host family, working hard in the fields all day, and not speaking English for weeks at a time. All this, I thought, would impress the folks back home and was not really such a big deal, because I felt so at home already with my friends in the village.

One night, as usual, I was reading in bed in my mud hut, under a mosquito net. I was also taking care of a dog that belonged to another nearby volunteer while he was away from the village traveling. The dog, Che, was a medium-sized plain Black Lab type of dog. Not the sharpest bowling ball in the bunch, but a faithful companion, and I liked having him around. Each night, I would take my eyeglasses off (I don't need them for reading), put them on the bedside table, grab my book, and tuck myself into the mosquito net, armed with a fifty-cent flashlight from the local market to read before sleep. Ah, I was all tucked under my net like a cocoon, reading a well-worn, yellow-paged Barbara Kingsolver book that had lovingly been passed from volunteer to volunteer. I was thinking that in the days of the Malian empire, books traded for more than gold in Timbuktu, and I thought of history repeating itself among the Peace Corp diaspora.

I suddenly became a bit distracted by Che's actions. He had been lying next to my bamboo-type bed quite contentedly. I sat up to observe him, with foggy focus because my glasses were outside the mosquito net. He was standing at attention with perky ears, body in geometrically perfect alignment, one paw raised straight. It was pointing toward an area right underneath my bottom, under the bed. *Hmmmm*...I thought. *I guess there is another mouse, or lizard under there. Ah, well, back to the book.* I dismissed Che like an underpaid lackey.

But Che was still pointing, like an English hunting dog, and I wondered admiringly where he had learned that trick. I decided to slowly pull the straw mattress back, so I could peek under the bed frame and scare the mystery critter out. As I peered about four inches under my precious buttocks, I saw a very large, beady-eyed, not-very-friendly looking rat the size of a camel. Like me, the rat became startled, Che became consumed by instinct, and my heart hammered against my ribs at an alarming rate. After that, as they say, it was all a blur. Literally. My glasses were still *outside* the mosquito net on the table, and I could not see beyond the distance of a book. I was too terrified to risk putting a limb out of my cocoon. I shook my flaccid flashlight, cursing the three-second life span of the batteries. The weak golden glow emanating from the torch was illuminating just enough of the drama in front of me to keep me curled up fetus-tight, protecting my buttocks and other extremities, my heart pounding.

I heard pig-like squeals, wolf-like growls, baby-like cries, and Hitchcockian screams. The two producers of this cacophony made their way to the corner of my bedroom, over to my makeshift concrete-block shelves in the corner. Whoa! There went three pair of underwear and a few pairs of socks, airborne over the rat/dog cyclone below. I squinted to see more of what was going on, and I caught a blurry glimpse of a small stuffed teddy bear, dressed in a lacy smock my mother had sent me in a recent care package. *How embarrassing that she did that to her twenty-three-year-old hippie daughter*, I thought at the time. But now that teddy was turning to shreds as it was doing acrobatics in the air above the scuffle, I became enraged at the rat for violating a symbol of love from my mom so far away. I was pissed. "Go, Che!" I cheered like a WWF fan. The screeches grew louder, undergarments still flying in the air. I was still squinting, and my hands clenched harder on the flashlight as it sputtered and ran out of juice.

Darkness. Silence. I waited, hearing my own accelerated breath. I heard Che's paws on the concrete floor coming closer to me. Courageously reaching my own paw outside the mosquito net, I reached for my lantern and eyeglasses. I struck the match to inspect the aftermath. O.K., my Peace Corps recruiter did not tell me about nights like this. My bedroom was a disaster area! Torn-up underwear and socks, a de-stuffed, de-smocked, de-headed teddy bear, and rat blood in puddles all over the floor.

Meanwhile, Che, all of a sudden, was a proud, A+ student who had just completed his final exam of Smart Dog Academy. The limp, lifeless rat at my feet was the assessment. He looked at me, begging for praise, and hoping for some sort of treat for his efforts. "Yeah, that's just frickin' great," I heard myself say out loud to him. "Good job. Now get that thing out of here! Out, out!" He was all of a sudden dunce dog again. He laid it closer to my feet and smiled a stupid smile. I think he drooled on purpose. "Arrrrrgggh!" I marched to the next room and got inventive. I returned with my rudimentary garden hoe and the dustpan. I scooped the rat up, tossed him into the dark yard for now, and returned to mop up the blood-soaked teddy bear stuffing.

As I was cleaning the room, thinking what-an-independent-strong-adventurous-woman-I-am-and-I'm-in the-middle-of-Africa-in-the-middle-of-the-night-all-by-myself-and-I'm-just-fine-cleaning-up-rat-blood, no-problem, I-am made-for-this-kind-of-challenge, but-I'm-getting-a-little-lump-in-my-throat. Che came *back* inside. He was portering the limp rat, and laid it at my feet as if to say, "I don't think you had your glasses on last time, so maybe you didn't see what a good boy I am." I noted the size of the rat. Big. I took a deep breath, patted his head, and tried to be sincere. "Good boy, Che." I tossed him a hunk of stale bread, and he happily trotted to the corner. I chucked the rat outside, and locked the door.

Somehow, I managed to clean up the room, put away some non-shredded clothes that survived the battle, have a good little homesick sniffle about the teddy bear, wash my hands about ten times, then curl back up with my book. I kept my glasses nearby this time. I slept well.

The next morning, I realized the rat did not just vaporize into rat heaven, and it was squarely in my path on the way to the cockroach latrine. Hmmm...I went over to my host family's hut across the dirt path from my hut for a much-needed intervention. I was surprised how much Bambara I knew, and couldn't believe I had acquired the vocabulary to explain the night's events satisfactorily to my host family's comprehension. I felt quite proud for a moment. They asked me if I was O.K., had a little laugh at my expense, then sent one of the older brothers over to my yard to take care of the rat.

Now, this older brother seemed to, from time to time, delight in shocking the new, naïve, *toubab* woman. This was one of those times. As he reached down to pick up the rat, he said casually, "Lunch."

I wanted to be sure I understood his Bambara. "Lunch?" I choked out. I eat lunch with the family every day.

He made sure to make eye contact with me, which is rare for gentle Malians. He locked into my eyes and said essentially, "Yup, and this is the best part." He held up the rat corpse, yanked off the testicles and held them up in his palm for me to see. I smiled back, trying as hard as ever not to show the complete horror I was sure was all over my face.

"Well, then, *bon appetit*," I said, and sent him on his way.

I stood there for a minute in my hot, dusty yard in Kangaba, Mali, where I felt so strangely at home, trying to figure out what lesson, what great meaning this event could bring to my life. I was feeling very sure that something profound was happening out of all this.

But then I shrugged my shoulders and strolled over towards my hammock to take a nap before lunch. "If it's not a good time, it's a good story," I told myself. That would be my mantra for the rest of the two years I lived in Mali.

Mary Noble got hooked on travel during her time living in Africa, and currently splits her time between Alaska and Thailand with her daughter and husband.

KATHRYN ABAJIAN

❧ ❧ ❧

Climbing the Coconut Tree

In the heat of the tropics the traveler finds herself the
object of young men's attention.

"I'VE BEEN WATCHING YOU ALL WEEK," HE SAID.
"You have a nice smile." And then, inexplicably,
"You are a good wife and mother."

He was a waiter at Aggie Grey's Hotel in Samoa and
I was on my last day in the country, lying by the pool,
trying not to think about leaving this paradise. He had
been standing in the sun's heat for forty-five minutes,
holding his tray and trying to convince me to meet him
in my hotel room.

When I pointed out the blinding difference in our
ages, he said, "For Samoans, age isn't important. Only
the love is important." I was amused, but not at all
tempted. He *was* beautiful—a tall Samoan with a generous smile and cocoa-colored skin. He was also younger

274

than any of my children and seemingly out of his mind. About six feet away an Australian couple lay silent, lapping it all up.

I've traveled to the South Pacific often, always to the tiny island nation of Samoa. The young men there, in all honesty, are ravishing. Before they settle into their village chiefdom where the size of their bellies reflects their status, they are gods of the rainforest. As boys they run barely clad through the taro plantations on errands for their elders. They tote water, palm branches, and baskets of coconuts suspended on poles that span their widening shoulders. And they climb coconut trees.

I watched an eight-year-old boy fetch my breakfast one morning: he tied one end of a rag to each ankle to keep his feet about ten inches apart; then he wrapped his arms around the hairy trunk and mounted the tree, scampering up in thrusts. Soon the blond *nui*, the youngest coconuts, dropped, rolling in all directions. It takes any kid on the island about ninety seconds to whack out a hole in the top of the fruit with his bush knife. The prize is sweet—creamy, cool, coconut milk.

These boys, whose small hands become deft handling bush knives as children, grow to young men with prominent calf muscles and broad backs, black hair, and flashing smiles. I'd see them at large along village roads, completely bare, except for the brightly colored sarong-like *lava lavas* knotted at their waists and the large hibiscus flowers stuck behind one ear. They seemed so comfortable in their bodies. I envied their robust capability.

These are young men who spend hours in the ocean spearing fish and octopus, who cut the grass by hand, their bush knives doing the mower's work. Many come of age by enduring weeks of tattooing, painfully earning the

tatau that covers every inch of their lower bodies in traditional patterns. They are works of art in their own natural
setting, Polynesian possibilities of the imagination.

Most fully grown women who travel outside the
U.S. know how easy it is to attract a man's lingering
glance far from home. Once away from the States' tire-
somely stylish and annoyingly fit females, normal-sized
American women who travel to other, more reasonable
cultures are valued for their natural and uncontrived
charms. It's fun and it's flattering. But when the attention comes from mere boys, it's always so surprising.

During one hour-long wait for takeoff at LAX on
a nearly empty plane, I desultorily resisted a young
Samoan man's invitations for me to sit beside him for
the nine-hour trip to Pago Pago. I had no desire to sit
beside anyone when I could have an entire row to myself
and mostly ignored him. But after he described the tour
of the island he had in mind for "us" on our arrival, I
finally asked, "Why are you interested in me? I'm probably your mother's age."

"But I like you."

I asked him if he was attracted to me "because I'm
palagi"—not Samoan.

He admitted to it, saying, "*Palagi* women have white
skin, and they know what they want." I thought he meant
they are self-directed, independent women who travel
alone and love it, as I do. Later, I wondered just what all
those other women wanted and how they knew it.

The attention kept coming. A young policeman in
Apia, the island's only town, stopped me while I was out
running early one morning. I trotted right over, thinking
he beckoned for official reasons. But he was wondering
the all-pervasive question, "How long are you staying?"

And then, "Do you go to the nightclub tonight?" There was Fia Fia, a nineteen-year-old I interviewed for ten minutes in an outlying village. A month after I returned home my mail brought a letter from him, telling me he "wanted to marry up" with me.

Amazing and amusing. It's not like this at home in Northern California. I *teach* nineteen-year-old boys at home. I grade their reading skills and encourage them to develop their essays with specific details; I've pretty much never thought about taking one home. I'd be happy if it were just a bit easier to get dates with a man close to my age—not necessarily older, but at least a few respectable years older than my thirty-year-old son. But such men aren't as quickly attracted.

Of course, the air's different in California. It's not nearly as heavy and erotically moist. The fish don't fly and glow in the moonlight just below the tranquil Southern Cross. On *my* west coast there's no pungent smoke from cooking fires early in the morning, redolent with hemp. The cab drivers aren't named "Rambo" and don't offer tours of the island "because you make my cab smell good."

After my last trip to the South Pacific, I went on to Bali in Indonesia, another tiny island. Though I wasn't really there to check out the men, I couldn't help but notice. Bali's well-known for its compelling beauty. And everything on the island—both nature's shapes and those made by the Balinese—seems a gift of a brilliant artist's hand. It's sensually stimulating, but not really sensuous. The Asian men I encountered there seemed so placid. Basically, they were men wearing skirts—men who drove and walked and talked with a sort of spent composure.

Until Nyoman, that is. At first Nyoman seemed like the other Balinese men, though he had a playfulness to

him I hadn't seen since Samoa. He was about twenty-
five years old and worked at La Taverna Hotel in Sanur.
He learned my name as soon as I arrived, and we spoke
a few times as he fetched beach towels or icy fruit drinks
for me.

Our conversation one evening started so gradually
I was completely unprepared. Standing in front of the
hotel in the dusk of the Balinese night waiting for my
cab, we were both watching some men who'd just arrived and who were excitedly speaking Balinese while
waving and pointing to the top of a huge coconut tree
right in front of us.

I asked Nyoman what they were saying. He told
me they were talking about climbing the tree to get the
coconuts.

"Do you ever climb coconut trees, Nyoman?" I
asked, filling the languid time with small talk.

"Yes, every night," he answered.

Thinking that was sort of odd, I replied, "Really?"

"Yes, sometimes seven times in one night."

I was still staring up, straining to see the actual coconuts in the branches. I immediately recalled those eager
boys and young men in Samoa with their easy strength,
mounting the coconut trees there. I couldn't turn toward
Nyoman; I couldn't let him see I knew what he was really saying. Then I thought, *what* is *he really saying*? Still,
I stared straight up while he said, closer now, right in my
ear, "I'd like to climb the coconut tree with you."

Then the cab pulled up and its door opened. I was
safe again from the absurd image of consorting with
one of my students. And now I remind myself there's
nearly always more happening than meets the eye and
apparently more going on with these men below the

surface—behind their ear flowers, their motor scooters, their bush knives and, of course, their skirts.

Back in the States, living as close to the very edge of the continent as I can afford, I fall into my regular lanes of travel to and from work and play. I think about Nyoman's hopeful appreciation and still laugh when I remember the waiter's persistence in Samoa. I've always admired the prowess of young men—all those years I watched Rudy Curinga quarterback my high school's games, the long white seasons I skied the slopes with a trove of guys in college, and the fearlessness of those backpackers I see in my travels. They easily sleep anywhere and explore anything.

I still spend the whole of my days from August through June accommodating young men's restlessness. I know them so well and feel affection for them—for their lanky sprawls, their amiable readiness, their effortless potential. But, like the ability most of us have to admire fine art without needing to own it, I can appreciate them as landscape.

And more and more lately, as the gravity of my own age nudges me, as I realize how limited women of my generation feel, I find I don't *really* want a nineteen-year-old boy of my own. I want to *be* one.

Whenever she's not listening to the breeze rattle palm branches, Kathryn Abajian can be found teaching writing and literature in the San Francisco Bay Area. She is the author of memoir and travel essays and arts reviews. Her first book, First Sight of the Desert: Discovering the Art of Ella Peacock, *traces her relationship with a woman who painted the "land she loved."*

ॐ ॐ ॐ

A Bridge Across Sand

Fate leads a wounded spirit off
the beaten track to healing.

*B*ORDERS. SCARS ON A MAP, BARBED WIRE RECREATIONS of the fault lines circumscribing our consciousness. As a wanderer, I'd run up against more than my share, but nowhere did they loom as baleful and unyielding as in Israel.

Prompted by a sudden surge of long-sublimated Jewish chauvinism, I first visited Israel in 1987, intending to connect with my roots. As I packed a suitcase, the Palestinian uprising began to make headlines. By the time my feet touched the hallowed tarmac at Ben Gurion Airport, armies of children had taken to the streets of Gaza City, Hebron, and Nablus.

Laying aside my Frommer's and instinct for self-preservation, I became a correspondent for a small news service. I moved to Jerusalem's Moslem Quarter, where donkey dung and tear gas canisters lay in sorry little heaps among the cobblestones. Daily, I followed the conflict to its flashpoint in the West Bank or Gaza Strip, numbly awaiting the inevitable eruption of nerves that would trigger the first volley of stones and rubber bullets. I watched baby-faced Israeli soldiers dynamite houses, rendering them rubble. I watched an eight-year-old Palestinian boy proudly pop his new glass eye into the palm of his hand and display it like a trophy. For two bitter winters, while the death toll mounted and fanatics on both sides played a vicious game of terrorism and retaliation, I fought a battle of my own. Each time I raised my Nikon to capture the image of a person crying or cursing or bleeding to death, I felt a piece of my heart turn to glass, as if my humanity were no more substantial than the lens of my camera, as if in pressing the shutter I severed a vital connection.

Sometime between the stabbings of old people on Jaffa Road and the demise of Rabbi Meir Kahane, I cut my press card to shreds with a pair of cuticle scissors. There are limits to how much misery a sentient being can absorb—having reached mine, I said my goodbyes and headed home.

Six years would pass before I returned, an interim of healing, during which I embraced—and found solace in—the Buddhist tenets of compassion and nonattachment. The teachings of the Dalai Lama, in particular, seemed to soothe my brutalized psyche.

I had always admired the exiled Tibetan holy man, his simplicity in speech and the elfin eloquence of his gestures, the lightness he embodied. Being no navel gazer, I had never courted a guru, but the Dalai Lama was different—he didn't collect disciples, didn't preach, didn't talk in riddles. Of any public figure, he came closest to transcending culture with his warm accessible demeanor and simply expressed vision of a future without borders.

When, in 1993, Rabin and Arafat shook hands on the White House lawn, all things seemed possible. For a scant few weeks the illusion of peace settled on an embattled land, and people the world over began again to believe in miracles.

My dharma fortified, I resolved to return to Israel, hoping through some vague retracing of steps to complete my healing. As I packed a suitcase, however, news of the Hebron Massacre blitzed the media: twenty Palestinians murdered in Abraham's tomb while in the act of worship, their Israeli assassin, a settler, unrepentant. I arrived in Israel to find the atmosphere no less charged, the hate rhetoric no less trenchant than before the signing of the peace accords.

Having changed journalistic hats, I skirted the conflict, diverting my gaze from the barricades to the tourist attractions just beyond them. Neither travel advisories nor blood-encrusted holy sites had kept the tour buses from Bethlehem or the Galilee. Nuns, backpackers, and souvenir hunters prowled every *souk* and ruin.

My assignment, an article on archaeological curiosities, engaged my interest only superficially. While my guide, Amir, rhapsodized about sieges and last stands, I escaped on birdsong, grateful to tears for each small copse of wildflower.

My research completed, I casually asked Amir who his next client would be. The Dalai Lama, he told me.

Instantly my lethargy lifted, replaced by the giddy anticipation of meeting the man whose teachings had lifted me above the mire of world events. I managed to finesse an invitation to the international ecology congress where the Dalai Lama was to be guest speaker and for the next four days positioned myself in his path each time he made an appearance. The venerable Tibetan moved with the graceful, energetic gait of a young man, face alight with a perpetual smile that dimpled his cheeks and gave his eyes an impish twinkle. Not even we journalists could sour his good humor. He responded to our questions, even the intentionally obnoxious ones, with unflagging candor. He didn't dodge our camera lenses or flinch in the face of our electronic flashes. Yet, one sensed he wasn't entirely there, that some inviolable part of him floated in the ether far above our heads.

"There is hardly the sign of a border from here," he intoned from the summit of biblical Mt. Yoash, looking out over Jordan, Egypt, and Saudi Arabia without acknowledging the military installations, electric fences, and barbed wire so jarringly visible to the rest of us. "From this I conclude that borders are a mental creation, sometimes troublesome, but in the mind."

That he was right, who would not have liked to believe, though the hardware of war seemed to shut out our view of the sun at every turn. We descended the mountaintop no less perplexed. The congress drew to a close and 150 environmentalists, all thoroughly depressed by one another's accounts of raped forests and desecrated rivers, headed for the nearest airport.

I traveled north by bus to Beersheba, cradling the hand the Dalai Lama had clasped, his words still resonating.

At Beersheba I joined a hardy group of trekkers bound for Eilat and the Red Sea. We were unlikely travel companions, eight in all—four Germans, four

Americans—herded along in loose formation by a blandly
convivial Israeli guide. Shlomo specialized in identifying
animal droppings; every few hundred feet he would
gather us around some pestilent muck or other and
poeticize its origins. It was springtime, hot by the time
the sun cleared the horizon. For five sun-blasted days we
immersed ourselves in the tenuous splendor of the Negev
Desert, hiking through red canyons and black canyons,
following ancient caravan routes to palm-studded oases,
riding camels through sandy expanses carpeted with tiny
seashells...a tableau marred only by random litter and
the relentless incursions of an army chopper. The group
got on as well as strangers with no common bond other
than sunburn and blistered feet might be expected to.
Once we had compared SPFs, inner soles, and itineraries,
conversation lapsed.

Our last night together coincided with the first night
of Passover, a holiday commemorating the Jews' exodus
from Egypt and celebrated with a seder, or ritual meal.

We had arrived in Eilat, an overbuilt touristic oasis at
the edge of the Sinai Desert. Across the Gulf of Aqaba,
city lights shone mauve-colored through the Jordanian
smog. Shlomo left us at a comfortable hotel, intending
to hitchhike home for the evening and rejoin the group
the following morning. Waving, we watched him jog
toward a dented soft drink truck and climb into the cab.
Forsaken in the hotel's crowded lobby, stranded between
two deserts, we stood staring at the black scar of highway
long after the truck had vanished from sight. All around
us well-dressed families streamed toward the brightly
lit dining room. I suggested we celebrate a seder of our
own, an idea received enthusiastically by the German
Christians in the group. The maitre d'hotel, obliging,

provided *hagaddahs* (prayer books), *matzot* (unleavened bread), and wine.

With Egypt only a few miles down the road, we retold the story of the Jews' delivery from slavery under Pharaoh, of their escape through the nearby Sinai with slabs of raw dough baking on their burdened backs. We broke the stiff sheets of *matzot* and blessed the sweet wine. When a German girl read from the *hagaddah* the first of the four questions, "How is this night different from all other nights?" I didn't need to consult the text for an answer. That Germans and Jews had crossed a biblical desert together, shared the bread of freedom, risen above the enmities imposed by politics and history—was this any less miraculous than a plague of frogs?

The next day as I headed north en route to Jerusalem, the landscape seemed somehow more benign, the borders less obvious. A soldier got down from the bus to pick me a wildflower. Perhaps the Dalai Lama had been right after all.

Germaine W. Shames is author of the critically acclaimed novel, Between Two Deserts. *Shames has written from six continents— soon to add the seventh—on topics ranging from the Middle East crisis to the plight of street children. Her essays and short fiction have been widely anthologized; her articles appear in such periodicals as* National Geographic Traveler, Hemispheres, *and* Success. *She was last spotted piloting a narrow boat up the Grand Union Canal, accompanied by an Anglicized gorilla.*

இ இ இ

Letter From Morocco

In Casablanca, a visitor learns to give
herself over to the unknown.

RAMADAN IS OVER, AND I HAVE EMERGED WITH
a new appreciation of the small pleasures of
food and drink, and of sleep: getting up before sunrise
to eat breakfast and then returning to bed is tiring and
confuses my body's clock. Wednesday was the 27th of
Ramadan, when the first part of the Koran was revealed
to Mohammed, and the mosques sang all night long, their
tune weaving into my dreams.

This morning, the *Eid il Fitr*, the end of Ramadan, I
walked out into streets cool and wet, smelling of rain.
People spilled into the street from the mosques in their
prayer, in the still morning.

To give yourself to an unknown is a wrenching experience. I was terrified to come here. To live in a place for

a year, to perhaps loathe it on first sight—entirely possible, arriving jetlagged and exhausted—to sleep there
and wake there, to breathe the scent of it and be chased
by its noises, to not only observe its shortcomings and an-
noyances but to belong to them, to say, this is what I have
chosen and it is mine. For the lives we live in are no less
physical and personal than the bodies we inhabit.

Now, I wish I could tell you the wonder of the *souks*
and marketplaces; the brilliant overflowing of spices,
olives, fabrics; the witchcraft stalls; the fishmongers;
the piles of mint and thyme scenting the air…and even
more than this is the wonder of its becoming familiar,
the sufficiency and contentment in knowing the names
of things, the words to tell the taxi drivers, the sense
and reason behind the lives of Moroccans. I've realized
that that is what I wanted all along, not to visit another
country, but to live in it, to find belonging and familiarity in the strange and exotic. E. M. Forster thought a
room with a view was a great thing—but I want more
than a view. Let others look out upon me—I will be the
one below the window, raising hands bright with saffron
and henna. I am lucky to have come here. Moroccans are
vivacious, dramatic, family-oriented, and so, so welcom-
ing. I want to see into their lives, and I cannot imagine
how hard it would be for me if I had come to a country
that would not let me in.

We go to the *hammam* once a week, with plastic stools
to sit on and plastic scoops to tip water over ourselves,
soap and shampoo, *khisses* (the black, finely nubbled,
abrasive mitts for scrubbing ourselves), and *sabon bildi*
(the soft, dark brown, olive oil soap used in the *hammam*). Beyond the changing room lie three hot, humid
rooms rising to vaults, lit by watery skylights. Around the

walls are stone cisterns, with a hot and a cold tap from the pipes running around the walls—the hot too hot to touch, the cold frosted and dripping. I wish I could paint for you the beauty of the girl standing beside the faucet. Her skin is shades of warm cocoa to milk-brown. She holds herself as easily as though she had never thought of being other than naked. Maybe she feels the gorgeous wholeness of herself every day, under her clothes, and it is like being naked in the *hammam*, before a careless audience of women. Silk-wet brown bodies sit or stand around us, and within minutes we, too, are shining with the heat and the laden air. *Sabon bildi* is musky and latherless and light on the skin. Having rubbed it into our skin, we must wait for the heat and moisture to do their work, so we sit in our nakedness in the languid heat, under the dim vault, in the soft echo of water and the murmur of women around us. Then we scrub, slowly and thoroughly, every bit of ourselves, and the dead skin and sweat and dust rolls off of us visibly. I have never been so clean. We dry ourselves, and walk home radiant with heat, through the streets with wet hair.

The vendors walk down our street with their carts, croaking, howling, hiccuping; the children in the half-seen courtyard behind us laugh and scream. The air is fragrant with wood-smoke. September turns into October; the days are bright and warm, with fresh, gusting winds from the sea; the nights are soft black, or tiled with bright stars.

Tuesdays and Thursdays I teach in an office that looks out towards the sea. In the foreground stands a beautiful church, set among palm trees, with a tiled roof as green as a mermaid's tail. The Atlantic is salt-clouded and iridescent, and the clouds shifting and luminous.

Home is made with small pleasures, small comforts and familiarities. This afternoon I climbed the stairs to the roof to hang my laundry. From the west came the tinny whine of the muezzin's call from the mosque next to our outdoor market, and then, more distinct, another from the south. Suddenly I could hear the words, the notes—a song. I stood among my blowing sheets in the afternoon sun, with the wind and the song of faith around me, and I was struck with the thought that I might really miss this place when it is time to leave. And I thought how every letter written from Earth should be a love letter; there is so much beauty in the world, and indeed this letter is one.

Melissa Manlove arrived in Morocco in the fall of 2001 to begin a year of teaching English just before 9/11. Moroccans, ones who knew her, as well as complete strangers, offered her their sympathies for her country's tragedy. Even after the U.S. reprisals began and the Muslim world was full of resentment against the U.S. government, Manlove says that Moroccans never once turned that resentment against her. Today she lives in Northern California.

ACKNOWLEDGMENTS

Thank you, James O'Reilly and Larry Habegger, for once again asking me on board for another adventure with Travelers' Tales. Thank you, too, to the many other people who found and read essays for this book, including Sean O'Reilly, Jennica Peterson, and Laura Kiniry. As usual, Susan Brady deserves the credit for producing this book, for keeping track of every single ball that the editors around her toss into the air, and for always being a professional, no matter what. Special thanks for additional editorial and production work goes to Jennifer Leo and Melanie Haage.

In this book that honors women I would like to add a special thank you to my mother, Elizabeth McKoy McCauley, for her strength and her ability to see the glass half-full; and to my sister, L. Elizabeth McCauley, for her friendship, support, and loving care, and for showing me what courage means.

ABOUT THE EDITOR

Lucy McCauley's travel essays have appeared in such publications as *The Atlantic Monthly*, the *Los Angeles Times, Harvard Review*, and Salon.com. She is editor of three previous Travelers' Tales anthologies—*Spain* (1995), *Women in the Wild* (1998), and *A Woman's Path* (2000), all of which have been reissued in the last two years. In addition, she has written case studies in Latin America for Harvard's Kennedy School of Government, and now works as a developmental editor for publishers such as Harvard Business School Press.

Women's Travel

A WOMAN'S EUROPE $17.95
True Stories
Edited by Marybeth Bond
An exhilarating collection of inspirational, adventurous, and entertaining stories by women exploring the romantic continent of Europe. From the bestselling author Marybeth Bond.

WOMEN IN THE WILD $17.95
True Stories of Adventure and Connection
Edited by Lucy McCauley
"A spiritual, moving, and totally female book to take you around the world and back."
—*Mademoiselle*

A MOTHER'S WORLD $14.95
Journeys of the Heart
Edited by Marybeth Bond & Pamela Michael
"These stories remind us that motherhood is one of the great unifying forces in the world."
—*San Francisco Examiner*

A WOMAN'S PATH $16.95
Women's Best Spiritual Travel Writing
Edited by Lucy McCauley, Amy G. Carlson & Jennifer Leo
"A sensitive exploration of women's lives that have been unexpectedly and spiritually touched by travel experiences....Highly recommended."
—*Library Journal*

A WOMAN'S WORLD $18.95
True Stories of World Travel
Edited by Marybeth Bond
Introduction by Dervla Murphy

Lowell Thomas Award
—Best Travel Book

A WOMAN'S PASSION FOR TRAVEL $17.95
True Stories of World Wanderlust
Edited by Marybeth Bond & Pamela Michael
"A diverse and gripping series of stories!"
—Arlene Blum, author of
Annapurna: A Woman's Place

Food

ADVENTURES IN WINE $17.95
True Stories of Vineyards and Vintages around the World
Edited by Thom Elkjer
Humanity, community, and brotherhood compose the marvelous virtues of the wine world. This collection toasts the warmth and wonders of this large extended family in stories by travelers who are wine novices and experts alike.

HER FORK IN THE ROAD $16.95
Women Celebrate Food and Travel
Edited by Lisa Bach
A savory sampling of stories by the best writers in and out of the food and travel fields.

FOOD $18.95
A Taste of the Road
Edited by Richard Sterling
Introduction by Margo True

Silver Medal Winner of the
Lowell Thomas Award
—Best Travel Book

THE ADVENTURE OF FOOD $17.95
True Stories of Eating Everything
Edited by Richard Sterling
"Bound to whet appetites for more than food."
—*Publishers Weekly*

HOW TO EAT AROUND THE WORLD $12.95
Tips and Wisdom
By Richard Sterling
Combines practical advice on foodstuffs, habits, and etiquette, with hilarious accounts of others' eating adventures.

TRAVELERS' TALES
THE POWER OF A GOOD STORY

New Releases

THE BEST TRAVEL WRITING 2005 $16.95
True Stories from Around the World
Edited by James O'Reilly, Larry Habegger & Sean O'Reilly
The second in a new annual series presenting fresh, lively storytelling and compelling narrative to make the reader laugh, weep, and buy a plane ticket.

IT'S A DOG'S WORLD $14.95
True Stories of Travel with Man's Best Friend
Edited by Christine Hunsicker
Introduction by Maria Goodavage
Hilarious and heart warming stories of traveling with canine companions.

A SENSE OF PLACE $18.95
Great Travel Writers Talk About Their Craft, Lives, and Inspiration
By Michael Shapiro
A stunning collection of interviews with the world's leading travel writers, including: Isabel Allende, Bill Bryson, Tim Cahill, Arthur Frommer, Pico Iyer, Peter Matthiessen, Frances Mayes, Jan Morris, Redmond O'Hanlon, Jonathan Raban, Paul Theroux, Simon Winchester, and many more.

WHOSE PANTIES ARE THESE? $14.95
More Misadventures from Funny Women on the Road
Edited by Jennifer L. Leo
Following on the high heels of the award-winning bestseller *Sand in My Bra and other Misadventures* comes another collection of hilarious travel stories by women.

SAFETY AND SECURITY FOR WOMEN $14.95
WHO TRAVEL
(SECOND EDITION)
By Sheila Swan & Peter Laufer
"A cache of valuable advice." —*The Christian Science Monitor*

A WOMAN'S PASSION FOR TRAVEL $17.95
True Stories of World Wanderlust
Edited by Marybeth Bond & Pamela Michael
"A diverse and gripping series of stories!" —Arlene Blum, author of
Annapurna: A Woman's Place

THE GIFT OF TRAVEL $14.95
Inspiring Stories from Around the World
Edited by Larry Habegger, James O'Reilly & Sean O'Reilly
"Like gourmet chefs in a French market, the editors of Travelers' Tales pick, sift, and prod their way through the weighty shelves of contemporary travel writing, creaming off the very best." —William Dalrymple, author of *City of Djinns*

Travel Humor

SAND IN MY BRA AND $14.95
OTHER MISADVENTURES
Funny Women Write from the Road
Edited by Jennifer L. Leo
"A collection of ridiculous and sublime travel
experiences."
       —*San Francisco Chronicle*

LAST TROUT IN VENICE $14.95
The Far-Flung Escapades of an
Accidental Adventurer
By Doug Lansky
"Traveling with Doug Lansky might result in
a considerably shortened life expectancy...but
what a way to go."
      —Tony Wheeler, Lonely Planet Publications

THERE'S NO TOILET PAPER $12.95
ON THE ROAD LESS TRAVELED
The Best of Travel Humor and
Misadventure
Edited by Doug Lansky   — ⋆ ⋆ ⋆ —

— ⋆ ⋆ ⋆ —   *ForeWord Gold Medal*
                Winner— Humor
Humor Book of the Year   *Book of the Year*
Independent Publisher's
Book Award

HYENAS LAUGHED AT ME $14.95
AND NOW I KNOW WHY
The Best of Travel Humor and Misadventure
*Edited by Sean O'Reilly, Larry Habegger & James
O'Reilly*
Hilarious, outrageous and reluctant voyagers indulge
us with the best misadventures around the world.

NOT SO FUNNY WHEN $12.95
IT HAPPENED
The Best of Travel Humor and
Misadventure
Edited by Tim Cahill
Laugh with Bill Bryson, Dave Barry, Anne
Lamott, Adair Lara, and many more.

WHOSE PANTIES ARE $14.95
THESE?
More Misadventures from Funny Women
on the Road
Edited by Jennifer L. Leo
Following on the high heels of the award-
winning bestseller *Sand in My Bra and other
Misadventures* comes another collection of
hilarious travel stories by women.

Travelers' Tales Classics

COAST TO COAST $16.95
A Journey Across 1950s America
By Jan Morris
After reporting on the first Everest ascent in
1953, Morris spent a year journeying across
the United States. In brilliant prose, Morris
records with exuberance and curiosity a time
of innocence in the U.S.

THE ROYAL ROAD $14.95
TO ROMANCE
By Richard Halliburton
"Laughing at hardships, dreaming of beauty,
ardent for adventure, Halliburton has managed
to sing into the pages of this glorious book his
own exultant spirit of youth and freedom."
       —*Chicago Post*

TRADER HORN $16.95
A Young Man's Astounding Adventures
in 19th Century Equatorial Africa
By Alfred Aloysius Horn
Here is the stuff of legends—thrills and
danger, wild beasts, serpents, and savages.
An unforgettable and vivid portrait of a
vanished Africa.

UNBEATEN TRACKS $14.95
IN JAPAN
By Isabella L. Bird
Isabella Bird was one of the most adventurous
women travelers of the 19th century with
journeys to Tibet, Canada, Korea, Turkey,
Hawaii, and Japan. A fascinating read.

THE RIVERS RAN EAST $16.95
By Leonard Clark
Clark is the original Indiana Jones, telling the breathtaking story of his search for the legendary El
Dorado gold in the Amazon.

Spiritual Travel

THE SPIRITUAL GIFTS $16.95 **OF TRAVEL**	**THE WAY OF** $14.95 **THE WANDERER**

THE SPIRITUAL GIFTS $16.95
OF TRAVEL
The Best of Travelers' Tales
Edited by James O'Reilly & Sean O'Reilly
Favorite stories of transformation on the road
that show the myriad ways travel indelibly
alters our inner landscapes.

PILGRIMAGE $16.95
Adventures of the Spirit
Edited by Sean O'Reilly & James O'Reilly
Introduction by Phil Cousineau

ForeWord Silver Medal Winner
— Travel Book of the Year

THE ROAD WITHIN $18.95
True Stories of Transformation
and the Soul
Edited by Sean O'Reilly, James O'Reilly &
Tim O'Reilly

Independent Publisher's Book Award
—Best Travel Book

THE WAY OF $14.95
THE WANDERER
Discover Your True Self Through Travel
By David Yeadon
Experience transformation through travel
with this delightful, illustrated collection by
award-winning author David Yeadon.

A WOMAN'S PATH $16.95
Women's Best Spiritual Travel Writing
Edited by Lucy McCauley, Amy G. Carlson &
Jennifer Leo
"A sensitive exploration of women's lives
that have been unexpectedly and spiritu-
ally touched by travel experiences....Highly
recommended."
— Library Journal

THE ULTIMATE JOURNEY $17.95
Inspiring Stories of Living and Dying
James O'Reilly, Sean O'Reilly & Richard
Sterling
"A glorious collection of writings about the
ultimate adventure. A book to keep by one's
bedside—and close to one's heart."
—Philip Zaleski, editor,
The Best Spiritual Writing series

Special Interest

THE BEST $16.95
TRAVELERS' TALES 2004
True Stories from Around the World
Edited by James O'Reilly, Larry Habegger &
Sean O'Reilly
"This book will grace my bedside for years
to come."
—Simon Winchester, from the Introduction

TESTOSTERONE PLANET $17.95
True Stories from a Man's World
Edited by Sean O'Reilly, Larry Habegger &
James O'Reilly
Thrills and laughter with some of today's best
writers, including Sebastian Junger, Tim Cahill,
Bill Bryson, and Jon Krakauer.

THE GIFT OF TRAVEL $14.95
Inspiring Stories from Around the World
Edited by Larry Habegger, James O'Reilly
& Sean O'Reilly
"Like gourmet chefs in a French market, the
editors of Travelers' Tales pick, sift, and prod
their way through the weighty shelves of
contemporary travel writing, creaming off the
very best."
—William Dalrymple, author of City of Djinns

DANGER! $17.95
True Stories of Trouble and Survival
Edited by James O'Reilly, Larry Habegger &
Sean O'Reilly
"Exciting...for those who enjoy living on the
edge or prefer to read the survival stories of
others, this is a good pick."
— Library Journal

365 TRAVEL $14.95
A Daily Book of Journeys, Meditations, and Adventures
Edited by Lisa Bach
An illuminating collection of travel wisdom and adventures that reminds us all of the lessons we learn while on the road.

THE GIFT OF RIVERS $14.95
True Stories of Life on the Water
Edited by Pamela Michael
Introduction by Robert Hass
"...a soulful compendium of wonderful stories that illuminate, educate, inspire, and delight."
—David Brower,
Chairman of Earth Island Institute

FAMILY TRAVEL $17.95
The Farther You Go, the Closer You Get
Edited by Laura Manske
"This is family travel at its finest."
—*Working Mother*

LOVE & ROMANCE $17.95
True Stories of Passion on the Road
Edited by Judith Babcock Wylie
"A wonderful book to read by a crackling fire." —*Romantic Traveling*

THE GIFT OF BIRDS $17.95
True Encounters with Avian Spirits
Edited by Larry Habegger & Amy G. Carlson
"These are all wonderful, entertaining stories offering a *bird's-eye view!* of our avian friends."
—*Booklist*

IT'S A DOG'S WORLD $14.95
True Stories of Travel with Man's Best Friend
Edited by Christine Hunsicker
Introduction by Maria Goodavage
Hilarious and heart warming stories of traveling with canine companions.

Travel Advice

THE PENNY PINCHER'S PASSPORT TO LUXURY TRAVEL $14.95
(2ND EDITION)
The Art of Cultivating Preferred Customer Status
By Joel L. Widzer
Completely updated and revised, this 2nd edition of the popular guide to traveling like the rich and famous without being either describes, both philosophically and in practical terms, how to obtain luxurious travel benefits by building relationships with airlines and other travel companies.

SAFETY AND SECURITY $14.95
FOR WOMEN WHO TRAVEL
(2ND EDITION)
By Sheila Swan & Peter Laufer
"A cache of valuable advice."
—*The Christian Science Monitor*

THE FEARLESS SHOPPER $14.95
How to Get the Best Deals on the Planet
By Kathy Borrus
"Anyone who reads *The Fearless Shopper* will come away a smarter, more responsible shopper and a more curious, culturally attuned traveler."
—Jo Mancuso, *The Shopologist*

SHITTING PRETTY $12.95
How to Stay Clean and Healthy While Traveling
By Dr. Jane Wilson-Howarth
A light-hearted book about a serious subject for millions of travelers— staying healthy on the road—written by international health expert, Dr. Jane Wilson-Howarth.

GUTSY WOMEN $12.95
(2ND EDITION)
More Travel Tips and Wisdom for the Road
By Marybeth Bond
Packed with funny, instructive, and inspiring advice for women heading out to see the world.

GUTSY MAMAS $7.95
Travel Tips and Wisdom for Mothers on the Road
By Marybeth Bond
A delightful guide for mothers traveling with their children—or without them!

Destination Titles

ALASKA $18.95
Edited by Bill Sherwonit, Andromeda Romano-Lax, & Ellen Bielawski

AMERICA $19.95
Edited by Fred Setterberg

AMERICAN SOUTHWEST $17.95
Edited by Sean O'Reilly & James O'Reilly

AUSTRALIA $18.95
Edited by Larry Habegger

BRAZIL $18.95
Edited by Annette Haddad & Scott Doggett
Introduction by Alex Shoumatoff

CENTRAL AMERICA $17.95
Edited by Larry Habegger & Natanya Pearlman

CHINA $18.95
Edited by Sean O'Reilly, James O'Reilly & Larry Habegger

CUBA $18.95
Edited by Tom Miller

FRANCE $18.95
Edited by James O'Reilly, Larry Habegger & Sean O'Reilly

GRAND CANYON $17.95
Edited by Sean O'Reilly, James O'Reilly & Larry Habegger

GREECE $18.95
Edited by Larry Habegger, Sean O'Reilly & Brian Alexander

HAWAI'I $17.95
Edited by Rick & Marcie Carroll

HONG KONG $17.95
Edited by James O'Reilly, Larry Habegger & Sean O'Reilly

INDIA $19.95
Edited by James O'Reilly & Larry Habegger

IRELAND $18.95
Edited by James O'Reilly, Larry Habegger & Sean O'Reilly

ITALY $18.95
Edited by Anne Calcagno
Introduction by Jan Morris

JAPAN $17.95
Edited by Donald W. George & Amy G. Carlson

MEXICO $17.95
Edited by James O'Reilly & Larry Habegger

NEPAL $17.95
Edited by Rajendra S. Khadka

PARIS $18.95
Edited by James O'Reilly, Larry Habegger & Sean O'Reilly

PROVENCE $16.95
Edited by James O'Reilly & Tara Austen Weaver

SAN FRANCISCO $18.95
Edited by James O'Reilly, Larry Habegger & Sean O'Reilly

SPAIN $19.95
Edited by Lucy McCauley

THAILAND $18.95
Edited by James O'Reilly & Larry Habegger

TIBET $18.95
Edited by James O'Reilly & Larry Habegger

TURKEY $18.95
Edited by James Villers Jr.

TUSCANY $16.95
Edited by James O'Reilly & Tara Austen Weaver
Introduction by Anne Calcagno

Footsteps Series

THE FIRE NEVER DIES $14.95
**One Man's Raucous Romp Down the Road of Food,
Passion, and Adventure**
By Richard Sterling
"Sterling's writing is like spitfire, foursquare and jazzy with
crackle...."   —*Kirkus Reviews*

ONE YEAR OFF $14.95
**Leaving It All Behind for a Round-the-World Journey
with Our Children**
By David Elliot Cohen
A once-in-a-lifetime adventure generously shared, from the
author/editor of *America 24/7* and *A Day in the Life of Africa*

THE WAY OF THE WANDERER $14.95
Discover Your True Self Through Travel
By David Yeadon
Experience transformation through travel with this delightful,
illustrated collection by award-winning author David Yeadon.

TAKE ME WITH YOU $24.00
A Round-the-World Journey to Invite a Stranger Home
By Brad Newsham
"Newsham is an ideal guide. His journey, at heart, is into
humanity."   —Pico Iyer, author of *The Global Soul*

KITE STRINGS OF THE SOUTHERN CROSS $14.95
A Woman's Travel Odyssey   *ForeWord Silver Medal Winner*
By Laurie Gough   — *Travel Book of the Year*
Short-listed for the prestigious Thomas Cook Award, this is an
exquisite rendering of a young woman's search for meaning.   —— ⋆ ⋆ ⋆ ——

THE SWORD OF HEAVEN $24.00
A Five Continent Odyssey to Save the World
By Mikkel Aaland
"Few books capture the soul of the road like The *Sword of
Heaven,* a sharp-edged, beautifully rendered memoir that will
inspire anyone."
                              —Phil Cousineau, author of *The Art of Pilgrimage*

STORM $24.00
A Motorcycle Journey of Love, Endurance,   *ForeWord Gold Medal Winner*
and Transformation   — *Travel Book of the Year*
By Allen Noren
"Beautiful, tumultuous, deeply engaging and very satisfying.   —— ⋆ ⋆ ⋆ ——
Anyone who looks for truth in travel will find it here."
                              —Ted Simon, author of *Jupiter's Travels*